THE COMPLETE FRANCHISE BOOK

**What You Must Know
(And Are Rarely Told)
About Buying or Starting
Your Own Franchise**

Dennis L. Foster

Prima Publishing
P.O. Box 1260BK
Rocklin, CA 95677
(916) 786-0426

Production by Christi Payne Fryday, Bookman Productions
Copyediting by Beverly Zegarski
Typography by ATG PrePress Services
Cover design by The Dunlavey Studio, Sacramento

Library of Congress Cataloging-in-Publication Data

Foster, Dennis L.
    The complete franchise book: everything you ever wanted to know about buying or starting your own franchise/Dennis L. Foster. —
Rev. and updated 2nd ed.
    p. cm.
    Includes index.
    ISBN 1-55958-316-9 (pbk.):
    1. Franchises (Retail trade) I. Title.
HF5429.23.F67 1993
658.8'708—dc20   93-9900
                                                   CIP

94 95 96 97 98 99   10 9 8 7 6 5 4 3 2 1

Printed in the United States of America by:
R.R. Donnelley & Sons Company

The Complete
Franchise Book

How to Order:

Single copies may be ordered from Prima Publishing, P.O. Box 1260BK, Rocklin, CA 95677; telephone (916) 786-0426. Quantity discounts are also available. On your letterhead, include information concerning the intended use of the books and the number of books you wish to purchase.

Contents

Part 3: FRANCHISING IN ACTION

APPENDIXES

Why You Need to Read This Book

Albert Driver's secret made him a popular host in the small rural community where he lived with his wife Jean and their three daughters. Many of his friends were co-workers at the aluminum plant where Albert had worked industriously for the past 11 years, and despite their persistent efforts to pry his secret from him, Albert's lips remained sealed.

The object of all this adoration and prying was his secret recipe for barbecue pork ribs. To Albert, it was more than a recipe — it was a family heirloom, passed down by his great grandmother who had immigrated to America from France.

One day, half-joking, Albert's next door neighbor, Harmon Stradling, offered to buy the recipe. Instead, Albert invited the Stradlings to dinner.

"Albert, you should open a restaurant," Harmon told his neighbor when the meal was finished, "and serve nothing but ribs. We'd make a fortune."

Albert laughed. "What do you mean 'we'?"

"We'll start a partnership," Harmon suggested. "I'll put up the money, and you barbecue the ribs."

"And what about my job at the plant?" Albert responded.

"Resign," Harmon countered.

1

"And my wife and kids? How will they eat?"

"Well," Harmon said, thoughtfully, "I suppose you could always feed them barbecue ribs."

The two friends laughed, but Albert did not quit his job to open a restaurant. However, two months later, the aluminum plant closed, and Albert found himself standing in the unemployment line.

Harmon approached his neighbor again about forming a partnership. This time Albert listened.

Frank Travis lived in the same rural community, but unlike Albert Driver, he had never been employed at the aluminum plant. Frank had served in the U.S. Air Force for nine years and opted for early retirement when the government closed the base where he was stationed.

After re-entering civilian life, it was not long before Frank decided to start a small business. Unlike Albert, Frank did not have a secret recipe or a neighbor with money to invest. In fact, his savings were relatively small. He did not know exactly what type of business he wanted to own, but he enjoyed working with people and entertaining guests. After studying his options, he decided the restaurant business was right for him.

Albert and Frank opened their restaurants at about the same time. Albert's eatery was located in a small retail strip just outside the town limits, whereas Frank's restaurant was housed in a new building in the best part of town. Together, Albert and his partner, Harmon Stradling, had invested nearly $50,000 of their own money to start the business. Frank had been able to start with just $15,000. Within three months, Albert's BBQ Ribs had closed. Yet Frank's restaurant was one of the most popular eateries in town and was already turning a profit.

Why did Frank Travis' enterprise succeed, while Albert Driver's restaurant failed? On the surface, Albert's business seemed to have everything going for it — working capital, an affordable location, and, of course, the secret recipe for barbecue ribs. In contrast, Frank did not have much money to invest, paid high rent, and knew almost nothing about cooking.

The answer is not as mysterious as it may seem. Albert and Harmon were not just in business for themselves — they were also in business by themselves. Frank, on the other hand, had lots of support; he had complete access to a professional marketing, advertising, financial, purchasing, and restaurant management staff.

Frank Travis had purchased a franchise to open a family style restaurant using the trademark, architectural designs, and menu of a well-known chain. To finance the business, he had received a government-guaranteed loan that was available to veterans investing in franchises. He had received thorough training, a set of comprehensive operating manuals, and assistance with building, staffing, and opening the restaurant.

Frank's franchisor had helped him select a site based on the company's prior experience in the restaurant business. They knew things about attracting customers that would have taken Albert and Frank years to learn on their own. After six weeks of intensive training at franchise headquarters, Frank shared much of that know-how.

Frank had purchased the same types of restaurant equipment as Albert and Harmon, yet had paid only about one-half the price. How? Frank's franchisor had already negotiated low prices from suppliers based on projected orders from a large number of franchisees. As a result, Frank paid wholesale prices for the same items that Albert and Harmon had to buy at retail.

For advertising, Frank paid a small percentage of his monthly income into a co-operating fund. By itself, this meager contribution would not have gone far to promote the restaurant, but combined with similar contributions from five hundred or so other franchises, Frank's payment helped finance television and radio campaigns, large advertisements in major newspapers, and prominent listings in the Yellow Pages. Albert could afford only to print up small fliers, which his daughters stuck on car windshields in supermarket parking lots.

In spite of their physical similarities, Albert's restaurant went bankrupt within weeks, while Frank's continues to thrive to this day. He is even thinking of opening a second restaurant in a nearby town.

Frank's case history illustrates some of the advantages enjoyed by the owner of a franchise business. The example of Albert, the unsuccessful entrepreneur, is indicative of some of the risks encountered by people who attempt to go it on their own.

According to the U.S. Department of Commerce, less than ten percent of all franchise businesses fail each year. In contrast, the Small Business Administration reports that over two thirds of all private enterprises eventually fail, most of them within the first year. Is it any wonder that, by the end of the current decade, franchises will account for over half of all U.S. retail business?

Still, although franchising is one of the most rapidly growing sectors of the economy, it is easy to overlook that potential perils and pitfalls do exist. The following is another case history, with a similar beginning but a very different ending.

Andrea Goodman's interest in cosmetology inspired her to start her own hairstyling salon. After researching the field, she decided to buy a franchise from a large chain. She was particularly impressed by an article in a small business magazine. In fact, the president of the hairstyling chain was on the front cover. According to the article, his chain had one of the fastest growth rates of any business in America. A franchisee interviewed by the magazine indicated that his hairstyling salon had become successful almost as soon as he had opened. In the previous three years, the chain had burgeoned from 200 outlets to over 3,000 franchises.

Swayed by the article, Andrea decided to apply for a franchise from the chain. To swing the investment, she paid an initial franchise fee of $30,000 and borrowed $50,000 more from relatives. She paid all but about $5,000 to the franchisor for architectural plans, fixtures, equipment, signs, initial advertising, and grand opening assistance.

After signing a franchise agreement, the franchisor had promised to send a representative to help with site selection, improvements, decoration, and grand opening activities. However, despite repeated telephone calls to franchise headquarters, the representative never showed up. Undaunted, Andrea oversaw the development of her salon herself. The business opened a full month behind schedule.

Two weeks later, the franchise corporation closed its offices and declared bankruptcy. The chain had grown so rapidly that it could not keep up with new outlet openings. In fact, it had sold more franchises than it could support. Most of the money from initial franchise fees was used to pay the company's debts, leaving insufficient funds for day-to-day operations. When the company ran out of money, 1,500 of the franchises it had sold were not yet open.

Without the training, marketing, purchasing, and other assistance she had been promised by her franchisor, Andrea's salon eventually closed.

As this case history illustrates, no business is immune to failure. Despite the relatively low failure rate of franchises, impressive statistics and laudatory magazine articles do not supplant the need for thorough research, adequate financing, and the diligent exercise of caution.

Franchising is often referred to as a dual-edged sword. At its best, it is capitalism's finest hour, a time for transforming simple ideas and bold ambitions into fulfilled dreams of personal enrichment and financial independence. At its worst, it is "vulture capitalism" run amok, in which every conceivable type of quick-buck scam and pyramid sales scheme is foisted on an unsuspecting public. The difference is often less visible than the writing on an oral contract.

This revised and updated edition of *The Complete Franchise Book* was written to help you sort out the facts about franchising today and to distinguish the signposts of success from the danger signals of fraud or failure. It begins with a broad self-evaluation of your mental, physical, and financial preparedness for franchising and concludes with a systematic procedure for evaluating a franchise opportunity.

Each chapter includes a set of self-tests, checklists, or work sheets to help you organize your search for the ideal franchise.

We'll examine just what franchisors can — and can't — do to influence a prospective franchisee to sign an agreement. We'll also take an in-depth look at the processes of researching opportunities and negotiating a franchise agreement. You'll learn about the psychological strategies that franchisors use to sell their franchises, then find out how to turn the tables to your own advantage.

We'll explore the mysterious regions of the Uniform Franchise Offering Circular (UFOC), translating it into plain English, then dissect a franchise agreement to see how it affects your rights as a business owner. You'll also examine the contents of a typical franchise operating manual and learn how this important tool both guides and governs the day-to-day operation of a franchise outlet. You'll also learn how to plan, finance, and organize a business, including things they won't tell you in franchise training school. Finally, we'll examine the critical factors that influence a decision to buy a franchise and ultimately determine the likelihood of success.

Along the way, this book will help you answer the following questions:

- Is franchising right for me?
- In what type of business will I be successful?

- How can I find the right franchise opportunity to fit my own objectives, budget, skills, and personality?
- How can I spot franchise come-ons and rip-offs, and avoid the usual pitfalls that typify a new busines start-up?
- How can I negotiate the most favorable franchise agreement?
- What should I look for in a franchisor's background?
- What kind of earnings can I realistically expect?
- What are my rights and obligations as a franchisee?
- What are a franchisor's rights and obligations?
- How can I raise the money to build and develop the business?
- What steps can I take to optimize my chances for success?

Most of the people who will read this book or have read the previous edition are considering investing in a franchise opportunity. However, some readers may already own or manage a successful business and want to evaluate the potential for developing a franchise system. For these erstwhile franchisors, *The Complete Franchise Book* will provide a personal tour of the ins and outs of planning, structuring, developing, marketing, and supporting a franchise organization.

Franchising: A Definition

Although the words "franchise" and "franchising" are widely used, many people have misconceptions about what these terms actually mean. In the most basic sense, a franchise is a right or privilege, such as the franchise to vote. In an economic sense, franchising is the practice of granting a license to use a specific trademark or business format. Technically, the word "franchise" refers to the license, not to the business outlet. Business format franchises include the exercise of ongoing rights and obligations under a franchise agreement.

Often, the term "franchising" is used interchangeably to denote the act of either buying or selling a franchise. In a more casual sense, the "franchising industry" refers to a large segment of the U.S. economy, accounting for nearly forty percent of all domestic retail trade.

A franchisor is a person or company that grants franchises to others. A franchisee is a person or company to whom a franchise is granted. For the rights granted by the franchise agreement, the franchisee pays a financial consideration — usually an initial fee and ongoing royalties assessed on the gross sales of the outlet.

The franchisee must supply the working capital to secure a site, construct the premises, and develop the outlet. To handle the initial investment, franchisees often borrow the funds or obtain financial assistance from an investor. The franchisee owns the outlet, but to a large extent, its operation is governed by the franchise agreement.

Franchising as a Growth Strategy

Franchising is not really an industry, but rather a method of distributing products or expanding operations. A company that wants to expand has four basic alternatives: (1) pursue vertical markets, (2) diversify (3) acquire or merge with another company, or (4) franchise.

Vertical marketing is based on the invention of new applications for existing products. For example, a manufacturer of residential air-conditioning equipment attacks vertical markets when it attempts to sell the same products to warehouses and farms. Another expansion strategy is to diversify the company's sources of income by introducing new products or entering new industries. For instance, a department store chain diversifies when it expands into the insurance, finance, and car rental fields. Often, both expansion objectives can be achieved by franchising.

As a growth strategy, franchising provides a business with the ability to rapidly enter and, sometimes, dominate new markets by increasing the number of distribution channels or outlets. Franchising also permits a company to diversify its sources of income by generating franchise fees and royalties.

To be successful in franchising, a company must have a unique or competitive product associated with a protected trademark. The business format must be well documented and easily replicated, so that it can be transferred to others. A typical franchise system has a training program for franchisees, architectural plans and product specifications, operating procedures, management controls, and assistance with purchasing, inventory, marketing, and advertising.

Since the economic boom years of the 1950s, the success rate of franchised businesses has been phenomenal. More than 90 percent of all franchise outlets survive at least five years, whereas two thirds of all other independently owned businesses fail, most in a year or less. The practice of franchising ideally taps the entrepreneurial motives of individuals who desire to be their own bosses, while generating an ongoing source of income to franchisors. From the franchisor's vantage point, franchising offers the ability to expand and diversify at reduced capital risk. From the franchisee's perspective, it offers self-esteem, an opportunity for self-management, and an asset of lasting value.

Part 1

The Anatomy of a Franchise

Chapter One

Made in the U.S.A.

The Franchise Revolution

In 1990, the first McDonald's outlet in Russia opened to a huge throng of hamburger-hungry Moscovites. Two years earlier, the world's largest Kentucky Fried Chicken restaurant opened in Beijing, China, on a corner of Tiananmen Square, within view of the Gate of Heavenly Peace.

One of the first sights greeting travelers to the remote South Pacific isle of Bora Bora is the yellow-and-black sign of a Hertz Rent-a-Car office.

The most crowded restaurants in Paris are not Maxim's or *La Tour d'Argent,* where every roast duck has a registration number, but McDonald's, Wendy's, and Burger King.

In King's Cross, the bustling tourism district of Sydney, Australia, the skyline is dominated by a flashing, twenty-story, electric Coca-Cola sign.

In many ways, these sights are symbolic of the pervasive cultural, as well as economic, impact of franchising in the modern world, for each of these famous brand names is a franchise trademark.

The word *franchising* conjures up a myriad of sometimes conflicting images. To the average American, a franchise means a sizzling burger on a sesame seed bun, a cardboard bucket teeming with crispy

11

fried chicken, or perhaps a deep-dish pizza topped with mozzarella cheese and pepperoni. However, mention the term to a pro football scout, and he'll probably think you mean a "franchise" player who can take a team from the cellar to the Super Bowl. A politician might think you're referring to the right to vote in a public election.

To an attorney, a franchise is a lengthy contract, but to an accountant, it is a financial relationship. To a banker, it is a relatively secure investment, but to a government regulator, it might be a red flag for consumer fraud.

From a cultural perspective, the franchise phenomenon is both a driving force and a reflection of public tastes in food, fashion, and lodging. In some way or another, franchising has managed to make its way into almost every corner of the earth. From Bangor, Maine, to Bangkok, Thailand, franchising has captured the public imagination and, in doing so, recruited to its ranks hundreds of thousands of erstwhile entrepreneurs.

An American Invention

Although franchising has gone international, it remains a uniquely American invention. Although the ancient Phoenicians invented money, it was Benjamin Franklin who first sold marketing rights to an exclusive product, territory, and trade name. He charged youths a franchise fee of ten cents to deliver *Poor Richard's Almanac* to subscribers in Philadelphia, thereby inventing both the newspaper route and the franchise. In 1851, Isaac Merrit Singer, the inventor of the modern sewing machine, also began selling marketing rights to enterprising individuals. In the timeworn jokes about traveling salesmen and farmers' daughters, the salesman was undoubtedly a Singer Sewing Machine franchisee.

The word *franchise* is derived from an Old French word, *franc*, meaning "free." Literally, a franchise is a right or privilege, as in the franchise to vote. As a method of business, franchising means granting, for a fee, the right to use a particular trademark or to market an exclusive product. In a larger context, franchising has come to mean much more. A modern franchise entails an entire business system in which every aspect, from the architecture of the building to the color of the stationery, is planned in elaborate detail. Many franchisors offer complete "turnkey" operations, fully stocked, equipped, and ready to run.

How important is the franchise method to the American free enterprise system? Consider this amazing statistic: according to the Industry and Trade Administration of the U.S. Department of Commerce, over 90 percent of the franchises that were open five years ago are still in business today.

Why are franchises so successful? A franchise is like a marriage between a perfectly matched couple; it weds a successful big-time operator with a motivated small-time operator who desires to be successful. Studies show that people who own their own businesses are more devoted to their jobs than are middle managers employed by large corporations. Franchisors benefit from the motivation and drive of their franchisees, while franchise owners benefit from the franchisors' trade secrets and industry knowledge.

Franchising and the Law

At a recent legal conference, I heard a franchise attorney proclaim that franchising is nothing more than a legal entity. Indeed, a franchise is a complex legal relationship between two parties — a relationship that is further complicated by reams of federal and state regulations. However, without its various financial, marketing, and operating systems, franchising — and, thus, franchise law — would not exist. No contracts would be written, no regulations would be enacted, and no attorneys would be retained if franchising was not, first and foremost, a successful business method.

If a franchise relationship does not work for both parties, ultimately, it will not work for either one. Unfortunately, not every franchise relationship has a happy ending, and much of the case law devoted to franchising involves unhappy franchisors or franchisees. Understanding the legal rights and obligations of both parties is a necessity in any franchise business.

In July 1979, sweeping franchise regulations were adopted by the U.S. Federal Trade Commission. Within thirty days, more than half of the franchises that were advertised in the *Wall Street Journal* before the regulations went into effect had disappeared. In this respect, regulation has had a favorable impact on the franchise industry by protecting unwary investors against potential abuse. However, like many government regulations, the franchise rules are not always followed and are sometimes difficult to enforce.

Still, anyone who contemplates a franchise investment — or works for a franchisor or franchisee — needs to have a sound understanding of federal and state regulations affecting the offer, sale, operation, and termination of franchises.

Franchising and Society

The behavior of people is influenced by the media. While it is true that franchise businesses reflect popular trends, franchises also influence public taste. The most obvious effect of franchising on Western cultures is the widespread popularity of fast food. According to the National Restaurant Association, 90 percent of all meals taken in public in the United States are eaten at fast-food restaurants. Is it any wonder that McDonald's is the most widely recognized brand name in the world?

Worldwide, no franchise product is more widely distributed than Coca-Cola, for which bottling franchises exist in almost every nation on earth. In foreign countries, the familiar red-and-white Coke trademark is virtually synonymous with American life and influence. Other well-known brands such as Ford, Hertz, and even the New York Yankees are also franchise trademarks.

In recent years, taking off the pounds has become as popular as putting them on. Health and fitness franchises such as Jazzercise, Diet Center, and Physicians Weight Loss have joined the ranks of Subway Sandwiches and Salads, Domino's Pizza, and Taco Bell.

In food service and other major industries, such as lodging, automotive services, retail sales, and personal services, franchises have become so influential that they often dictate consumer trends, fashions, and pricing.

14

The Security of Sameness

Sameness is a basic component of consumer consciousness. Few fears are more pronounced than the fear of the unknown. Who has not balked at turning into an unknown fast-food stand by the highway or driven past an anonymous motel in quest of a recognizable brand name? Whose imagination has not conjured up nightmarish images of grease-encrusted grills, derelict washrooms, and unscrupulous, cigar-puffing managers?

Consumers patronize known establishments, in part, from fear of the unknown. A franchise attracts customers because it is a known commodity. If you've had one Big Mac, you've had them all. But who knows what unsavory ingredients lurk between the buns of a "Bruno's Bar and Grill" burger? If you've slept in one Holiday Inn, you have a pretty decent idea of what it's like to sleep in any of them. But who knows whether the plumbing even works in the "Downtown Motel?"

Franchisors often refer to their franchise systems as "cookie cutters," stamping out near-clones of their original "flagship" businesses. A franchise outlet wraps consumers in a security blanket of sameness. We expect a Big Mac to taste the same in Portland, Oregon, as in Portland, Maine — or Port Moresby, Papua New Guinea, for that matter.

From chocolate chip cookies to computers, from togs to tacos, the most popular products are those that cater to the common denominator in public taste. Franchise outlets, with their uniform operating standards and cookie-cutter designs, are the very essence of that common denominator.

Franchising and the Economy

McDonald's stock first appeared on the New York Stock Exchange on 15 April 1965 at about seventeen times the company's earnings for the prior year. Within weeks, the price soared from $22.50 to $49.00 a share.

Because of the successful track record of franchise businesses, major corporations involved in franchising are highly prized as investments. At various times, the stock of McDonald's, Coca-Cola, Hilton, and other franchisors has attracted financial institutions as well as independent investors. In addition, absentee investment in franchise businesses has become a virtual mainstay of venture capital groups and fund managers.

With the high success rate of franchise outlets, lenders are more willing to finance franchise start-ups than other small businesses. Commercial finance companies, venture capitalists, profit-sharing funds, and banks provide over two-thirds of the total capitalization of retail franchises.

According to the U.S. Department of Commerce, franchises represent over one-third of all U.S. retail trade, accounting for an estimated $600 billion in gross sales in 1993. More than 2,000 franchise chains employ over seven million members of the work force. Half a million Americans currently own franchise outlets, and the number of people who are actively interested in investing in a franchise opportunity has never been greater. A new franchise outlet is opened every eight minutes of every business day.

According to the Department of Commerce, franchising is the average American's most viable means of owning a business. *Time* magazine predicts that, by the year 2000, franchises will generate 60 percent of all retail sales.

On the one hand, business owners do sacrifice some measure of independence to become franchisees. They also sacrifice a percentage of their income — a royalty on all gross revenues. On the other hand, the average franchise owner earns 20 percent more than another small business owner. A franchise is also four and one-half times more likely to succeed than any other form of business.

However, franchising is about more than retail sales, employment, and small business survival. It is also about self-fulfillment, personal expression, and creativity. A person who invests in a franchise does not just buy himself or herself a job. Franchisees are people motivated by accomplishment and driven by a dream — the dream of self-management, financial independence, and personal enrichment.

Chapter Two

The Franchise Formula

A Strategy for Growth

It is often said about life in the ocean — and in business — that "little fish are eaten by big fish." As straightforward as that saying may sound, it is far from the truth. One of the most successful fish in the sea is the cleaner wrasse, which spends most of its life between the jaws of a big fish. The wrasse's diet consists of tiny parasites that live in the mouths of larger fish. Big fish actually encourage the wrasse to dine in their mouths. From this relationship, the cleaner wrasse enjoys a prosperous livelihood, and the big fish maintains its good health.

Biologists call this type of behavior a symbiotic relationship — one in which each party is dependent on the other for survival. Replace each species with a business, and you have a franchise relationship.

Franchising is a method of owning a business in cooperation with others. It is also a major contributor to the U.S. economy. More important, franchising is a strategy for personal and financial growth.

In the most basic sense, a "franchise" is a right or privilege to conduct a particular business using a specified trade name. Trade secrets and a packaged business format are usually part of the deal. The "franchisor" is the company that offers the franchise to others. The person who buys a franchise from a franchisor is the "franchisee."

Franchising enables a franchisor to enter new geographical mar-

17

kets quickly and expand its sources of revenue. To a small business owner, franchising offers a ready-made format for a business and improved odds for survival.

For the benefits and advantages of a franchise license, the franchisee pays an initial fee, an ongoing royalty, or both. In this way, the franchisor receives a continuous supply of working capital to expand and develop the organization.

The most fundamental type of franchise is a license to use a distinctive trademark or to market an exclusive product. A sales territory is often included with the license. For instance, during the Civil War era, a Singer franchisee obtained a license to sell sewing machines within an established geographic area. This type of arrangement is referred to as a trademark or distributor franchise.

Trademark Franchising

The best way to understand a trademark franchise is to study a famous case history.

In 1886, a Georgia pharmacist, John S. Pemberton, blended together ground cola nut, oils from the coca leaf, a pinch of caffeine, and miscellaneous herbs. Although he promoted his elixir as a hangover remedy, it did not become popular until a soda fountain clerk mistakenly mixed the syrup with carbonated water. Pemberton named the concoction Coca-Cola and advertised it as the "Intellectual Beverage and Temperance Drink." His bookkeeper, Frank Robinson, a talented caligrapher, created the distinctive curved-letter logo.

Shortly before Pemeberton died, he sold the rights to his tonic to an Atlanta drugstore owner, Asa Candler, for $1,200. Candler was an astute businessman and expanded the distribution of the soft drink to soda fountain operators across the country. He sold nationwide bottling rights to two young Chattanooga attorneys, Benjamin Franklin Thomas and Joseph Brown Whitehead, for the sum of one dollar. Thomas and Whitehead eventually resold their franchise to a syndicate of three banks for $25 million. Robert Woodruff became president of Coca-Cola in 1923 and began establishing Coca-Cola bottling factories around the globe to supply American troops with "the pause that refreshes."

Throughout the company's history, the recipe for the Coca-Cola syrup has remained a carefully guarded secret passed between family members. The soft drink is produced by independent bottling companies operated under franchise agreements with the franchisor, nicknamed "Big Coke" by franchisees. A hallmark of the Coca-Cola franchise is an exclusive territory granted to the franchisee "in perpetuity."

Today, the Coca-Cola franchise empire is one of the most influential business organizations in the world. Although the company enjoys a 29 percent share of the U.S. soft drink market, 60 percent of the chain's sales originate from overseas franchises. "Big Coke" has even received applications for franchises on the moon.

The heart of the Coca-Cola franchise is its famous trade name and the secret recipe for the syrup. However, a franchise does not have to have a secret recipe, or even an exclusive product, to be successful. Most modern franchises are based on the "cookie-cutter" concept, known more formally as business format franchising.

Business Format Franchising

There is no better way to visualize a business format franchise than to study the world's most successful franchise system, McDonald's. Although much has been written about the McDonald's organization, many people do not realize that the company experienced a series of false starts, pitfalls, and failures before a successful franchise system finally was developed. In fact, the founders, Maurice and Richard McDonald, had very little to do with the chain's success and, at one point, decided not to sell franchises.

The McDonald brothers opened their first eatery, a drive-in restaurant, in Pasadena, California, in the late 1930s. With three uniformed carhops who served customers in their automobiles, the outlet sold not hamburgers but hot dogs. In 1940, the McDonalds opened a larger drive-in in nearby San Bernardino, with twenty carhops and parking for 125 cars. The new restaurant specialized in beef and pork sandwiches and hickory-smoked ribs.

By 1948, the brothers' success had exceeded their most ambitious expectations. However, the headaches of operating a congested drive-in facility left them with little time to enjoy their newfound riches. Exasperated, the McDonalds closed the lucrative restaurant and, three months later, reopened the outlet as a streamlined hamburger stand designed for high volume and speedy service. The outlet's advertising symbol was a cartoon cook named Speedy. The new system of hamburger preparation was dubbed the "Speedy Service System." By the mid-1950s, the San Bernardino outlet had become a virtual fast-food profit factory.

In 1952, the two brothers sold their first franchise to Neil Fox in Phoenix, Arizona. A local neon sign maker, George Dexter, came up with the final design for the huge, yellow arches that would become the restaurant's symbol for the succeeding three decades. Fox paid a fee of $1,000 for his franchise.

The cautious restaurant operators sold nine franchises before they began to have second thoughts about creating a hamburger chain. The idea of trekking across the country from one motel to another in search of restaurant managers did not appeal to either brother. Because their hearts were not in franchising, the expansion effort stalled.

In 1954, the San Bernardino outlet was visited by a malted milk machine salesman named Ray Kroc. Impressed by the assembly-line efficiency of the San Bernardino outlet, Kroc negotiated the rights to sell licenses for the brothers' Speedy Service System. McDonald's System, Inc. was incorporated on 2 March 1955.

Kroc surrounded himself with raw, hungry talent and guided the franchise chain to national prominence. Although his contract restricted him from altering the Speedy Service System in any way, Kroc unilaterally began to modify the McDonald's business format. As the chain proliferated, the relationship between Ray Kroc and the McDonald brothers began to sour. In 1961, the McDonalds sold Kroc all their interests in the hamburger business for $2.7 million, enough to pay each brother $1 million after taxes.

In 1963, the "Speedy" chef logo was replaced by "Archie McDonald," to avoid confusion with "Speedy Alka Seltzer." In December of the same year, Willard Scott, who had previously played Bozo the Clown on television, appeared as another clown, Ronald

McDonald, destined to be the hamburger chain's symbol for the next thirty years. In 1988, the company trotted out a new mascot, "McMan-in-the-Moon," in an attempt to appeal to more upscale, cosmopolitan consumers.

Despite numerous challenges by imitators, plagiarizers, and heavily financed competitors, the success of McDonald's in captivating the fast-food consumer remains unparalleled, with 9,500 outlets, including 2,300 located overseas.

What made McDonald's so successful? The McDonald brothers did not have a secret recipe or, for that matter, a unique product. Instead, they devised an assembly-line-style system for producing hamburgers. That system enabled the restaurant to maximize production while minimizing labor costs, thereby tripling profits. Still, the chain did not expand significantly until the distinctive McDonald's trademark was developed and the company invested heavily in media advertising.

Three elements were integral to the chain's phenomenal success: a refined business format, a recognizable trade name, and an ongoing support system for franchisees. By themselves, these components have a tangible value, yet without one other element they would still not be enough to create a successful franchise.

That element is know-how. A successful franchisor knows what to do — and what not to do — to succeed in a small business. The early failures of the McDonald brothers and the various problems encountered by Ray Kroc were invaluable lessons to franchisees opening new outlets. One important benefit of investing in a franchise is avoiding the trial-and-error pitfalls that doom most small businesses.

However, a franchise chain like McDonald's does not become successful just by providing franchisees with know-how, a business format, and a well-known product to sell. Without the ambition, drive, and entrepreneurial spirit of franchisees, no franchise chain could hope to succeed over the long haul.

Franchising and the Entrepreneur

The following case history illustrates the importance of the entrepreneurial spirit in franchising.

Mayo and Nick Boddie grew up during the Great Depression in Nash County, North Carolina. Their father, Nicholas, a tobacco and cotton farmer, was forced off his land in 1933. Before its sale, the family farm had dwindled from 10,000 acres to fewer than 700.

After a year in college, Mayo went to work for the elder Boddie, who had gone into the service station business, and Nick hired on with their aunt, who ran a small family hotel. In 1961, the two brothers pooled their savings to acquire several small businesses, including three gas stations, two laundromats, and a hotel.

The Boddies's accountant was an old schoolmate, Leonard Rawls, who also kept the books for Wilbur Hardee, who owned a hamburger restaurant in nearby Greenville. Rawls and an acquaintance, Jim Gardner, had negotiated the rights to franchise Hardee's system for selling fifteen-cent, charcoal-broiled hamburgers.

The Boddie brothers bought four Hardee's franchises. Their company, Boddie-Noell Enterprises, Inc. (BNEI), presently operates 208 franchise outlets in five states, grossing $210 million annually. Eventually, the Hardee's chain became one of the largest fast-food organizations in the world. The Boddie brothers are credited with much of that success.

As the story of the Boddie brothers illustrates, it is possible for a franchisee to become quite wealthy. In fact, some franchisees have become more successful than their franchisors. However, as the following case history points out, most people enter franchising to pursue a dream of independence and self-management.

Jack Peterson had worked for fourteen years as a regional sales representative for a major book publisher. Each year, he earned a substantial bonus in addition to his salary. When he had saved enough money, he decided to start a business of his own. After careful consideration, he invested in a franchise offered by an established printing chain.

At the time Jack signed the franchise agreement, the franchisor had over 1,300 outlets specializing in "quick-print" services. The chain was well known in the business community and advertised extensively on the radio, in business journals, and in major newspapers. If he had tried opening a print shop on his own, he would have had to invest a small fortune in advertising and promotion to attract customers. Instead, on the day Jack's outlet opened for business, customers began walking through the door.

Jack's franchise was up for renewal after ten years. During the first term, his average earnings were slightly less than what he had made as a sales representative. However, when ten years had passed, he did not hesitate to renew the franchise agreement. Furthermore, he did not regret one minute of his life as a franchisee. For Jack, the entrepreneurial freedom he enjoyed as an independent business owner was the most valuable reward of owning a franchise.

Jack Peterson's case is not unique. According to a Gallup Poll, 75 percent of existing franchisees believe their investments have met or exceeded their expectations. In the same survey, 75 percent also indicated that, if given the same opportunity, they would invest in the same franchise again.

As each of these case histories emphasizes, a key factor in the success of any franchise is the franchisee's entrepreneurial spirit.

When a franchise company recruits franchisees to join its organization, the franchisor is keenly interested in the applicant's personal ambition. As a rule, people who own their own businesses are more dedicated to success than are middle managers or department heads. That dedication translates into more satisfied customers and increased productivity. Franchising works for franchisors not just because it works for franchisees but also because franchisees work for *it*.

Someone who buys a franchise receives a business package that would otherwise take years to develop and refine. Franchisees also benefit from a strengthened ability to compete in the marketplace. Contributions collected from all the licensed outlets can be used to finance major advertising campaigns that an independent operator could never afford. From these campaigns, each franchisee derives the image and marketing power of an industry giant. In addition, a franchisee obtains collective purchasing power, the envied status of self-management, and the know-how to avoid the costly mistakes that doom most small-time operators.

But what about the franchisor? Why should a successful company hand out its trade secrets and put others in business for themselves?

A franchisor's motives are not much different from those of a franchisee. By franchising, a company gains the potential of building a business empire worth many millions from a relatively small investment. A franchisor receives ongoing royalty payments from the outlet's combined gross sales but may also produce revenues from selling supplies or equipment to franchisees.

The Regulatory Atmosphere

Despite the enormous influence of franchising today, buying a franchise was once a risky venture. Practically anyone with an idea for sale, where proved or not, could sell so-called franchises to eager, unsuspecting buyers. Many of these buyers ended up with little more than empty pockets and broken dreams.

As an example, consider the story of Mary Dearborn, who wanted to transform her hobby — fitness exercising — into a small business of her own. The idea first came to her when she saw an ad for a "franchise opportunity" in the back of a health magazine. The words "huge profits" were draped across the top of the ad in big, bold print, and a stream of dollar bills descended along both sides. She called the phone number at the bottom and talked to the "franchisor" in person. The suave, articulate salesman convinced her to mail a check for $3,000 to purchase an "opening inventory" of exercise equipment.

Three weeks later, a delivery agent dropped several boxes of unassembled parts in Mary's driveway. There were no assembly instructions, no sales training manuals, no business guides. She dialed the number in the ad to discover the "franchisor's" phone had been disconnected.

Overnight, Mary — and hundreds of other fitness enthusiasts — were each $3,000 poorer, with nothing but a garage full of useless parts to show for their investments. Because of such abuses, in 1980 the federal government stepped in to protect the public against fly-by-night scam artists by regulating the offer and sale of franchises.

In today's strict regulatory environment, franchisors must comply with a long list of disclosures and requirements. The Federal Trade Commission introduced extensive franchise reform in 1980. The FTC regulations were modeled after the 1971 California Franchise Investment Protection Law, which in turn was adapted from a paper created by a convention of Midwestern securities commissioners.

The first of the "full and accurate disclosure" laws governing franchise opportunities was passed by the California legislature in 1971. Today, thirteen states have similar laws on their books. Franchisors who sell franchises in these states must comply with a standardized format for disclosing information to prospective franchisees. A similar requirement is enforced by the Federal Trade Commission for all franchisors operating in the United States.

This disclosure format is called the Uniform Franchise Offering Circular, or UFOC. The UFOC is a document designed to inform prospective franchisees about the background of those offering the franchise and the mutual obligations created by the franchise ageement. In some states, this information must be filed with an agency responsible for monitoring franchises. A state regulator may have to approve the offering before it can be promoted to prospective franchise buyers.

The FTC requires franchisors in every state to provide a UFOC to prospective franchisees before the contract can be signed or any payment can be made. If a franchise salesman asks a prospect to pay a deposit before the prescribed time period has elapsed — and most assuredly, there are some who do — it may be in violation of state or federal law.

In most states with specific franchise laws, franchisors must also comply with the opinions of state-employed regulators. Such authorities have almost unlimited power over who may and may not do business in their states.

Even in unregulated states, a franchisor must follow the FTC's requirements for full and accurate disclosure in the form of a UFOC. A potential buyer may not be coerced, persuaded, or tricked into signing until all the facts have been disclosed and clarified.

Other regulations affect what happens after a contract is signed. In 1992, Iowa legislators enacted the Franchise Relationship Law, which gives franchisees specific rights above and beyond those stated in a franchise agreement. Among other things, the Iowa law requires franchisors to permit franchisees to transfer their ownership and restricts a franchisor's ability to locate additional outlets within an existing franchisee's market area. After the Iowa law was enacted, eighteen other states proposed similar legislation.

At the federal level, two new bills were introduced in the U.S. Congress in 1992. The first bill, titled the Franchise Disclosure and Consumer Protection Act, would require franchisors to disclose a range of specific information, including the potential earnings of a franchisee, in plain language. The second bill, titled the Federal Fair Franchise Practices Act, would prohibit a franchisor from terminating a franchisee's rights without a good business reason.

The International Franchise Association (IFA), a trade association of major franchisors, opposes all of the proposed state and federal laws. The IFA fears that complying with the new regulations would be costly to franchisors. People in favor of the regulations include unhappy investors who have lost money or businesses to a small group of unscrupulous franchisors.

It should be emphasized that the overwhelming majority of franchisors are honest, and only a small percentage of the franchise investments that are made each year result in complaints or lawsuits. Still, the number of disputes, abuses, and outright frauds continues to increase every year. Some legislators and attorneys argue that the present regulations do not go far enough to protect investors. Others insist that voluntary self-regulation of the franchising industry is preferable to enacting new laws.

Rules and regulations are but one aspect of a franchise investment. In the remaining chapters, we will examine the psychological, ethical, sociological, legal, and financial forces that make franchising work, while exploring the subtle, sometimes volatile, chemistry that governs the franchise formula.

Chapter Three

To Franchise or Not to Franchise

A Self-Evaluation

A franchisor of drycleaning stores received applications from two prospective franchisees who wanted to open an outlet in the same market area. One applicant, Robin L., had owned a drycleaning store before and knew a great deal about the business. The other applicant, William C., had recently retired from the armed services and had no previous experience in either drycleaning or business management. Robin was independent-minded and self-willed. He considered himself a leader, not a follower, and did not like taking instructions from other people. In contrast, William did not believe he could run a successful business without help. He was capable of leading others, but, to some extent, he also wanted to be led.

It may surprise you to learn that the franchise was awarded not to independent-minded Robin but to evenhanded William. The franchisor believed Robin would not be satisfied giving up a portion of his independence, whereas William actively sought the type of assistance the franchisor had to offer.

Although many people would like to be their own boss, not everyone who wants to own a business would make a successful franchisee.

If you buy a franchise, you will have to sacrifice some measure of your entrepreneurial independence. If you don't fancy yourself obeying a laundry list of mandatory policies and procedures, your experience in franchising will be an unhappy one.

Franchising is a bold and exhilarating adventure involving numerous decisions, both rational and emotional. If you are considering a franchise investment, you must recognize from the outset that such a decision is not an exclusively intellectual consideration. There is an emotional side to every important decision, particularly one that will so profoundly affect your life, career, and well-being, yet it is important to balance that emotional part against the purely rational aspects of where you are now, where you want to be in the future, and how you are going to get there.

As you listen to your brain, remember to give your heart equal time. No matter how logical a franchise choice might seem initially, unless you truly love the work, your commitment to success will be something less than total, and in a franchise, nothing less than total commitment will do. In any line of business, the perfect franchise is the one that best matches your personality, desires, abilities, and budget.

Most people considering a franchise investment ask the obvious question: Is franchising right for me? However, it is equally important to ask: Am I right for franchising? Despite franchising's track record of creating successful small business owners, it is not the perfect method of entrepreneurship for everybody. Not everyone who would like to invest in a franchise would make a good franchisee.

Before you embark on this bold adventure, devote some serious thought and time to self-evaluation. Exactly why should you consider franchising rather than making a go of it on your own? After all, 20 percent of independent business owners succeed on their own, and you might be one of them. Then again, maybe your personality, aptitudes, and skills more closely match those of America's half-million franchise owners.

After you sign a franchise agreement, your franchisor will call many of the shots. Can you live with the obligations and restrictions of a franchise agreement?

A franchisor will provide training and guidance, but you will also be saddled with an array of mandatory policies and procedures. However, as a franchisee, you will be an independent business owner, ultimately accountable for your own success or failure. Are you willing to shoulder this burden?

A good place to start your self-evaluation is to compare yourself with successful small business operators who have already made the franchise decision.

Who Invests in Franchises?

The traits of successful franchisees were the subject of a seven-year study by The Development Group, a consulting firm that works with franchise organizations. The consultants created a questionnaire designed to obtain demographic information about people who apply for franchises. This questionnaire became part of the franchise application sent out by The Development Group's client firms during the study period.

The consultants studied the questionnaires and compiled the table in Figure 3-1.

Figure 3-1

Sex	Male	76%
	Female	24%
Education	College graduate	64%
	High school graduate	34%
	Dropouts	2%
Marital status	Single	24%
	Married	76%
Income	Less than $20,000	8%
	$20,000 to $34,999	22%
	$35,000 to $49,999	36%
	$50,000 or more	34%
Previous managerial experience	Less than 1 year	12%
	1 to 5 years	58%
	5 years or more	30%

Previously owned a business	Never	44%
	Within last 5 years	42%
	Longer than 5 years ago	14%
Most important reason for investing in a franchise	Desire to be own boss	52%
	Increase earnings	38%
	Acquire training	6%
	Other	4%

The most interesting result from this study is that, for more than one-half of the applicants, the main reason for investing in a franchise is the desire to be one's own boss. Like Jack Peterson, the former book salesman who invested in a print shop franchise, they seek an opportunity for self-management and self-expression. Some may be frustrated with their current job and on the lookout for independence. Others may be pursuing a personal dream to own a successful business.

Many franchisees actually sacrifice a portion of their earnings potential as wage earners for the opportunity to own their own businesses. Some of the applicants in this study had good incomes before setting out on their own, yet decided on franchise opportunities that they knew would not earn them as good a living as their former occupations.

You might think: well, who wouldn't want to be his own boss? You may be surprised to find that many people would rather not have the headaches that come with the territory. Every platoon has only one commanding officer but many rank-and-file soldiers who would rather follow orders than formulate them. A franchisee is better suited to be a leader, but he is neither a private nor a general but rather something closer to a captain — capable of leading others but also capable of following the broad objectives and general guidance of a superior.

As you might guess, the second reason people invest in franchises is the quest for financial growth and, ultimately, riches. Many franchises are purchased strictly for investment purposes, like a diamond or security is bought for its speculative value. In fact, according to the Department of Commerce, about 15 percent of franchises have absentee owners — people who buy a franchise for its investment value but hire someone else to manage the business.

Of course, everyone who goes into business for himself or herself is pursuing a dream of financial independence and security. Someone who invests in a franchise most likely expects more from life than the seeming drudgery of a wage-earning career. He or she has a high level of ambition and an irrepressible belief that the rewards outweigh the risks. So, although money may not be the number-one consideration in the minds of franchise owners, it's still high on the list.

People also invest in franchises from a desire to be a winner. Most of us have a longing for a positive self-image and heightened self-esteem. Franchisees enjoy the identity of success and, through their tie-in with a large organization, the industry dominance that accompanies the business. In the seven-year study, one owner of a restaurant franchise said he gladly paid an "exorbitant" franchise fee because the franchisor was "dripping with success." Many people buy franchises in the hope that some of their franchisor's successful image will rub off on their small businesses.

People also invest in a franchise to obtain training and guidance from an experienced insider. Franchisees are more likely than other entrepreneurs to recognize their own limitations. They know it takes a broad range of insights and skills to develop a successful business. After all, who among us is a competent chief executive, industry expert, creative advertising executive, skilled financial officer, and experienced personnel director, all rolled into one?

Franchise buyers seek know-how and support in the crucial aspects of running a business, especially advertising, accounting, and industry practices. The owner of three hairstyling franchises reported that he wanted "a big head start — no pun intended." Asked why he invested in a franchise rather than simply opening his own hair salons, the entrepreneur responded, "I planned to open these salons anyway. With a franchise, I have at least a three-year head start."

A franchise is an asset of lasting value. Franchise businesses are commonly resold by the original owner, often for a substantial profit. Most independent businesses are lucky to survive five years, whereas a franchise agreement has an average term of ten years and is almost always renewable.

Another signficant finding of the seven-year study was a dramatic increase in the number of female franchisees between 1988 and 1992. During this period, the percentage of franchises owned by women more than doubled. This statistic points out the increasing importance of female entrepreneurs in franchising.

No matter what your gender, if you are motivated to be your own boss, want to build a business that will have a lasting value, and are willing to sacrifice a portion of your independence to obtain a competitive edge, you may be a prime candidate for a franchise investment. However, even with a franchisor's help, starting a business is not exactly a pleasure cruise. Before you take another step, you must take inventory of your mental, physical, and financial preparedness for the challenging tasks ahead.

Foster's Five F's

The personal ingredients for success in franchising can be summarized in five words beginning with the letter F:

- foresight
- flexibility
- fitness
- financing
- franchiseability

Ask yourself if you possess all — not just some — of these essential traits. The following case studies may help you determine the answer.

Foresight

Ellen Clark owns a highly profitable clothing store. She invested in a franchise after spending twelve years as a devoted housewife and mother, but even before she married, she envisioned herself someday owning a business in the fashion field. She worked part-time for a local department store, putting aside as much money as she could to help finance her dream. At first, she tried going it on her own. The first store Ellen opened failed after a few months, but she did not abandon her dream. She took another job, continued saving, and, together with her husband, obtained a second mortgage on their home. This time, she invested in a franchise from an established chain that had ties with major suppliers. Her new store was an unqualified success.

One reason Ellen finally succeeded was her foresight and planning, which, little by little, translated her dream into a reality. She clearly defined her objectives and goals and, whenever the occasion arose, took concrete steps to attain them.

Do you have a vision of where you would like to be five or ten years from now? Do you have a dream of owning your own business and being your own boss? Do you organize and plan for the future or merely take things as they come? Do you have the persistence and self-confidence it takes to succeed in your own business?

Flexibility

After working in advertising for eight years, Gerald Levitt invested in a franchise to open a portrait studio. He knew how to handle a camera, but when he attended his franchisor's three-week training course, he was asked to forget everything he knew about photography. He was taught that handling people was the most important part of the portrait business. He had never supervised people before and had to learn a great deal about hiring, training, and motivating employees.

To operate his business successfully, Gerald was forced to accept some very basic changes in his environment — changes in his attitude, point of view, personal acquaintances, and daily routine. Also, he had to be willing to learn new concepts and adopt new ideas.

Do you accept change readily and willingly? Do you adapt well to new people in your environment? Are you sensitive to the needs and desires of other people, or are you mainly concerned about your own well-being? Are you willing and able to learn new concepts and techniques?

Fitness

Lewis Markoff thought starting his own computer store would be a snap. He certainly had the initiative; he had always been willing to work long hours with minimal supervision. Furthermore, in over ten years he had not missed a day of work due to illness. After signing a franchise agreement, he quit his job and set about developing his new store. Lewis had always believed the best way to accomplish things was to do everything himself. He worked seven days a week, twelve to eighteen hours a day, often skipping meals. Nothing was more important to him than getting his business off the ground. The day his computer store was scheduled to open, Lewis became seriously ill. He spent the entire Grand Opening week in the hospital, suffering from pneumonia.

Lewis had not taken into consideration the fact that major life changes often cause hidden mental and physical stress. His neglecting to eat, sleep, exercise, and relax properly was an open invitation to a serious illness.

Can you handle the stress that occurs with starting a new business? Are you in excellent health, both physically and mentally? Do you have a healthy life-style balanced by proper nutrition, regular exercise, and planned periods of relaxation?

Franchiseability

Mark Lacey had run his own bookkeeping business for ten years before he signed a franchise agreement with a company famous for preparing tax returns. In the past, Mark had usually been able to make ends meet, but his business was hindered by an unexpected downturn in the economy. He hoped a famous trademark would attract enough extra clients to keep him in business for himself. The franchisor provided Mark with a franchise operating manual packed with policies and procedures. Feeling he already knew enough about the business, Mark put the manual aside.

Six months later, a franchise representative questioned Mark about certain deductions he had entered on a client's tax return. "It's none of your business," Mark replied angrily. When the franchisor demanded to inspect his financial records, Mark refused to cooperate with the auditor. Not long after that, his franchise was terminated, and lawsuits were filed on both sides.

Needless to say, neither party benefited from this short and unhappy affair. In this instance, the relationship unraveled because Mark wasn't "franchiseable."

Are you willing up to give up at least a portion of your independence in return for the benefits of a franchise? Do you have the leadership abilities and "people" skills it takes to succeed? Are you willing to learn, or do you think you're too old or too experienced to be taught anything new? Are you receptive to the advice and opinions of others, or do you usually think you know more than everyone else?

Financing

Glenda Meyer wanted to be her own boss. It wasn't so much that she was frustrated in her current job; what she really wanted was to start a business in a field in which she had a keen personal interest. She was looking for a way to transform her hobby into a successful business. She had the desire, the will, the personal courage. What she didn't have was any spare cash to invest. However, she knew there was money available for new businesses. She borrowed some money from a relative and applied for a small business loan from her bank. She also found a franchisor that was willing to finance part of the investment.

It took Glenda seven years to pay off all the money she had borrowed. The payments were so high that there was barely enough money after expenses to pay herself a small salary. At one point, she considered closing or selling the business. Gathering her courage, she decided to stick it out. She has now paid off all her debts and is the owner of a successful interior decorating store.

The reason Glenda finally succeeded is because she managed to obtain adequate financing. Besides the money to open the store, she also needed enough to support herself until the business began to turn a profit. According to the Department of Commerce, the main reason most new businesses fail is inadequate financing.

How do you propose to finance your business? Can you handle the risk of failure? Will you need financial assistance, and, if so, where will you find it? Will you be able to obtain additional financing if you should need more later on?

Evaluating Your Mental Preparedness

Mental preparedness involves more than a desire to be your own boss or the willingness to shoulder responsibility. It also involves some more elusive traits, such as your level of self-confidence, your individual resourcefulness, and your overall attitude about people.

The following self-test may help you sort out your mental preparedness for investing in a franchise. Answer each question as frankly as possible (the only person you can cheat is yourself). Each possible answer has an assigned point value, which is shown in the scoring table at the end. To determine your total score, add up the point values of all the answers you selected. For example, for question 1, give yourself 2 points if you answered "A" or 6 points if you answered "B." Then read the interpretation that corresponds to your score.

Are You Mentally Prepared for Franchising?

1. True or false? Bosses have more headaches than their employees.
   a. True
   b. False
2. True or false? There is no reward without risk.
   a. True
   b. False
3. How often is your work the main topic of conversation at the dinner table?
   a. Often
   b. Occasionally
   c. Never
4. How upset are you when your work is performed well but nobody seems to notice?
   a. Very upset
   b. Somewhat upset
   c. Not upset in the least
5. Do you feel that you do more work in less time than other people or do more than your share?
   a. Yes
   b. No
6. How often do you feel that you could do your boss's job better than he or she?
   a. Often
   b. Occasionally
   c. Never
7. How would you characterize your work habits?
   a. I am meticulously organized.
   b. I am generally quite organized.
   c. I'm sloppy, but who has time to organize?

8. Would you call yourself a perfectionist?
   a. Yes
   b. No
9. When you are solving a problem or carrying out a job, how do you go about handling it?
   a. I forge ahead without stopping until the problem is solved or until the job is finished.
   b. I dedicate myself to the task when things are going smoothly but know when to stop if the going gets rough.
   c. I have too many problems to solve or too many jobs to do to do any of them the way I think they should be done.
10. How willing are you to stake your savings on a business of your own?
    a. Totally willing
    b. Somewhat willing
    c. Not very willing
11. How long does it take you to adapt to a new boss, a new employee, or new coworkers?
    a. I readily accept new people and changing conditions in my work environment.
    b. It takes a while, but eventually I accept change.
    c. I have difficulty accepting new people and changing working conditions.
12. How would you describe your attitude about people in general?
    a. I enjoy working with people, and they seem to enjoy working with me.
    b. I get along with most people and have relatively few enemies.
    c. There are more important things in life than pleasing other people.
13. How do you feel about working on a project by yourself?
    a. I prefer having total responsibility for a project.
    b. I like tackling projects alone but with some advice and assistance from others.
    c. I would rather work on a project as a member of a team, given clear and specific instructions.

14. How would you react if you started a business and it failed?
    a. I would learn from my mistakes and start over from scratch.
    b. It would set me back temporarily, but eventually I'd recover.
    c. I'm not a gambler; I never make a move if there's a risk of failure.
15. How do you feel about hard work?
    a. I'd rather supervise hard work than take it on myself.
    b. I'm not allergic to hard work, but I'd just as soon avoid it, if possible.
    c. I enjoy my work and believe that worthwhile results can be achieved only through serious effort.
16. How much experience have you had as a manager, supervisor, teacher, or trainer?
    a. Five years or more
    b. From one to five years
    c. Less than a year
    d. None
17. Have you ever owned a business?
    a. Yes
    b. No
18. Do you feel you need more income to achieve your personal goals?
    a. Yes
    b. No
19. If you started a business, how would your family and friends react?
    a. They would be supportive, and, if possible, I would try to involve them in the business.
    b. At first, they would resent it if I devoted too much time to a business, but eventually they would adjust.
    c. My desire to succeed in business is more important to me than my family or friends.

20. How would you feel about going back to school at your present age and employment level?
    a. I would rather be making money on the job than wasting time in a classroom.
    b. I might be uncomfortable, but I would do whatever was necessary to pass the course.
    c. I would enjoy the opportunity to learn new ideas, concepts, and techniques.

Scoring

1. A-2 B-6
2. A-6 B-2
3. A-5 B-2 C-1
4. A-5 B-2 C-1
5. A-6 B-2
6. A-5 B-2 C-1
7. A-4 B-3 C-1
8. A-5 B-3
9. A-5 B-2 C-1
10. A-5 B-2 C-1
11. A-5 B-2 C-1
12. A-5 B-2 C-1
13. A-3 B-4 C-1
14. A-4 B-3 C-1
15. A-1 B-2 C-5
16. A-3 B-2 C-1 D-0
17. A-5 B-3
18. A-6 B-2
19. A-6 B-4 C-0
20. A-0 B-2 C-6

Interpretation

84–101 *Full speed ahead!*
You have the entrepreneurial spirit, self-confidence, flexibility, and perspective to be a successful franchisee. You're exactly the type of individual that most franchisors are looking for. What's more, you have many of the same attitudes and ideals that characterize people who are successful in business.

69–83 *Look both ways before crossing the street!*
You do have many of the attributes that typify people who succeed in a franchise business, but be careful to select a franchise that is backed by a well-established organization with a strong track record. Let your decision be guided by the franchisor's ability to lead the way and assist you in every aspect of the business.

25–68 *Proceed with caution!*
Your level of self-esteem, ambition, and flexibility could use some improvement before you leap into a franchise investment. But that doesn't necessarily exclude you from the field. Ask yourself if you'll really be happier shouldering the responsibilities of owning your own business and risking your financial future. If, after reading this book, you're convinced that franchising is right for you, prepare yourself psychologically for the hard work, dedication, and effort that it will take to succeed.

Evaluating Your Physical Preparedness

Aside from the obvious question of your present physical health, other factors are also involved in your physical preparedness for a franchise. One of the most important is stress.

Major life changes make the body susceptible to physical illness. An individual experiencing a number of major life events in rapid succession has a higher risk of succumbing to a major illness than do other people. Changes such as the death of a family member, a divorce or separation, accidental injury, a job change, or departure of a family member from the household all contribute to personal stress. Less profound changes affect us, too: vacation activities, changes in social activities and acquaintances, changes in living conditions, and changes in our financial situations.

The influence of job and work is an important factor in both mental and physical health. Getting a new job or leaving an old one, trouble with the boss or others in the company, deadlines, pressures, and problems provide a constant stream of stressors and anxieties.

The effect of life changes on physical health was the subject of an investigation by Adolf Meyer, a psychiatrist at Johns Hopkins Medical School. Dr. Meyer charted the social changes of his patients to see if there was a relationship between life events and illness. His charts revealed that his patients' illnesses generally coincided with major events in their personal lives.

This trend was confirmed by a behavioral scientist at Cornell University, Harold Wolff. In a study of 5,000 patients, he found that just before a major illness, there was a series of major life changes. The changes plotted by Dr. Meyer and Dr. Wolff included job-related stressors and social changes ranging from getting a traffic ticket to changing jobs.

Leaving a job to start a new business is by itself a significant source of stress. Conducting a franchise search, negotiating a contract, and arranging financing will compound the potential effects on your physical well-being.

There are many ways to cope with stress effectively. Sound nutrition is one of the most important. People who handle stress effectively get to bed early enough the night before work to enjoy proper rest but avoid oversleeping. They get up early and eat a leisurely breakfast. They manage their time effectively and schedule their workday to leave room for unforeseen developments. They take breaks, get a nutritious lunch away from the workplace, and stop working at a reasonable hour. They also set aside time for rest and recreation.

People who are best able to cope with stress have a good support system made up of family and friends. They also have hobbies and social interests outside their jobs. They exercise regularly, maintain a stable weight, and have a nutritious diet.

Take a few minutes to answer the questions in the following self-test designed to gauge your physical preparedness for investing in a franchise and starting a new business.

Are You Physically Prepared to Handle the Stress of Starting a Franchise Business?

1. How do you manage your time?
   a. I manage my time effectively and feel a sense of accomplishment.
   b. I try to be organized, but sometimes my schedule is disrupted by unexpected crises.
   c. I take things as they come.
2. How would you describe your sleeping habits?
   a. I often stay awake at night solving problems or thinking about work.
   b. I fall asleep quickly and get enough sound, satisfying sleep each night.
   c. I go to bed late and get up early, but I rarely get sleepy during the day.
3. In the last month, have you had a serious disagreement with your boss?
   a. Yes
   b. No
4. Has your financial situation changed much, either for better or worse, in the last six months?
   a. Yes
   b. No
5. Were you fired from your last job?
   a. Yes
   b. No
6. Have you changed your working hours in the last ninety days?
   a. Yes
   b. No
7. Have you changed jobs or been given new or different responsibilities in the last six months?
   a. Yes
   b. No
8. How health-conscious are you in your daily life?
   a. I follow the rules of good health and nutrition.
   b. I sometimes exercise and try to eat properly, but I often skip meals.
   c. Who has the time to exercise or eat properly?

9. Do you do more work or less work than other people in the company with similar responsibilities?
   a. More
   b. Less
   c. About the same

10. If you went to a party, would most of the people there be
    a. people you know because of your job
    b. people you know outside your job

11. How do you feel about your relationships with others?
    a. I work to make my personal relationships harmonious and satisfying.
    b. I have a limited social life, but I basically like people.
    c. Life isn't a popularity contest.

12. Has any member of your immediate family been taken seriously ill or been seriously injured in the last six months?
    a. Yes
    b. No

13. Have you taken out a bank loan or a mortgage in the last three months?
    a. Yes
    b. No

14. Do you have mostly different friends now than before you went to work?
    a. Yes
    b. No

15. Have you experienced any sexual difficulties in the last three months?
    a. Yes
    b. No

16. Have you disagreed with your spouse, roommate, or best friend over any financial or household matters in the last three months?
    a. Yes
    b. No

17. Do you ever have more than one alcoholic drink per day?
    a. Often
    b. Sometimes
    c. Never

18. Do you have a doctor's prescription for a tranquilizer, sedative, or sleeping pill?
    a. Yes
    b. No
19. Do you work toward your personal goals at least some time each day?
    a. Yes
    b. No
20. How do you cope with the stress in your life?
    a. I recognize the stressors in my life and use effective methods for dealing with them.
    b. I know when I am experiencing stress, but I am usually too busy to do anything about it.
    c. I have never really thought about it.

Scoring

1. A-0 B-2 C-5
2. A-5 B-2 C-0
3. A-5 B-1
4. A-5 B-1
5. A-5 B-1
6. A-5 B-1
7. A-5 B-1
8. A-0 B-2 C-5
9. A-5 B-3 C-1
10. A-5 B-1
11. A-0 B-2 C-5
12. A-5 B-1
13. A-5 B-1
14. A-5 B-1
15. A-5 B-1
16. A-5 B-1
17. A-5 B-2 C-0
18. A-5 B-1
19. A-1 B-5
20. A-0 B-3 C-5

Interpretation

71–100 *Somebody call an ambulance!*
You're not listening to your body's stress signals. Change your life-style by learning to relax and take better care of yourself. It is important to realize that it is impossible to eliminate stress from one's life. However, with conscientious effort, the negative effects on health and well-being can be reduced. You're worth the effort.

35–70 *En garde!*
You're not a walking time bomb, but keep your guard up. Beware of health-threatening life events and changes. Work hard but learn to relax. Follow the rules of good health and nutrition. Be sure you manage your time effectively and have interests outside your work.

14–34 *Congratulations!*
You are treating your body very well. You are probably rewarded by good health, but give yourself some praise anyway. Keep up the good work!

Evaluating Your Financial Preparedness

Besides being mentally and physically prepared, you must also be prepared to handle the financial obligations of buying a franchise and sustaining the business until it becomes profitable.

Financial preparedness doesn't mean you have to have a large capital sum to invest in a franchise. Many franchisors offer financial assistance. Moreover, numerous third parties, such as banks, venture capital groups, and small business investment companies, may be able to help you finance the investment.

Still, you must be ready to accept the financial responsibility. Investing in a franchise may minimize your risk, but as in any business venture, there is a chance of failure. If your new business should fail despite your best efforts and those of your franchisor, would you be able to recover? If you cannot answer "yes" to this question, you're not financially prepared for a franchise investment.

The degree of financial readiness that will be required depends on many factors, including the nature of the business you have in mind. After you have identified one or more franchises as potential investments, refer to the guidelines in Chapter Eight to determine how much financing is required — and how much you can realistically expect to earn.

Before you begin your search, ask yourself the following questions:

What is the maximum investment I am willing to undertake, including possible financial assistance from someone else?

Am I willing to sign a personal guarantee for a business loan or other financial assistance?

What is the type and amount of collateral I have available to back a loan request?

If I don't have enough collateral, am I willing to give up a share of ownership in the business to a partner or investor?

Will I have to focus my search exclusively on franchisors who offer financial assistance?

What is the maximum investment I can handle without financial assistance?

Chapter Four

A Balance of Power

The Anatomy of a Franchise

To most people, a franchise is a place where double-decker hamburgers or Southern-fried drumsticks are served from behind a brightly lit counter. Technically, a fast-food restaurant is not a franchise at all, but rather a franchise outlet. In this case, the term *franchise* refers to the right or privilege to conduct a particular type of business. The outlet's owner receives this privilege by purchasing a franchise from the franchisor, a company that sells franchises to qualified entrepreneurs.

As an example, consider someone who purchases a franchise to open a Holiday Inn hotel. The franchisor, a British company named Bass, owns the Holiday Inn trademark along with all the plans, blueprints, designs, and operating methods associated with a Holiday Inn hotel. To own and operate a Holiday Inn, an investor must first obtain a franchise from Bass. The investor, who is called the franchisee, pays a fee to the franchisor and puts up the money to build the hotel. In return, the franchisor permits the investor to use the company's trademarks, plans, blueprints, and signs and puts the franchisee through a training program.

Franchises are not limited to the hotel and food service industries. Retail stores, amusement parks, auto repair shops, car rental agencies, real estate companies, banks, travel agencies, and trade schools all can be opened and operated under franchises granted by large chains.

In a technical sense, franchising is the practice of granting franchises in conjunction with standardized operating, marketing, or management methods. In a tradename-only franchising, a franchisor grants only the right to sell a trademarked product or service. In contrast, a business-format franchise involves a combination of a trademark, a training program, an operations manual, systematic management procedures, and other "significant control or assistance" by the franchisor.

In 1986, the International Franchise Association (IFA) commissioned John Naisbitt, the author of *Megatrends,* to conduct a study on franchising trends. The author concluded that tradename-only and product franchising has declined steadily since 1972, while business-format franchising has increased. His list of the ten most popular formats included restaurants, nonfood retail outlets, lodging establishments, convenience markets, business services, automotive products and services, retail food outlets, car rental agencies, construction and home improvement outlets, and recreational and travel services.

Components of a Franchise

A modern business format franchise has four basic components:

- an identity, usually based on a registered trademark
- an operating system or business format, consisting of specifications, quality standards, and prescribed products or methods of operation
- a support system, usually consisting of training and ongoing assistance with marketing, advertising, purchasing, and other operational aspects of the business
- a continuous financial relationship, usually a lump sum paid in advance plus an ongoing royalty based on an established percentage of gross revenues

The identity and business format are normally owned by the franchisor. In some cases, a franchise opportunity may be based on marketing rights to an exclusive product rather than a business format. The franchisee is an independent business owner who contracts with the franchisor to obtain the right to put these components to use. The franchisee provides the working capital to establish and develop the outlet. In many franchise opportunities, the difference between success or failure lies in the ongoing services provided to franchisees.

Here's how the International Franchise Association defines a franchise:

> JFA franchise is a continuing relationship between franchisor and franchisee in which the sum total of the franchisor's knowledge, image, success, manufacturing, and marketing techniques are supplied to the franchisee for a consideration.

The franchisee pays a financial consideration to the franchisor and invests the money required to start the business. The franchisor supplies an optimized business system or exclusive product, a recognizable identity, and know-how. The franchisee must usually abide by the franchisor's quality standards and product specifications, yet, despite this relationship, a franchisor and a franchisee are not legal business partners. The franchisee is the exclusive owner of the business.

In many cases, purchasing a franchise means acquiring a prepackaged business. However, although the franchisee owns all the assets, the franchisor may have a strong voice in how the business is run. The cornerstone of every franchise is a contract that defines the rights and obligations of the franchisor and the franchisee.

Business Format Franchises

A typical business format franchise has the following components:

- licensed trademark
- training program
- operations manual
- specifications, blueprints, and designs
- advertising systems
- ongoing assistance

Licensed Trademark

The franchisee receives the right to use the franchisor's trademark, name, logo, or other commercial symbol, thus taking advantage of the parent company's reputation and image. For example, a franchisee licensed to use the McDonald's trademark benefits from major national television advertising and the image of an industry giant.

Training Program

The franchisee receives training in operating the franchise business, usually at the franchisor's headquarters or at a designed site. Industrywide, franchise training programs range from two days to six months. A typical curriculum consists of the following subjects: industry background; outlet development; accounting, purchasing, and inventory methods; product preparation, manufacturing, or merchandising; sales and marketing; advertising and promotion; and staff hiring and training. Additional technical or industry-specific training may also be offered, depending on the business and the franchise.

Refresher courses, periodic seminars, and annual conferences may also be offered by the franchisor.

Operations Manual

The franchisor's trade secrets, know-how, and experience are usually documented in a confidential operations manual loaned to franchisees for the term of the franchise. A good manual includes detailed policies, procedures, and techniques for starting and developing the outlet, ordering initial supplies and inventory pricing and merchandising, preparing or selling products, outlet management, hiring and training staff, personnel policies, bookkeeping techniques, and technical aspects of the business.

Many franchise operations manuals are divided into series, with separate volumes devoted to daily operating procedures, management policies, marketing and advertising, technical operations, and so forth.

Specifications, Blueprints, and Designs

Franchisors often provide specifications and designs for building and operating the outlet. Examples include architectural plans, construction blueprints, and designs for fixtures and signs. Franchisors may also provide approved supplier lists, suggested or mandatory opening inventory lists, and detailed specifications for equipment and ingredients, where applicable.

Food service franchisors commonly provide franchisees with secret recipes or ingredients, such as premade dough for bakery goods or patented syrups for bottled soft drinks.

Advertising Systems

More than half of franchisors administer or provide for a cooperative advertising fund, to which franchisees contribute a small percentage of their outlets' gross revenues. This pool is generally used to finance major national or regional campaigns to the benefit of all franchisees.

Franchisors may also assist individual outlet owners through the preparation of standard advertising materials, such as fliers, commercials, or camera-ready artwork for newspaper or magazine advertisements. Most franchise agreements force franchisees to abide by their franchisors' advertising standards and to use only artwork and language approved by the franchisors' advertising departments.

Ongoing Assistance

A typical business format franchise includes provisions for ongoing assistance, such as on-site troubleshooting and guidance by a field manager or consultant. Franchisees may also have access to company advisers via a toll-free "hotline."

As franchisors improve their business systems and operating methods, they invariably share innovations with their franchisees or upgrade the image of their outlets.

The Legal Definition of a Franchise

Various federal regulations and state laws include the word *franchise*. However, the word may have a different meaning depending on the regulation or law. The federal definition of a franchise is found in Federal Trade Commission Rule 436.2, Paragraph 6160, as follows:

> (a) The term "franchise" means any continuing commercial relationship created by any arrangement or arrangements whereby . . . a person offers, sells, or distributes to any person . . . goods, commodities, or services which are: (1) identified by a trademark, service mark, trade name, advertising or other commercial symbol . . . or (2) directly or indirectly required or advised to meet the quality standards prescribed by another person where the franchisee operates under a name using the trademark, service mark, trade name, advertising or other commercial symbol.

What does this mean in plain English? The first component is a trademark, logo, or name that is owned by the franchisor and licensed to the franchisee. For example, a franchisee who acquires a franchise from McDonald's Corporation receives the right to put up a McDonald's sign on the restaurant. Likewise, other franchisees receive the right to operate under such well-known trade names as Kentucky Fried Chicken, Hertz, or Hilton.

The second component is a set of quality standards. For example, a fast-food franchisor usually sets standards relating to the cleanliness of the outlet and the grooming of employees.

The federal definition of a franchise also includes the following qualification:

> The franchisor exerts or has the authority to exert a significant degree of control over the franchisee's method of operation, including but not limited to, the franchisee's business organization, promotional activities, management, marketing plan or business affairs; or (2) the franchisor gives significant assistance to the franchisee in the latter's method of operation.

Thus, a franchise must also involve "a significant degree of control" and "significant assistance" by the franchisor. A franchisor may exert control by setting mandatory procedures, product specifications, and so forth. A franchisor may provide assistance in the form of a training program, an operations manual, and ongoing help with advertising, inventory planning, and purchasing.

The third component of a franchise under the FTC definition is a continuous financial relationship, explained as follows:

> The franchisee is required as a condition of obtaining or commencing the franchise operation to make a payment or a commitment to pay to the franchisor, or to a person affiliated with the franchisor.

Simply stated, any business relationship or opportunity is legally a franchise if it includes a trademark license, quality standards, management controls, operating assistance, and a fee.

A Valued Identity

Foremost, a franchisor offers its good name in the industry. A successful identity is one of the hallmarks of a franchise offering. Therefore, the franchisor must be capable of substantiating its value.

Much of the value of a franchise identity is derived from the recognition, reputation, and goodwill of the franchise organization. People buy products from vendors that are familiar to them.

Likewise, people who invest in franchises are looking for a successful image. If you take on a franchise, your franchisor's identity, in effect, will become your identity. You may be John Smith or Jane Doe when you sign the franchise agreement, but when the sign outside your business lights up for the first time, you'll suddenly become Mr. Pizza Parlor, Ms. Computer Store, or Mr. and Mrs. Car Rental Agency.

Trademarks are protected on both federal and local levels. Federal protection is secured by registering a trademark with the Registrar of Patents and Trademarks. Before a trademark is registered at the federal level, a search is conducted to ascertain whether the same trademark has been previously registered by another party. If no prior registration is found, the trademark recieves "applied for" status, permitting the applicant to use the symbol "TM" in association with the trademark. A one-year waiting period, in which the trademark may be contested by others, is required before the trademark is officially "registered," and the owner may use the ® symbol in conjunction with the trademark.

Trademarks are often registered at the state or county level as well. In disputes over trademark rights, the earliest registration, whether local or federal, generally applies in a particular locality. For example, even though a trademark may be registered at the federal level, another party who obtained a local registration for the same trademark on an earlier date may be entitled to trademark in his or her locality.

A section of the Uniform Franchise Offering Circular (UFOC) is devoted to trademarks and trade names. In Section 13 of that document, franchisors are required to describe "any trademark, service mark, trade name, logotype or other commercial symbols to be licensed to the franchisee." Each mark, name, logo, or symbol that the franchisee will be entitled to use must be identified. In addition, the UFOC must state whether any of the trademarks and service marks have been registered with the United States Patent and Trademark Office or whether an application for registration is pending.

A license to use a trademark or trade name does not, by itself, constitute a franchise, but a trademark license is an integral element of any franchise relationship. The name must be exclusive, but it may apply either to the products distributed by the franchisee or to the business itself.

Control and Assistance

Typically, the types of control and assistance exerted by a franchisor include an exclusive territory, training in the operation of the business, site selection or approval, streamlined production or selling techniques, personnel policies, assistance with advertising and promotion, and quality standards. Such controls and assistance are often referred to as "a community of interest" between the franchisor and franchisee.

The franchise agreement, the formal contract between the franchisor and the franchisee, spells out the rights and obligations of both parties. For example, the franchise agreement may obligate the franchisor to provide a training program and restrict the franchisee from owning another business that competes directly with the franchise outlet.

The franchisor's advice, specifications, and quality standards may be contained in a publication called the franchise operating manual. Among other subjects, a typical operating manual covers bookkeeping practices, maintenance procedures, sales techniques, advertising policies, personnel hiring and training, inventory control, and purchasing.

The franchise operating manual is the franchisor's "bible." It documents the business format and sets forth the standards and policies that all franchisees are expected to follow.

One of the most important considerations of a franchise opportunity is the ease with which the business format can be transferred to the franchisee. If you buy a franchise, you will acquire more than just a trademark; ideally, you will obtain a finely tuned business system.

Some franchisors go so far as to provide a complete "turnkey" business; in such a case, when you graduate from franchise training school, you will receive a fully developed outlet. However, it is more common for a franchisor to provide blueprints, manuals, specifications, and training, relying on the franchisee's initiative to get the business established.

The franchisor usually loans the operating manual to the franchisee for the term of the franchise agreement. On expiration or termination of the franchise, the book must be returned to the franchisor. This requirement helps to protect the franchisor's trade secrets and maintain the aura of secrecy about the business system. After all, if the formula weren't secret, why would you pay good money to obtain it?

Fees and Payments

In return for the franchisor's valued identity and finely tuned operating system, the franchisee pays a fee. Typically, franchise fees are of three types:

- an initial fee, due on signing the franchise agreement
- an ongoing royalty charged on the gross revenues of the outlet
- other royalties or fees for advertising, consultation, or other assistance

A new franchise opportunity or a franchise offered by a small chain may charge a relatively low initial fee. Conversely, the larger the chain, the more you can expect to pay for the privilege of joining. For example, the first Burger King franchises sold for as little as $300, and the first McDonald's franchisee paid an initial fee of just $1,000. Today, a franchisee might pay as much as $30,000 for either of these franchises.

Why is an established franchise more valuable than a new one? For one thing, an experienced franchisor has a demonstrated track record. For another, the sheer number of outlets maximizes such collective benefits as cooperative advertising and volume purchasing.

Note that, in the FTC definition, a business relationship is not a franchise unless a financial consideration is paid by the franchisee. Specifically, the total payment or obligation during the first six months of the franchisee's operation must be more than $500. If this condition is not met, the arrangement is not a true franchise under FTC requirements and thus might be exempt from at least a portion of the federal rules.

Franchising by Any Other Name

When is a franchise not a franchise? And when is a so-called business opportunity really a franchise offering? In some cases, investments that are promoted as franchises do not have all the essential components. The term *franchise* implies backing, support, and a strong likelihood of success, yet many so-called franchise offerings are little more than trade name licenses or highly priced sales territories. Do these types of offerings fall under franchise regulation?

Some states, such as California, consider an investment offering to be a franchise whenever the word *franchise* is used in promotion. But what about the carefully named "business opportunity" that seems to have the components of a franchise but is promoted as a completely different type of investment?

A franchise does not have to be called a franchise to come within the scope of state laws or federal regulations. In fact, franchise regulators in some states spend the greater part of their time investigating franchiselike opportunities in order to identify unethical operators attempting to skirt the law.

In most states that regulate franchise sales, any business that sells the right to a trade name or business format and receives a payment for that right is a franchise, no matter what term the promoter may use to describe the investment. Be wary of any promoter who claims not to be a franchisor but offers you the right to use a trade name for a fee.

The FTC considers any business relationship to be a franchise if the following qualifications are met:

- The franchisee is obligated to sell goods or services supplied by the franchisor or to purchase supplies from vendors designated by the franchisor.
- The franchisor selects a site for the outlet, establishes a territory, or solicits customers for the franchisee.
- The franchisee pays a fee of more than $500 within six months after the franchise business has opened.

This requirement covers such businesses as product distributors and vending machine routes, even though a trademark is not included in the arrangement. If a business relationship involves any form of "significant control or assistance," such as a marketing plan, operating manual, or training program, the federal franchise rules apply.

Exemptions to the Rules

Both federal and state rules and laws exempt certain types of business relationships and enterprises from the franchise regulations. At the federal level, these exceptions include employer-employee relationships, general partnerships, cooperative associations, and departments within a department store.

In addition, a franchise that accounts for no more than 20 percent of the gross sales of the franchise holder is also exempt from FTC rules. This type of franchise is called a "fractional" franchise. For example, a franchise to sell flavored ice within a convenience store would be exempted if the receipts were no more than 20 percent of the store's total revenues.

Different exemptions are granted by various states. For example, California law exempts gasoline service stations and bank credit card services.

Evaluating the Components of a Franchise

If you begin to search for an ideal franchise business, you will probably be startled by the dramatic variation in the level of image, refinement, and sophistication among franchise organizations. Some franchisors will seem aggressive, organized, and professional. Others may strike you as methodical, plodding, and rough-edged. Still others may come across as slick, rigid, or too anxious to close a deal.

Remember that the franchise decision has three aspects: rational, emotional, and financial. The following worksheet will help you organize your thoughts, keep the franchise search in perspective, and refrain from making a costly mistake:

Franchise Identity

Is the trade name sufficiently well known to attract customers?

If the identity is not well known, is it catchy or unique enough to justify buying a franchise?

Is the name so similar to another business name or trademark that it might cause confusion?

Is anyone else already using the same name or a similar trademark in your market area? If so, can you obtain the right to use the name or trademark from the party already using it? How much will it cost?

Is the image of the business conducive to your own personality and self-image?

How do you feel about becoming the "owner" or "president" of this business?

Control and Assistance

Does the franchisor offer a training program? If so, how long is it? What topics are covered?

Will the franchisor help you select a site for the business?

Will the franchisor provide a franchise operating manual? If so, which of the following subjects are included?

    ___ grand opening

    ___ setting up books and records

    ___ accounting and reports

— advertising and publicity
— purchasing and inventory
— marketing and sales
— daily operating procedures
— cleanliness and grooming
— employee policies and procedures
— technical information

Will the franchisor provide predesigned signs, menus, fixtures, decorations, etc.? If not, will the franchisor help you procure these items from reliable suppliers?

Will the franchisor help you purchase equipment, supplies, or inventory at a discount? Is it really a discount?

Will you be required to purchase products or supplies only from suppliers designated by the franchisor?

What controls will the franchisor impose on the daily operation of the business?
— business or working hours
— use of advertising and signs
— outlet maintenance and appearance
— employee grooming or uniforms
— bookkeeping and banking procedures

Will you be restricted from selling to customers outside a designated territory?

Will you be restricted from owning another business or selling other types of products?

Does the assistance promised by the franchisor outweigh the restrictions and controls?

Fees and Payments

How much is the initial fee?

Does the initial fee vary from one location to another? If so, what is the amount of the fee for the location or territory you have in mind?

How does the initial fee compare to that paid by other franchisees in the same industry?

How much is the ongoing royalty? Is it a fixed amount or a set percentage?

Does the franchisor charge a cooperative advertising royalty in addition to the basic franchise royalty?

Is the cooperative advertising royalty fixed for the entire term of the franchise, or can it be raised or lowered in the future?

Who will determine how advertising royalties are spent — the franchisor or the franchisees?

What other types of royalties or fees are charged?

    __ consulting fees

    __ bookkeeping fees

    __ computer use fees

    __ equipment lease fees

Chapter Five

The Price of Admission

Franchise Fees and Royalties

In a capitalist economy, every product has at least two price components: cost and profit. For example, a grocer buys a loaf of bread for
fifty cents and resells it for a dollar. In addition to the fifty cents he
paid to the bakery, the grocer has also incurred other costs in conjunction with the loaf — delivery, labeling, stocking, etc. Let's say this
"overhead" amount is ten cents per loaf on the average. Therefore, the
first sixty cents of the resale dollar covers the grocer's product costs.
The remaining forty cents is profit.

Contrary to popular belief, the price of a franchise is not unlike
the grocer's price for a loaf of bread. Many believe the initial fee paid
by a franchisee is a source of profit for the franchisor. In reality, the
initial fee represents the cost component of the franchise. It is by collecting ongoing royalty payments from franchisees that a franchisor
hopes to derive profits.

Almost any form of payment by a franchisee to a franchisor is
considered a franchise fee, including any fee for training, advertising,
deposits, signs, or royalties. However, in most business format franchises, the price includes three components: the initial fee, ongoing
franchise fees (royalties), and advertising fees.

Initial Fees

The initial fee is normally paid by the franchisee upon signing the franchise agreement. The fee is not as arbitrary as it may seem. Franchisors don't sit around with their feet propped up on their desks, thinking, "Well, maybe I can get $10,000 . . . or who knows? Maybe, $20,000." (To be frank, a small percentage of franchisors do just that, but, in the long run, they usually fail.)

In theory, the initial fee is designed to compensate the franchisor for the costs of putting the franchisee in business. Typically, the fee is applied by the franchisor toward the costs of recruiting and training the franchisee and assisting with business planning and start-up.

Some state laws require the cost components of the initial fee to be itemized to minimize the amount of "blue sky," or unjustifiable costs, included in the total. In addition, the Securities Exchange Commission prohibits corporations that sell franchises from including initial fees as income until the fees "are fully earned" by the franchisor. In other words, the franchisor must fulfill all its obligations to the franchisee before the money can be counted as income.

Initial fees charged by franchisors range from a few hundred dollars for a newspaper route to more than a hundred thousand for a well-known hotel or resort franchise. The average initial fee is $16,200.

Most initial fees take into consideration the following factors:

- the value of the business, or its goodwill
- the value of the market or territory
- the average cost of recruiting a franchisee
- the average cost of training a franchisee
- the cost of signs, ads, plans, or other aids

The Value of the Business

When a franchising company starts out, it has no franchises sold or open. Consequently, it must rely on intelligent guesswork to place a value on its franchises. In most franchises, at least part of the initial fee represents the value of goodwill.

Goodwill refers to the reputation of the business and its ability to attract new or repeat customers. As such, goodwill is considered an asset of a business, because when the business is sold, its goodwill will be transferred to the new owner.

However, in franchising, the value of goodwill is often perceived, not calculated. Thus, it nearly always equals demand. In other words, goodwill is never less valuable than the maximum amount anyone is willing to pay for it. For instance, how much more valuable is the right to own a restaurant named McDonald's than the right to own one named Fuddrucker's? It's basically whatever people are willing to pay.

Nonetheless, there are some ways to place a fair price on goodwill. An investment broker often estimates goodwill at 4 to 12 percent of the market value of the business. He calculates the market value by multiplying annual profits times two and one-half.

For example, assume a business generates $100,000 per year in profits. The market value may be calculated as follows:

$$100,000 \times 2.5 = 250,000$$

In this example, the business should theoretically be worth about $250,000. Figured at 12 percent, a high — but not necessarily unreasonable — rate, the value of goodwill would be calculated as follows:

$$250,000 \times .12 = 30,000$$

In this instance, the value of goodwill is about $30,000. At 4 percent — a more common yardstick — the value would be $10,000.

The value of a new franchise is essentially hypothetical. Hence, demand almost always dictates the value. Based on the maximum price the seller can command, the same franchise may sell for different prices at different times or in different parts of the country. Bear in mind that in the case of an established franchise, the seller may not be the franchisor but rather a franchise broker or franchisee reselling his outlet.

As a general rule, the more outlets, the higher the initial fee. For example, a franchisor might start out offering franchises at an initial fee of only a few hundred dollars. Some franchises might be fronted without charging any initial fee, simply to build momentum.

If you are considering a franchise that is just getting off the ground, a "sweetheart" deal is not out of the question. No matter how successful the franchisor's original business, if he does not yet have a track record in franchising, the initial fee should be considered negotiable. If you invest in such a franchise, you will be assuming a proportionately higher risk and are justified in expecting some form of compensation or compromise.

The fees and royalties checklist at the end of this chapter includes some important questions about how the value of a franchise is justified.

The Value of the Market

Besides the intangible value of the identity and goodwill, the initial fee often reflects the value of an exclusive territory or trading area. In this case, the franchisor may base part of the fee on population statistics, demographics, or sales surveys to estimate the relative worth of a specific territory. For example, some real estate franchises charge a set amount for each 100,000 people in the territory.

The franchisor may carve out franchise territories of equal value or vary the initial fee based on the relative worth of the market.

We'll see how franchise territories can be appraised later in this chapter.

The Cost of Putting the Franchisee in Business

The remaining cost components of an initial fee — those attributable to putting the franchisee in business — are more tangible. For example, the average cost of recruiting a franchisee can be estimated with a fair degree of accuracy. This amount might include costs attributable to advertising, lead processing, administration, and accounting. Similarly, the franchisee training program has an identifiable cost that must be integrated into the initial fee. In addition, the franchisor may need to recover the costs of printing the franchise operating manual, preparing architectural plans, and assisting with site selection, signs, and other activities.

As an example, let's say a franchisor, Golden Opportunities Franchise Corporation, plans to sell fifty franchises in the forthcoming fiscal year. If the company's annual advertising budget is $100,000, it will cost an average of $2,000 to recruit each franchisee. Let's say the company's annual operating budget includes $250,000 to run the franchisee training school. Thus, the average training cost will run $5,000 per franchisee. As you can see, this franchisor must already charge at least $7,000 per franchise just to cover its costs. Add to that figure such costs as the franchise operating manual, site selection assistance, communications, etc., and it is not difficult to see why initial fees of $15,000 or more are common.

Figure 5-1 illustrates the cost components of the initial fee for a hypothetical franchise.

Figure 5-1

Average advertising cost per franchisee	$2,000
Average training cost per franchisee	5,000
Average administrative cost per franchisee	3,600
Architectural plans and blueprints	1,200
Franchise operating manual	700
Site selection and grand opening costs	2,500
Goodwill	5,000
Total initial fee	$20,000

As Figure 5-1 illustrates, the initial fee compensates the franchisor for the cost of putting the franchisee in business. The only "blue sky" is the value of goodwill, which can often be verified by analyzing the sales of comparable outlets.

If a franchisor has very few outlets, you would be justified in expecting the initial fee to be relatively low — just enough to cover recruiting, training, and administrative costs. With an established franchisor whose name is well known, you would expect a disproportionate value to be placed on goodwill and intangibles — a value you might be willing to pay.

The following are some examples of initial fees in various industry categories, based on recent franchise offerings:

Automotive

Jiffy Lube	$35,000
AAMCO Transmissions	30,000
Midas International	20,000
Budget Rent-a-Car	15,000
Goodyear Tire Centers	15,000
Novus Windshield Repair	2,900

Food service
Dunkin' Donuts	40,000
Mrs. Fields Cookies	25,000
McDonald's	22,500
A&W Restaurants	15,000
Domino's Pizza	6,500
Baskin-Robbins	None

Personal services
Jenny Craig	50,000
Pearle Vision	30,000
Supercuts	25,000
Jazzercise	325

Bear in mind that initial fees may vary depending on the location or the type of outlet.

Ongoing Franchise Fees

Besides an initial fee, most franchise investments also involve an ongoing fee. In most cases, a royalty is charged on the gross sales or net revenues of the franchisee's outlet or business. Gross sales are the total receipts before expenses are deducted. Net revenues are the total sales after expenses are deducted. Needless to say, the difference is significant.

Franchise royalties range from one-half of 1 percent to 15 percent of gross sales. The average franchise royalty is 5 percent of gross sales. A typical franchise agreement defines gross sales as "the actual receipts of the outlet, after deducting any refunds, returns, and taxes collected." In other words, royalties are not charged for sales tax paid by customers or for purchases that are refunded or returned.

The percentage of franchisors that base the franchise royalty on net sales is relatively small.

In lieu of a royalty, a fixed fee may be payable at weekly or monthly intervals. In some cases, the ongoing fee is hidden in the franchisor's markup of goods or supplies that the franchisor sells to franchisees.

66

A franchise royalty, like the initial fee, should reflect both the worth and maturity of the organization. The first franchises sold by a franchisor are often offered at a relatively low royalty. As more outlets begin to open, the initial fee and royalty may be increased. To illustrate, assume Golden Opportunities Franchise Corporation first sets the initial fee at $7,500 and the monthly royalty at 3.5 percent of gross sales to attract franchisees. At this appealing price, the franchisor rapidly sells six franchises, thereby increasing the actual and perceived value of the business. The franchisor is now justified in hiking the initial fee to $12,500 and the monthly royalty to 5 percent.

Now, that does not mean that the existing six franchisees have to pay more than they originally bargained for. The franchisor is obliged to honor the existing franchise agreements but is free to institute the new fees to all subsequent franchisees. (Both the initial fee and the royalty are required to be disclosed in the franchisor's offering circular, so any increase requires a new UFOC as well as an amendment to the application for franchise registration in regulated states such as California, Illinois, or New York.)

Let's say Golden Opportunities sells another twelve franchises at the higher price. The value of the franchise has increased still more, so the franchisor raises the initial fee to $15,000 and the royalty to 7.5 percent. Golden Opportunities now has six franchisees who paid $7,500 each in initial fees and continue to pay a royalty of 3.5 percent of gross monthly revenues and another twelve who paid $10,000 in initial fees and are paying out 5 percent of their gross incomes. Anyone else who buys a franchise from Golden Opportunities will have to pay the new amount — $15,000 plus 7.5 percent.

Figure 5-2 illustrates how franchise fees and royalties tend to increase with the number of outlets.

Figure 5-2

An example of an ascending scale for initial fees and franchise royalties

	Outlets 1–29	Outlets 30–77	Outlets 78 +
Initial fee	$15,000	$17,500	$20,000
Royalty	5%	6.25%	7.5%

In Figure 5-2, the first twenty-nine outlets are sold at an initial fee of $15,000 with an ongoing royalty of 5 percent of gross sales. However, the thirtieth outlet is sold at an initial fee of $17,500 and a royalty of 6.25 percent. The initial fee and royalty are raised again after seventy-seven outlets have been sold.

As you can see, higher initial fees and royalties generally indicate a more mature organization. When franchise opportunities are evaluated, a franchisor's fees should be compared with those of other franchishors in the same field. Contrast the size, experience, and recognition of the franchise chain with those of the others. Ask yourself: Are the fees justifiable in relation to competition? Do they accurately reflect the franchisor's number of years in the industry? Does the franchisor have more outlets than franchisors that command lower fees?

Royalties vary significantly from one franchise to another. A Budget car rental franchisee pays 7.5 percent of gross monthly sales to the franchisor. A Holiday Inn franchisee pays 5 percent. The owner of a Baskin-Robbins ice cream parlor pays from just .5 to 1 percent. Besides a franchise royalty, many franchisors also derive profits from the sale or lease of products, supplies, or equipment to franchisees. Thus, although a royalty may seem low superficially, the total cash outlay to the franchisor in fact may be substantial.

Advertising Fees

An advertising fee is a separate payment by the franchisee for promotional assistance. Typically, advertising fees may be accrued in a joint national or regional fund to finance major promotional campaigns on behalf of all the contributing franchisees. The most common type of advertising fee is a royalty on the gross sales of the franchisee's outlet. In some cases, a set fee is assessed for promotional assistance.

Typically, advertising fees are paid into a cooperative fund. Monies accruing in this fund are pooled to finance national and regional advertising campaigns for the benefit of all franchisees.

A cooperative advertising fund benefits an individual franchise owner by financing major advertising programs that would be otherwise unaffordable. The franchisor benefits from increased exposure of the trade name and business, thus increasing the value of both its product and franchise.

Note that not all franchisors maintain a cooperative advertising fund. Many franchise systems require franchisees to conduct and pay for their own promotions. Unhappily, this practice sometimes leads to a loss of control over the business image. It also tends to alienate franchisees if advertising standards deteriorate. After all, it is the security of sameness that attracts consumers to franchise establishments in the first place.

Advertising royalties are not always placed in a cooperative fund. In some cases, the money ends up in the general operating fund of the franchise corporation. Some franchise agreements empower the franchisor to spend franchisees' advertising royalties any way the franchisor chooses. For a franchisee, that's not necessarily a bad arrangement. Often, a franchisor does not know the most effective way to promote its outlets. Still, when evaluating a franchise opportunity, it is worth investigating where advertising fees go and who controls how they are spent. Some advertising funds are controlled by a committee of franchisees.

Advertising royalties range from a fraction of 1 percent to several percentage points. Haagen Dazs franchisees pay ten cents per gallon of ice cream sold, whereas Travelodge franchisees pay 4 percent of room sales. Manhattan Bagel franchisees pay .5 percent of their gross revenues. One franchisor in the building construction field charges $100 per month for advertising.

Like franchise royalties, advertising royalties may be subject to periodic increases. However, a cooperative advertising fund benefits all outlets equally, and so charging different franchisees different rates might be viewed as a dubious practice.

There is a tendency, when investigating a franchise opportunity, to focus on franchise fees and royalties, overlooking a much more meaningful price component: the total initial investment.

The Initial Investment

On the surface, a franchise with an initial fee of $10,000 might seem like a bargain compared to one offered for $35,000. But a more meaningful comparison is to contrast the total initial investments. How much will it cost to start the business? What is the cost of equipment, supplies, and inventory? How much money will be required to sustain the business until it begins to return a profit?

The Uniform Franchise Offering Circular (UFOC), which every franchisor is required to provide, must include a breakdown of the franchisee's initial investment. A typical breakdown shows the initial fee plus the cost of procuring and developing a site. It must show the cost of all equipment, leases, fixtures, and inventory required to operate the business. It may also include working capital for out-of-pocket expenses before the business becomes profitable. Franchisors are not obligated to follow a specific formula for estimating working capital requirements.

Figure 5-3 is an example of the initial investment breakdown for a typical retail outlet. In Chapter Ten, we'll take a closer look at the actual costs of getting into a franchise business.

Figure 5-3

An example of a franchisee's estimated initial investment breakdown

Item	How Paid	Amount	When Due	Paid To
Initial fee	Lump sum	$25,000	Signing of agreement	Franchisor
Equipment	As ordered	27,000	As ordered	Vendors
Lease deposits	As agreed	3,600	As agreed	Lessor
Improvements	As agreed	9,000	As ordered	Vendors
Inventory	As ordered	35,000	As ordered	Suppliers
Licenses and permits	—	1,000	As agreed	Licensing body
Insurance	As ordered	1,800	As agreed	Carrier
Working capital	—	9,000	—	Various
Total		$111,400		

Many factors affect the total initial investment, including the location, industry, local wage scale, and state of the economy. Franchisors often provide high and low estimates for the same type of outlet, realizing that it might cost 50 percent more to develop a business in San Francisco, California, than to develop one in Greensboro, North Carolina.

Figure 5-4 compares the total initial investment for various franchises, based on information disclosed by the franchisors:

Figure 5-4

Janiking	$1,500 minimum
Decorating Den	$8,630 to $31,230
Gymboree	$13,000 to $26,000
Subway	$38,200 to $70,400
Sir Speedy	$120,000 (typical)
Blockbuster Video	$365,000 to $659,000
Arby's	$525,000 to $850,000

Franchise Organization and Fees

Franchise fees may be influenced by how a franchise system is organized. If you buy a franchise from a subfranchisor, your royalty payments may be shared by both the subfranchisor and the original franchisor. A subfranchisor, also called a master franchisee, has the rights to sell franchises within a specified territory under a master franchise agreement with the franchisor.

The organization of a franchise system is called the ultrastructure. A satellite system is the simplest form of ultrastructure. Like moons revolving around a planet, each franchise is an independent satellite operating under the global influence of the franchisor. In this type of organization, each outlet is directly accountable to the franchisor. There are no subfranchisors or other marketing levels between the franchisor and the franchisee. Likewise, the initial fee and franchise royalties are paid directly to the franchisor by each franchisee.

If you buy a franchise in a satellite system, you may also obtain an exclusive territory in which the franchisor promises not to sell another franchise outlet. Some states have laws on their books requiring all franchisors operating in those states to protect the marketing territories of franchises.

By granting a territory and agreeing not to compete with you within that territory, a franchisor creates value for the franchise. What is a franchise territory worth? The answer to that question depends, among other things, on the nature of the business, the size of the territory, and local economic conditions.

Evaluating a Franchise Territory

A savvy franchisor knows only too well that each area of the country has a different value as franchise territory. For example, retail sales in Los Angeles, California, are about ten times higher than in Providence, Rhode Island. If a franchisor grants an exclusive territory, the boundaries may be based on such factors as population, demographics, or sales. A typical franchise territory may be as large as a country or as small as a city block.

Figure 5-5 is an analysis of the relative value of the top 100 franchise markets, based on three factors, each of which were given equal weight: population, sales, and the local economy. Each market represents a standard metropolitan statistical area (SMSA). Each index shows the relative value of the SMSA in comparison to a hypothetical base SMSA with an arbitrary value of 1. Thus, New York has a population 23.2 times greater than Charleston, South Carolina, and so forth. The sales index is based on total expenditures by consumers and businesses. The local economy index is based on the average pretax income per household.

This relative value scale can be used to compare the worth of each SMSA. For instance, the value of New York City is about twice that of Philadelphia and ten times that of New Orleans. Thus, if franchise rights to the New Orleans market are worth $10,000, the rights to the New York City market would be worth $100,000, and so forth.

This scale can also be used to project the maximum number of franchise units that can be established in a market. For example, if it is assumed that one unit can be established in Charleston, a maximum of twenty-nine units could be established in New York, twenty units in Los Angeles, three units in Phoenix, etc. Similarly, a franchisor might expect to sell three times as many outlets in Chicago as in St. Louis.

Figure 5-5

The relative value of the top 100 franchise markets

Rank	Market	Population	Sales	Economy	Rel. Val.
1	New York	23.2	31.0	32.0	28.7
2	Los Angeles	18.1	22.2	18.5	19.6
3	Chicago	17.7	17.3	14.6	16.5
4	Philadelphia	12.1	17.3	12.2	13.9
5	Boston	9.8	10.0	9.3	9.7
6	San Francisco	8.2	10.5	9.1	9.3
7	Detroit	10.7	8.7	8.4	9.3
8	Washington, DC	7.9	7.6	7.0	7.5
9	Dallas–Ft. Worth	7.0	6.6	5.6	6.4
10	Cleveland	4.7	7.4	6.8	6.3
11	Houston	7.5	7.2	3.7	6.1
12	Nassau–Suffolk, NY	7.0	5.2	4.9	5.7
13	St. Louis	6.1	5.3	5.1	5.5
14	San Diego	5.5	6.6	4.2	5.4
15	Minneapolis–St. Paul	5.3	5.6	5.0	5.3
16	Anaheim–Santa Ana	5.2	7.1	3.7	5.3
17	Pittsburgh	5.5	5.6	4.1	5.1
18	Miami	4.5	5.8	4.5	4.9
19	Baltimore	5.6	3.6	5.6	4.9
20	Atlanta	4.9	5.0	4.8	4.9
21	Newark	4.8	5.3	3.3	4.5
22	Seattle	3.7	4.9	4.2	4.3
23	Tampa	3.9	4.6	3.8	4.1
24	Hartford–New Haven	4.6	3.5	3.5	3.9
25	Denver	4.1	3.9	3.4	3.8
26	Indianapolis	2.9	4.4	4.0	3.8
27	San Jose	3.4	4.4	3.6	3.8
28	San Bernardino	3.7	4.3	3.1	3.7
29	Milwaukee	3.6	3.6	3.3	3.5
30	Phoenix	4.5	3.1	2.8	3.5
31	Cincinnati	3.4	3.3	3.3	3.3
32	Kansas City, MO	3.1	3.7	3.1	3.3

33	Sacramento	2.6	3.8	3.4	3.3
34	Portland, OR	3.1	3.3	3.3	3.2
35	Columbus	2.7	3.1	2.8	2.9
36	San Antonio	4.0	2.2	2.3	2.9
37	New Orleans	3.0	2.8	2.7	2.8
38	Buffalo	3.2	2.6	2.2	2.7
39	Memphis	2.3	2.8	2.9	2.7
40	Nashville	2.1	2.9	2.9	2.6
41	Providence	2.1	2.8	2.9	2.6
42	Ft. Lauderdale	2.5	3.1	1.8	2.5
43	Orlando	2.0	3.0	2.3	2.4
44	Salt Lake City	2.3	2.4	2.4	2.4
45	Charlotte	1.6	2.8	2.8	2.4
46	Louisville	2.2	2.4	2.4	2.3
47	Oklahoma City	2.1	2.6	2.2	2.3
48	Bridgeport–Stamford	2.1	2.5	2.1	2.2
49	Dayton	2.0	2.4	2.3	2.2
50	Norfolk	2.1	2.2	2.4	2.2
51	Birmingham	2.1	2.3	2.2	2.2
52	Toledo	2.0	2.1	2.1	2.1
53	Raleigh–Durham	1.4	2.2	2.5	2.0
54	Greensboro	2.1	1.9	2.0	2.0
55	Albany	2.0	2.1	1.9	2.0
56	Honolulu	2.0	2.2	1.7	2.0
57	Rochester	2.5	1.6	1.6	1.9
58	Richmond	1.6	2.0	2.0	1.9
59	Tulsa	1.6	2.0	1.9	1.9
60	Jacksonville	2.0	1.9	1.7	1.8
61	Gary–Hammond	1.6	2.4	1.1	1.7
62	Wichita	1.0	2.1	1.9	1.7
63	Syracuse	1.7	1.5	1.8	1.7
64	Mobile	1.1	1.9	1.9	1.6
65	Little Rock	1.0	1.9	1.9	1.6
66	Knoxville	1.2	1.8	1.8	1.6
67	Omaha	1.5	1.7	1.6	1.6
68	Shreveport	1.0	1.8	1.9	1.5
69	Fresno	1.3	1.7	1.6	1.5
70	Austin	1.6	1.9	1.0	1.5
71	Allentown	1.6	1.8	1.1	1.5
72	Akron	1.6	1.7	1.1	1.5

73	Flint	1.3	2.1	0.9	1.4
74	Des Moines	0.9	1.8	1.7	1.4
75	Youngstown	1.3	1.4	1.4	1.4
76	Roanoke–Lynchburg	0.9	1.5	1.7	1.4
77	Albuquerque	1.1	1.5	1.5	1.4
78	Grand Rapids	1.5	1.5	1.0	1.3
79	Green Bay	0.5	1.7	1.7	1.3
80	Cedar Rapids	0.8	1.5	1.6	1.3
81	Davenport	1.0	1.4	1.4	1.3
82	Chattanooga	1.0	1.4	1.4	1.3
83	Wilmington	1.3	1.4	0.9	1.2
84	Spokane	0.9	1.4	1.4	1.2
85	Springfield, IL	0.5	1.6	1.4	1.2
86	South Bend	0.7	1.4	1.4	1.2
87	Tucson	1.3	1.1	1.1	1.2
88	Portland, ME	0.6	1.4	1.4	1.1
89	Jackson, MS	0.8	1.3	1.4	1.1
90	El Paso	1.2	1.1	1.0	1.1
91	Lansing	1.4	1.1	0.8	1.1
92	Baton Rouge	1.2	1.0	1.1	1.1
93	Columbia, SC	1.0	1.0	1.1	1.1
94	Peoria	1.0	1.2	1.1	1.1
95	Las Vegas	1.1	1.4	0.6	1.0
96	Springfield, MO	0.7	1.1	1.2	1.0
97	Lexington	0.8	1.1	1.1	1.0
98	Evansville, IN	0.7	1.1	1.1	1.0
99	Lincoln	0.5	1.2	1.2	1.0
100	Charleston, SC	1.0	1.0	0.9	1.0

Area Franchising

Large market areas are sometimes granted in association with master franchises or area franchises. In this strategy, the franchisor licenses to a "master" or area franchisee subfranchising rights to a large territory — for example, a state or region. The area franchisor receives the right to sell satellite franchises in the territory. The master franchise agreement may restrict the number of subfranchises that can be sold. However, in some cases, the master franchisee is free to establish as many outlets as he can sell.

Area franchising is commonly used in the real estate industry. For example, the Century 21 real estate system was built on this concept. A master franchisee who purchased area rights to a large geographical territory received the right to subfranchise many Century 21 offices. The individual outlets function as satellites of the master franchise. The franchisor, in turn, controls the master franchisees. Each satellite pays initial fees and royalties to the area franchisor, who then pays royalties to the franchisor.

To maintain control over the various levels and sublevels of the franchise system, the franchisor has a team of "area controllers." However, the master franchisee shoulders the burden of recruiting and, in some cases, training franchisees.

By area franchising, a franchisor maximizes greatest short-term cash flow while minimizing overhead. Consider a franchisor planning to sell 300 franchises in one year. The recruiting and administrative costs alone would be staggering. Instead of selling and supporting individual outlets, the company might opt to sell off subfranchising rights to several large regions.

Let's say this franchisor finds a master franchisee willing to pay $100,000 for subfranchising rights in one of the regions. With one transaction, the franchisor may realize as much income as he would have by selling ten individual outlets, yet the company also avoids the costs of recruiting, training, and putting the franchisees in business. In this way, the franchisor sacrifices a share of the long-term cash flow to produce a higher short-term income.

Trade-Name Franchising

Another hybrid form of franchising is the trade-name franchise. In a trade-name franchise, the franchisor licenses a franchisee to use a particular name or trademark in conjunction with the distribution of a particular product or service. Coca-Cola, Pepsi-Cola, and Seven-Up are probably the most recognizable trade-name franchises. Bottlers buy the right to use the soft drink trademark and obtain access to the recipe or syrup from which the product is made, but they do not receive a comprehensive business format. In fact, a typical soft drink bottler may have contracts with more than one franchisor. Thus, in some markets, the same company that has the Coca-Cola franchise might also bottle Dr. Pepper and Orange Crush.

Obviously, a trade-name franchise must have a well-recognized brand name or trademark to justify its value.

Evaluating Franchise Fees and Payments

When a franchise opportunity is evaluated, it is important to determine exactly what type of franchise is being offered as well as what type is best for the investor.

Do you need training? Is a prepackaged business format important? Or is a famous trademark enough? Do you want direct access to the franchisor, or would you be content dealing with a subfranchisor or master franchisee?

The following checklist is designed to help you ask — and answer — these and other important questions about the price of admission to franchising.

Fees and Royalties: An Evaluation Checklist

Initial Fee

___ What is the amount of the initial franchise fee?

___ Does part of the fee represent goodwill? If so, how much?

___ How was the value of goodwill determined?

___ Is the price of goodwill reasonable? (To find out, take a look at the potential annual profits of the business, then multiply the projected annual profits times 2.5 to estimate the market value. Now, if the franchisor is well established or widely known, is the price of goodwill no higher than 12 percent of the market value of the business? If the franchise system is small or new, is the price of goodwill no higher than 4 percent of the market value?)

__ Does part of the initial fee represent the value of a marketing area or sales territory? If so, what is the amount?

__ How does the territory price compare with those of other franchises in different territories?

__ What formula or other means did the franchisor use to price the territory?

__ How much of the initial fee represents the franchisor's cost of
    __ recruiting and training
    __ site selection assistance
    __ grand opening assistance
    __ franchise operating manual
    __ signs and other aids
    __ accounting and administration

__ Does any part of the initial fee represent "blue sky" — money that cannot be justified as a cost component?

__ Is the initial fee higher or lower than those of other comparable franchises in the same industry and with the same number of outlets?

Franchise Royalties

__ How does the franchise royalty compare with royalties offered by other franchises in the same industry and with a comparable number of outlets?

__ Is the royalty based on gross sales (total receipts before expenses) or on net revenues (after expenses)?

__ Is the royalty fixed for the entire term of the franchise, or can the franchisor raise or lower the royalty during the term of the franchise?

__ If the royalty is not fixed, what factors will the franchisor use to adjust the percentage or amount?

__ If the royalty is based on a set amount rather than a percentage, what will be your total monthly obligation? Based on reasonable sales estimates, what percent of the outlet's gross sales would that represent?

__ Is the same franchise royalty paid by all franchisees? If not, how does the franchisor determine how much each franchisee must pay?

___ Will you pay the royalty directly to the franchisor or to a master franchisee or subfranchisor?

___ What services will you receive?

Advertising Fees

___ Does the franchise agreement require you to pay an advertising fee or royalty in addition to the franchise royalty? If not, will part of the franchise royalty be used to promote your outlet?

___ Who will have control over how and where advertising fees are spent?

___ Besides ongoing advertising fees, will you be obligated to spend other monies on advertising and promotion? If so, how much?

___ Are advertising fees deposited in a separate cooperative fund or mixed with the franchisor's general operating fund?

___ What portion of the advertising fees is actually used to advertise franchisees' outlets?

___ How much does the franchisor spend to advertise and promote its franchise outlets each year?

___ What advertising media are used? How will these media reach customers in your market?

___ Is the advertising fee a fixed amount, or will it be based on a percentage of sales?

___ Does the franchise agreement permit the franchisor to raise the fee during the term of the franchise?

___ Do all franchisees pay the same advertising royalty? If not, what formula or other means does the franchisor use to determine how much an individual franchisee must pay?

Part 2

The Franchise Quest

Chapter Six

The Dangling Karat

How Franchisors Recruit Franchisees

In *The Adventures of Tom Sawyer,* Ben Rogers, munching contently on an apple on his way to the old swimming hole, comes across Tom Sawyer busily whitewashing his aunt's fence.

> "Hello, old chap," says Ben. "You got to work, hey?" Tom wheels suddenly and says: "what do you call work?"

Ben decides he'd like to try his hand at the whitewashing, but Tom denies him the privilege. Frustrated, Ben offers Tom his apple core. One by one, other boys drop by to negotiate.

By midafternoon, "Tom was literally rolling in wealth," and, on top of that, his friends had finished whitewashing the fence. In addition to a kite and a dead rat on a string, his newfound fortune consisted of "twelve marbles, part of a jew's harp, a piece of blue bottleglass . . . a tin soldier, a couple of tadpoles, six firecrackers, a kitten with only one eye, a brass door-knob," and various other boyhood treasures.

What made Tom such a successful entrepreneur? It was a franchise sales strategy well known in marketing circles today. Tom had discovered "a great law of human action":

> In order to make a man or boy covet a thing, it is only necessary to make the thing difficult to attain.

Franchisors use a variety of strategies to motivate qualified people to invest in franchises. None is more successful than the technique known as reverse selling — the art of making a product difficult to attain.

As an example, consider the case of Claire Thompson, who noticed an ad for a Bijou Video franchise in the Wednesday edition of the *Wall Street Journal*. Claire had thought about starting her own business, and a videocassette rental store seemed like just the right opportunity. At the bottom of the ad, in small print, was a phone number to call for more information. It was a long-distance toll call.

Why, Claire wondered with pique, would any self-respecting corporation, in an era of global communications, not use a toll-free telephone number? Yet despite the nuisance, Claire called to inquire about a franchise and to request a copy of the franchisor's offering circular, which, as discussed earlier, informs prospective franchisees about the franchisor's background and the mutual obligations created by the franchise agreement.

Instead of an offering circular, Claire received a packet of brochures, photographs, and application forms. The brochure contained an upbeat description of the benefits of becoming the "president" of a Bijou Video company. Claire liked the sound of that: president of her own company.

Accompanying the brochure was a photograph showing someone about Claire's age standing happily in front of a wall covered with shelves of videotapes. Yes, Claire nodded, that could easily be her standing in front of those shelves. It seemed like a pretty good place to spend time.

When Claire unfolded the set of application forms, her heart sank. There were forms about her personal background, forms about her bank and credit accounts, one for listing her assets, another for her debts and liabilities, still more with essay-type questions about her life ambitions and personal qualifications.

Already, the seemingly simple task of looking into a franchise opportunity was considerably more complicated — and more demanding — than she had ever imagined.

It took Claire three weeks to finally complete all the forms and questionnaires. When she mailed them back, she hoped for a prompt response. But when two weeks went by without an acknowledgment, she impatiently called the long-distance phone number. The telephone representative assured Claire that someone would be getting back to thank her for her application and to ask a few personal questions about her job, family, and finances.

Six weeks later, Claire received by registered mail a Bijou Video offering circular and a copy of the franchise agreement. The cover letter invited her for a personal interview at the franchise headquarters in Chicago.

Claire was dismayed. She had been expecting a Bijou Video representative to call on her in her hometown. Now she was faced with the prospect of spending a sizable sum on round-trip airfare for herself, her husband, and possibly her attorney as well as food and lodging for the entire party.

By the time Claire had her first eye-to-eye meeting with the franchisor, she would have already committed numerous hours of self-evaluation and a substantial amount of hard-earned cash. Those commitments alone would make it hard for her not to invest in a franchise.

Like Tom Sawyer, Bijou Video knew only too well the "basic law of human action." To attract qualified investors, the franchisor intentionally made its franchises difficult to obtain.

The Ideal Franchisee

The most successful franchisees are those who have a pronounced desire to be their own boss and seek to derive self-esteem from the business. A savvy franchisor grooms its investment offering to stimulate these motives. Still, the ideal franchisee is someone who does not possess all the know-how and skills that it takes to start, develop, and operate a viable business. After all, why else would anyone invest in a franchise?

In preparation to sell franchises, a franchisor first creates a profile of a hypothetical "ideal" franchisee. Most franchisors know specifically what age, education, personal traits, and professional background an individual must possess to be successful in their line of business. Franchisees often come from an industry related to the franchise, but many have little previous experience in the business, so the franchisor also tries to identify what type of current job or business a good prospect might have.

The process of attracting potential franchise owners is called *franchisee recruitment marketing*. Just as the U.S. Marine Corps tries to recruit "a few good men," a franchisor hopes to recruit an elite corps of qualified investors who have the right attributes to be successful.

A recruitment marketing program targets people who are likely to fit the ideal franchisee profile (IFP). The program must capture their attention, motivate them to apply, stimulate them to invest, and sustain their motivation after they sign. From the franchisee's point of view, the process of applying and interviewing for a franchise can be difficult and time-consuming. From the franchisor's vantage point, sustaining an applicant's motivation from start to start-up is no minor challenge.

To do so, a franchisor must be able to fulfill both the rational and emotional needs of prospective franchisees. Franchisors know that a prospect must literally fall in love with the business, investing not just working capital but also loyalty, devotion, and self-esteem.

If you open a franchise, you will devote the majority of your working hours to the business. You will spend more time in the franchise outlet than in your home. The business will become an extension of your personality and, as such, your primary source of pride and self-image. Aware of this aspect of your decision, franchisors work hard to develop the emotional aspects of the franchise search.

Not everyone who has the financial resources to buy a franchise has the desired supervisory, entrepreneurial, and managerial qualities. A franchisor must be able to pinpoint the precise segment of the population that has the right behavioral qualifications, is compatible with the franchisor's management style and personality, and qualifies financially. To accomplish these objectives, franchisors focus their advertising and recruiting on people who fit the profile.

The Franchisee Profile

Who are the "ideal" franchisees? As you discovered in Chapter Three, a typical franchise owner has at least five years of managerial experience or two or three years in a teaching or training position. Franchisees must be competent learners but also good motivators and trainers. As the chief executives of their own businesses, they have the ultimate responsibility for hiring, training, and motivating employees. Without skills in these areas, in most businesses a prospective franchisee has little hope of succeeding. Many franchisees with management backgrounds come from the industry in which the franchisor does business.

Franchisors also decide what type of education and marital background their franchisees should possess. Consider, as an example, a franchise to sell toiletries door-to-door. The franchisor may prefer a married female with no children. The reasoning is that a wife seeking a second source of household income is most likely to be successful at this kind of business. Furthermore, a married woman without children may be more career-oriented than a working mother.

As another example, consider a franchise to operate a retail hardware store. The franchisor might give preference to married male applicants with children on the supposition that the entire family will help run the business. Married fathers tend to be more stable than single males.

It should be clear by now that, when it comes to equal opportunity, a franchise is quite different from an employer-employee relationship. A franchise may set arbitrary standards on the types of persons with whom it enters into a franchise agreement. A franchisee is an independent contractor, not an employee or agent of the franchisor. Certainly, no franchisor should base an investment decision on ethnic or sexual prejudice, but franchisors are generally free to select the parties with whom they sign contracts without regard to the criteria that govern employment situations.

Besides demographics, franchisors weigh other, less obvious aspects of a franchisee's behavior. In some businesses, verbal communication skills, mechanical aptitude, and math skills are important to success. Most franchisors look for evidence of basic organizational skills and strong personal integrity.

If you apply for a franchise, your previous background will weigh heavily in the franchisor's decision to grant you a franchise. Besides management or teaching experience, a franchisor may also be on the lookout for an applicant who is already familiar with the industry in which the franchisor operates. For instance, one franchisor of computer stores considers only applicants who have at least three years of experience in the electronics industry.

Other franchisors, however, may study a prospect's background with the opposite view in mind: to eliminate applicants with preexisting experience in the franchisor's field. For example, some franchisors in the fast-food industry automatically disqualify applicants who have restaurant backgrounds. These franchisors take the position that a freshly trained recruit from outside the industry is more likely to make a successful franchisee. For one thing, such a franchisee is less apt to bring to the business habits and prejudices inconsistent with or even prohibited by the franchisor's system. For another, the franchisee's primary source of industry expertise will be the franchisor, further reinforcing the important psychological bond between the parties.

Marketing Strategies

The methods that a seller uses to persuade customers to buy a product are called *marketing strategies*. The ways in which a customer responds to these strategies are called *buying behavior*. Merely offering a product for sale does not, by itself, produce sales. For example, if a franchisor fails to run a recruitment advertisement, it is quite possible nobody will apply for a franchise. Running an ad might attract some prospective franchisees, but this action, by itself, will not persuade someone to invest in the franchise.

A recruitment ad may make people aware of the franchisor and its business, but awareness alone is insufficient to create buying behavior. Buying behavior consists of a series of actions and reactions. A customer's reactions often provide signals as to what type of behavior will occur next. An action or event that triggers a particular behavior is called a *stimulus,* and the reaction is called a *response*. Potential responses may be either positive or negative. For every stimulus, there is an identifiable — and sometimes predictable — response.

Until a customer buys a product, she or he is a prospective customer, or *prospect*. The main objective of franchisee recruitment marketing is to create prospects and convert them into franchisees. To effect this conversion, the franchisor must be capable of guiding the prospect's buying behavior to a favorable outcome.

Before a transaction will occur, a prospective franchisee must make three basic types of commitment: rational, financial, and emotional.

The Rational Commitment

Every prospect must have a logical reason why he or she is willing to invest in a particular franchise. If you are a prospective franchisee, you must come to grips intellectually with the realities of starting, developing, and operating a business. You must accept rationally the long hours, extra effort, operational headaches, and burdensome paperwork. You must understand and be willing to accept the performance standards, restrictions, requirements, and operating procedures imposed by the franchisor. You must be prepared to sacrifice a measure of freedom in exchange for the benefits of the franchise. When you actually apply for a franchise with the intention of investing, you must demonstrate your understanding and acceptance.

Most investors are searching for a well-designed business format with a strong likelihood of producing a profit. They also have set goals and objectives related to their careers, financial status, and personal lives. Only by fulfilling the logical needs of investors can a franchisor create a rational commitment to buy, but without a rational commitment, buying action will never take place.

The Financial Commitment

Besides a rational commitment, every prospect must also make a financial commitment. Every product has a price, which usually limits the type and number of buyers. Customers must be able to afford to pay the price before they can purchase a product. However, no one buys every product they can afford or only those products they can afford. Before deciding to invest in a franchise, a prospect must have a set budget and a firm commitment to spend the necessary funds.

The Emotional Commitment

There is an emotional aspect to every type of investment. Whereas a franchise business has a logical foundation, there is also a highly developed sense of adventure, excitement, challenge, and self-esteem in starting a business. There is also an emotional aspect to selecting a specific franchisor. Everyone prefers to do business with people they feel comfortable with.

If you are considering a franchise investment, you must assess your emotional investment in the business. Project yourself into the franchise environment. How do you feel about spending the majority of your working hours there? How do you feel about the sign, the building, the store, or the office? Do they inspire pride, enthusiasm, self-esteem? Will you be proud to call yourself the owner of the business, or the president of the company? How do you feel about the franchising company and its staff? Do they inspire loyalty, motivation, confidence? Will you be able to work with — not against — the franchisor for the entire term of the agreement?

If you must answer "no" to any of these questions, the franchise is probably not right for you. All three commitments — rational, financial, and emotional — are essential to making a sound franchise decision. If even one of these commitments is absent, the best decision is a "no" decision.

Reverse Selling

A franchisor is constantly searching for evidence of successful franchising behavior in prospective franchisees. Franchisors look to psychological marketing strategies to narrow the field of applicants and produce a small set of highly qualified, strongly motivated prospects — the *creme de la creme*. The instrument of this strategy is the technique we referred to earlier as "reverse selling."

Reverse selling motivates the prospect to do the selling, effectively reversing the roles of customer and salesperson. The customer assumes the active role, and the salesperson takes the resistive role. It's not that the franchise sales representative doesn't want to sell the franchise. He simply wants the prospect to demonstrate enthusiasm, commitment, and perseverance, all essential franchising behaviors. A successful franchisee has to be a good salesperson, and the first challenge is to sell himself or herself to the franchisor.

For these reasons, a franchisee recruitment program is often designed as a series of psychological obstacles. The prospect must overcome each one in order to advance to the next level. Only after conquering all the obstacles and demonstrating both an intellectual and an emotional commitment does she or he make the franchisor's list of best-odds franchise holders. If a prospect fails to respond appropriately at any point, her or his name is automatically scratched from the list.

Investment Obstacles

The commitments that are required to succeed in a franchise business are influenced by a variety of factors. For example, people are swayed by television commercials, fashion fads, and social trends, among other things. People of different ages, backgrounds, and social status are subject to different influences. Franchisors are interested not only in the factors that produce buying action but also in the factors that motivate prospective franchisees to select a particular franchisor.

Franchise buying behavior can be influenced by such factors as cost, individuality of design, physical location, and the franchisor's image. But just as some factors influence buying behavior in a positive way, other factors may pose potential obstacles to the sale.

Potential obstacles exist to even the simplest sale. Sales obstacles fall into five general cateories: space, time, knowledge, value, and ownership. A space problem exists if the location or territory you are interested in is unavailable. A time problem exists if you cannot arrange financing within the time frame stipulated in the franchise agreement. Knowledge is a potential obstacle if the franchisor does not disclose enough information for you to make an intelligent decision. A value obstacle exists if the total initial investment exceeds your expectations or pocketbook. Ownership is an obstacle if you can't arrange sufficient financing to handle the investment.

Investment Benefits

Often, a potential obstacle to a franchise investment can be overcome by a benefit. Like obstacles, franchise benefits fall into five categories: monetary, location, time, sensory, and psychological.

Monetary value is the most obvious benefit of a franchise investment. In a basic sense, value is the relationship between the quality of a product in relation to its price. In a franchise investment, value is the relationship between the profit potential and the total initial investment.

Some people are more budget-conscious than others, but given two products of about the same quality and location, most people will buy the one with the lower price. The same premise is often true in franchising. Given two comparable franchise opportunities, most investors will select the one that has the higher profit potential or the one with the lower fees and royalties.

Most prospective franchisees have a particular location or market area in mind. Some prospects place a high emphasis on certain demographics or features, such as a high-income residential area, whereas others may insist on a location in or near their hometown. Although it may not be the primary concern, location has a definite influence on a franchise decision.

In a franchise investment, time benefits may also be important. Most people have set schedules, and if a deal is not closed by a set deadline, they may search elsewhere for a solution.

Sensory benefits are derived from sights, sounds, smells, and taste. The overall impression created by the sensory benefits of an outlet is called *ambience*. Many customers patronize a store, hotel, or restaurant on the basis of ambience alone. Likewise, sensory benefits can have a major impact on how a prospective franchisee reacts to a franchisor. A clean, tastefully furnished office or an upscale retail outlet filled with customers is certain to create a positive reaction, but a franchisor that seems haphazard and disorganized will not impress many prospective franchisees.

As mentioned previously, a franchise investment also offers psychological benefits such as self-esteem, self-image, and the satisfaction that comes with being one's own boss.

From a franchisor's standpoint, it is important to overcome potential obstacles while stressing the benefits of a franchise investment. As a prospective franchisee, it is important to identify potential obstacles early on and attempt to overcome them before making a final decision. Try to define clearly the monetary, location, time, sensory, and psychological benefits of the franchisor's offering. When you have completed your investigation, if any obstacles remain, or if any benefits are missing, don't go any further.

But if all the obstacles have been overcome, and if the value, location, timing, image, and psychological benefits ideally match your objectives, needs, motives, and desires, you are already well down the road to franchise success.

In the next chapter, we'll examine in detail the processes of applying for a franchise and preparing for the emotional roller-coaster ride on the path to a franchise agreement. Meanwhile, the following worksheet contains some important questions to help you gauge your financial, intellectual, and emotional commitments; identify potential obstacles; and define the essential benefits of a franchise opportunity.

Assessing Your Franchise Buying Behavior

Evaluating Your Financial Commitment

Overall, does the business seem worth the initial investment?

Do you think the initial fee fairly reflects the franchisor's costs of putting you in business?

Are you willing to pay the franchise royalty every month from your gross revenues?

After deducting your royalty payments, will you still be able to earn a decent profit?

Evaluating Your Rational Commitment

What does the franchisor offer that you can't otherwise do or acquire by yourself?

Will the value of the business appreciate — increase over the years?

Does the franchisor have a solid track record?

Are other franchisees of the franchisor satisfied with their investments?

Evaluating Your Emotional Commitment

If you invest in the franchise, will you be proud to be its owner?

If you had your choice of any business to enter, would you pick the one in which the franchise is engaged?

Do you have a special interest or hobby related to the business?

Are you excited about belonging to this field?

Identifying Obstacles and Defining Benefits

Is a franchise available for the location, territory, or market that you are interested in? How flexible are you about the location of the franchise?

Will the franchise agreement allow you enough time to arrange financing and develop the business? How flexible is the franchisor about timing?

Do you know enough about the franchise to make an informed decision? Have you checked out the franchisor's background?

Can you handle the investment?

Do you have sufficient credit or collateral to arrange financing? Will you have any partners, stockholders, or other investors?

Is the franchisor's image conducive with that of a successful business? Is it conducive with your own self-image and self-esteem?

Chapter Seven

Decisions, Decisions

The Franchise Roller Coaster

At times, investigating a franchise opportunity is like riding a roller coaster. One moment, you'll be skyrocketing with anticipation; the next you'll be plummeting into remorse. In a split second, you may go from being excited and ambitious to being reserved and cautious. In one instant, you may be ready to sign anything; in another you may find yourself glancing around, looking furtively for an exit.

The Psychological Challenge

In Chapter Six, you saw how the technique known as "reverse selling" is often used to motivate prospective franchisees to assume an active role in making an investment decision. To stimulate this behavior, a franchisor may pose a series of psychological obstacles that the prospect must overcome to obtain the franchise.

The obstacles may range from minor nuisances to significant commitments. For instance, as a prospect, you might be required to inquire about the franchise opportunity at your own expense. The reasoning behind this tactic is that someone who is unwilling to commit to even the small expense of a long-distance phone call is unlikely to invest in a franchise or, for that matter, to be successful in running one. There's a lot to be said for this idea.

On the opposite side of the reverse-selling coin, a franchisor who uses persuasive selling tactics may have something to hide. Most likely, he sells franchises to anyone willing to buy one. *Beware of the franchisor who makes it too easy to buy a franchise.*

The Buying Decision

Understanding how prospective franchisees make buying decisions will help you organize your research and pursue your investigation. It will also help you understand how franchisors recruit and motivate franchisees.

Buying decisions may be viewed in three basic categories: complex, low-involvement, and repetitive. The following case histories illustrate these types of buying decisions.

David Carter was interested in investing in a franchise, but he was unsure exactly what type of business to start. He consulted several directories of franchise opportunities and searched in the classified listings of the *Wall Street Journal* and *USA Today*. Based on his findings, he considered several options.

David contacted each franchisor on his list to obtain information. Each franchisor sent him an information package describing the opportunity and itemizing the start-up costs. He selected a dozen franchises that he felt would best fit his objectives and budget. After discussing the options with his wife, he narrowed the field to three franchisors.

David then made plans to visit a typical outlet of each franchisor. After touring the facilities and talking with the owners, he arranged to meet with the sales representative of a transmission repair chain.

Charlotte Weber managed a small bookstore for a large chain. She had worked for the company for three years when she was approached by the vice president in charge of retail operations. The executive told her the company had decided to begin franchising and to sell off the outlet she managed. Charlotte was offered an option to buy the store. After carefully considering the offer, Charlotte became a franchisee of the company.

Carol Keith was a regular customer of health and fitness clubs. Her job required her to stay overnight in many different cities. As a result, she became something of an expert on various fitness chains. One chain in particular seemed to be the most consistent in terms of facilities, services, and rates. When a franchise opportunity opened up in her hometown, she immediately called the chain's headquarters to apply for a franchise.

Complex Buying Decisions

Selecting a franchise from a wide field of potential opportunities is an example of what management scientists call a complex buying decision. Such a decision may involve numerous factors that must be carefully evaluated before a transaction will take place. A complex buying decision has five stages:

1. need arousal
2. information processing
3. evaluation
4. selection
5. outcome

Need Arousal

Need arousal means recognizing that you have a need or want to be fulfilled. This is the first step in making any decision, whether it is simple or complex. The instant you say to yourself, "I want to start a business," you have become a prospective franchisee.

Behind virtually every franchise decision is the basic need for financial growth. A desire for a change of occupation or employment is sometimes important in need arousal. For example, some franchise opportunities attract investors who simply are bored with their present jobs.

97

Information Processing

After identifying your needs, you are ready to initiate a search for the available solutions. One way is to gather the information deliberately — for example, by contacting a franchise broker or consulting a directory of franchise opportunities. Information may also be received incidentally — for example, in a magazine or newspaper advertisement.

Information processing consists of three basic phases:

1. specification
2. information gathering
3. comprehension

Before beginning to gather information, you must break down your overall needs into more specific needs. What type of business do you have in mind? What size investment can you handle? Where do you want to locate the business? Your specific needs will immediately set the boundaries for the search process. Among other things, your needs will establish the investment range, a specific location, and, often, the type of business.

After specifying your needs, you are ready to begin gathering information. One way prospective investors gather information is by consulting reference sources such as a business journal or a directory of franchise opportunities. You will find a good list of sources in Appendix A.

Figure 7-1 illustrates a typical franchisee recruitment ad for a fictitious franchisor. It is a composite of various advertising strategies used by different franchisees. In states that regulate franchise sales, a franchise ad must pass bureaucratic inspection. Guarantees of success or vague claims of financial windfalls are specifically prohibited.

Ads like the one in Figure 7-1 appear every day in business and financial publications. The *Wall Street Journal* and *USA Today* have classified advertising sections devoted specifically to franchise opportunities. Periodicals such as *Inc., Venture,* and *Entrepreneur,* which target entrepreneurially motivated individuals, also run franchise ads. Some franchisors may run ads in a trade publication or special interest magazine to reach people experienced in a particular industry.

Figure 7-1 illustrates several psychological aspects of a typical recruitment marketing program. To cater to the reader's desire for self-esteem, the ad may refer to the franchise as the "president" or "owner" of his own business. After all, the word "franchisee" has a bland, legal sound, whereas the word "president" is dripping with prestige.

Figure 7-1

Wanted: Company President

We're looking for a qualified entrepreneur to own a successful retail widget business. Your store will feature fine, name brand widgets and widget-related products. Widget World Franchise Corporation will provide assistance with nearly everything you need to start your own business and keep it operating.

Widget World company presidents benefit from the proven reputation and nationally recognized name of Widget World. Store owners also receive continuing local support and help with financing as their business grows. So, you won't be alone in your quest for success. Our trainers and field support personnel will be there to help you every step of the way.

So, if you think you have what it takes to own and operate a successful retail business in an exciting, growth-oriented industry, you're invited to explore the Widget World franchise opportunity. It's your opportunity to achieve self-management, growth, and personal enrichment!

Contact: Director of Franchise Sales, Widget World Franchise Corporation.

A recruitment ad is not an offering, and, except for the prohibition against false claims and success guarantees, the franchise company can say almost anything it wants in a recruitment ad. More reliable information can be gathered from sources such as *The Rating Guide to Franchises,* which condenses the franchise offering circulars of major franchisors and rates their opportunities according to such criteria as financial strength, fees and royalties, training and services, and industry experience.

Identifying opportunities is only the first step in information gathering. The next step is requesting information kits from selected franchisors. We will take a close-up look at franchise information kits later in this chapter.

This step initiates the next phase of information processing — evaluation. Evaluation involves interpreting the information you have gathered and, if necessary, gathering additional data. For example, like David Carter, you might narrow the selection and then visit representative outlets to obtain empirical data about the franchises. (Empirical data is based on firsthand observation or experience, as opposed to merely reading or hearing about a product. Perceptual data is based on advertisements, reviews, or recommendations by other parties.)

Evaluation

The evaluation stage of a complex buying decision takes place when you analyze your options. The options range from deciding not to invest to deciding on a particular franchise that seems to fulfill your needs. I use the phrase *seems to* here because evaluation is largely a matter of perception. For example, you may read a review in a magazine stating that a particular restaurant has excellent food, but, until you actually eat in that restaurant, the information is only perceptual.

Whether you realize it or not, your personal beliefs and attitudes have a strong influence on the evaluation process. For example, some people want to start a large business and are willing to invest more money. Others are mainly interested in a low investment and would be satisfied with a simple business. People who belong to certain religious or political organizations may give preference to franchises that are associated with their groups. Be aware that you have such influences and try to determine how they will affect your selection decision.

Whether your attitudes are logical or not, they are important. If you are not entirely comfortable with your decision, or if you experience the slightest degree of negativity, will you have the total commitment it takes to succeed?

Selection

The selection phase occurs when you make a decision to proceed with one of the options. Usually, this phase consists of a series of smaller decisions. You might decide to reject all of the options, or, alternatively, you might decide to seek yet another solution. For example, if you were considering opening a family-style restaurant, you might decide to open a fast-food outlet instead.

As a prospective franchisee, the first selection you must make is the decision to proceed. A prospective franchisee enters the selection phase by requesting an information kit from one or more franchisors.

Outcome

When a buying decision is made, the outcome may be either positive or negative. If the franchise adequately fulfills your overall and specific needs, and you are satisfied with the investment, the outcome may be considered positive.

In franchising, the true measurement of an outcome is franchisee satisfaction. With few exceptions, no franchisor can survive over the long term by selling only to new franchisees. A satisfied franchisee is a walking advertisement for the franchise, but a dissatisfied investor spreads ill will for the franchisor and all of its franchisees.

Low-Involvement Buying Decisions

The example of Charlotte Weber, who bought the bookstore she had managed for three years, illustrates a low-involvement buying decision. In this situation, the prospect was not highly involved in the information gathering, evaluation, or selection processes. In fact, the franchisor had already developed the entire business before it was offered to Charlotte as a franchise. Still, the final decision rested with Charlotte, who might have elected to invest in a different franchise. If she had so decided, the search for an alternative franchise opportunity would have initiated a high-involvement buying decision.

Repetitive Buying Decisions

The example of the loyal customer who invested in her favorite franchise illustrates a repetitive buying decision. Most people do not regularly change their behavior, and this principle is also true of buying behavior. People adopt a regular pattern of behavior out of convenience. We learn from our experiences and form our behavior on the basis of what we have learned. Thus, a satisfied customer has a reason to believe that his or her satisfaction will be repeated in the future.

Investing in a favorite franchise when the occasion arises transforms a complex buying decision into a relatively low-involvement decision.

Cultural Influences

Investors do not make franchise decisions solely on the basis of information processing and evaluation. They are also influenced by cultural factors, people, and life-style. *Culture* refers to the basic customs and beliefs of a community, religion, or ethnic group. The traits that characterize a particular culture are called *cultural values* and are passed from one generation to another. For example, in some Asian cultures, people consider cows to be sacred and, therefore, do not eat beef or dairy products. Because of this cultural value, steakhouses and ice cream parlors have difficulty marketing to these groups.

Most households in America have indoor toilets, and very few American travelers would select a hotel that does not have this feature. However, in some developing countries, indoor plumbing is found only in the residences of wealthy citizens, and, therefore, virtually any lodging establishment with a toilet is considered a first-class hotel. Yet, by American standards, the same property might be considered primitive or unacceptable.

More refined values exist within each culture. For example, in the United States, elderly people with fixed incomes often have different cultural values than a young, professional couple with children. Low-investment chains often direct their marketing efforts to families, retirees, and blue-collar individuals, whereas high-investment chains often focus on executives and affluent couples without children.

Be aware of the cultural influences that affect your investment decisions. They are a real part of you, and you cannot afford to ignore them. But also be aware that the business world is made up of people of diverse cultural backgrounds.

Reference Groups

Besides cultural values, prospective franchisees are also influenced by other people. The people who provide information or offer opinions that influence someone else's buying behavior are called a *reference group*. For example, a student is influenced by other people in his or her class, and an office worker receives information from coworkers. The most influential reference groups are families and friends.

Members of a reference group may be one of three basic types:

- information sources
- influencers
- key decision makers

An information source is anyone who provides information that affects the investment decisions of others. For example, a happy franchisee may tell friends or relatives about his business. In this respect, every franchisee is an information source for other prospective franchisees.

An influencer is a person other than the prospective franchisee who has control over some aspect of the investment decision. Examples of influencers include family members, friends, business associates, and advisers such as an accountant, banker, or attorney.

A key decision maker is the person who is ultimately responsible for the investment decision. If the franchise will be owned by a corporation, the chief executive may be the key decision maker. In a family situation, marital bliss — and franchise success — may depend on both spouses sharing both the investment decision and the commitment to succeed.

A wise investor researches information sources and seeks the counsel of family, friends, associates, and professional advisors. If you are considering a franchise, realize that it is not your decision alone.

Whether your investment will be based on a complex, low-involvement, or repetitive decision, the adventure of starting and running a business will in some fashion affect your relationships with your family and your friends. Like the proverbial attorney who is a fool because he has himself for a lawyer, you would also be foolish not to seek out and rely upon qualified counsel.

The Lead Processing Labyrinth

After selecting a franchise and starting an investigation, you will open a door and enter a corridor. It will not be straight, like a tunnel, with a light visible at the end. Instead, it will continually branch in different directions and at times seem dimly lit. Like a lab mouse searching for a piece of cheese, it will take dedication, persistence, and possibly ingenuity for you to make your way through the labyrinth. A reward awaits you at the end, but only if you make all the right choices.

This weaving, branching, sometimes puzzling, maze enables the franchisor to select only those franchisees who have what it takes to make it in a franchise. Owning a business requires more than a desire to be one's own boss. It also requires a burning desire to succeed. In franchise brochures, that quality may be referred to as a "dedication to self-accomplishment" or the "willingness to do whatever it takes to succeed."

From a franchisor's point of view, every person who inquires about a franchise opportunity is a "lead." The labyrinth that leads from inquiring about a franchise to being offered a contract is called "lead processing." Franchisors reason that, if you don't have the perseverance to make it through the lead processing labyrinth, your chances of succeeding in a business are slim.

Lead processing begins when a prospect first inquires about a franchise opportunity — usually by dialing a telephone number or mailing a letter. The franchisor usually responds by mailing out an information package, referred to as a franchise "kit."

A typical kit contains a word-processed cover letter, a color brochure, reprints of newspaper or magazine articles about the franchise or industry, and a set of application forms. It may also include photographs and samples of product advertisements. Most franchisors wait until the applications are returned before offering circulars to selected prospects.

A franchise kit may tell you a great deal about the franchisor. To some extent, its depth, detail, preparation, and professionalism are telltale signs of the franchisor's own self-image, personality, and management skill.

A typical franchise kit consists of the following parts:

- a history of the franchising company and its predecessor
- an overview of the franchise offering, stressing the benefits to franchisees
- a list of qualifications for becoming a franchisee
- credibility devices, such as reprints of newspaper articles, sample ads, photographs, and product samples
- application forms

The history is usually told in a brief and colorful description of the founding, growth, and development of the parent firm. What is said is often less relevant than what is *not* said. For example, a new franchise may be described as being "short on history" but "long on future." What this really means is the franchisor does not have much of a track record. When a franchise venture is so new that it has no history, the franchisor's hired ad men search their repertoire of superlatives to create convincing images. For example, you might find that, instead of the history of the company, the kit contains a history of the industry or possibly even the history of franchising.

The history of the franchisor often focuses on an individual, such as the founder of the company or a famous public figure associated with the franchise. The idea is that a franchisee can relate more easily to a human being than to a company. Franchisors know that, as a prospective franchisee, you will project your own identity into the business. The historical individual serves as a role model for you to follow. The premise of a "father figure" at the helm of the franchising corporation is an important element of many recruiting schemes.

The father figure exudes wisdom, inspires confidence, and warms the heart. In some cases, it is a "grandmother" figure — the person who baked the first cookie, blended the first pizza sauce, or plucked the first chicken. In other cases, the figurehead may be a celebrity — for instance, a famous singer, actor, cowboy, or athlete.

Before you place too much faith in figureheads, it might pay to check on their background and credentials. Is she or he the real architect of the franchise or just some token celebrity under contract to promote the business?

A typical franchise overview includes a breakdown of the initial investment. It may also enumerate the ostensible benefits of the franchise while only lightly touching upon the obligations and restrictions. These "negatives" are often left to the offering circular, which, in most cases, only the most highly qualified applicants receive. (The exact legal requirements for disclosing the information in an offering circular are discussed in Chapter Eight.)

Applicants for a franchise must contend with a glut of paperwork, much of which may seem irrelevant on the surface. As discussed earlier, this documentation helps the franchisor eliminate tire-kickers and motivate those prospects who have a serious interest in the franchise. It also provides a concrete tool for testing a prospective franchisee's organizational and communication skills.

For example, how you answer an essay-type questionnaire reveals much about your character and personality. For example, if your answers seem poorly prepared with no definite objective, the franchisor will think you are a poor organizer or a hesitant decision maker. If the answers are handwritten with bad grammar and incomplete sentences, you will be perceived as a poor communicator. Worse, the franchisor will assume you have a poor self-image. If you don't care what kind of image your work conveys to others, what kind of image would you project for a franchise system?

In contrast, if your application forms are well thought out, neatly typed, grammatically correct, and concise but informative, you will be perceived as a competent organizer with solid communications skills and serious intent. What's more, you'll convey a high degree of confidence, self-image, and self-esteem.

If you were a franchisor, which type of applicant would you rather have as a franchisee?

Figures 7-2 through 7-4 are examples of a typical franchise application form, net worth evaluation sheet, and questionnaire. As illustrated in Figure 7-2, the application form usually consists of two parts: personal data and references. A typical franchise application looks a lot like an employment application, with spaces for the applicant's name, personal and business address and telephone, birth date, and other personal data about the prospective franchisee. Most applications require the applicant to provide details regarding education and prior business background, including names, places, dates, and degrees or titles.

Figure 7-2

Franchise Application

The Board of Directors requires that this application be completed prior to further consideration as a franchisee for our company. All information will be kept in the strictest confidence.

Geographical Preference: _____

NAME	Last	First	Middle			Social Security Number	

PRESENT ADDRESS	Street	City	State Zip	Own Rent	Length of Time	Phone	

FORMER ADDRESS	Street	City	State Zip	Own Rent	Length of Time	Phone	

	Birth Date	Marital Status	Number of Children	

Citizenship	Have you ever been convicted? If so, give date and offense.	

Father	Full Name	Present Address	Occupation	Employer
Mother				
Spouse				

REFERENCES	Name	Address	Firm	Position	Years Known
1.					
2.					
3.					

EDUCATION	School Name & Location	Last year attended	Graduated	Degree
High School				
College				
Graduate				

EMPLOYMENT	Employer	Address	Position	How long?	Phone
1.					
2.					
3.					
4.					
5.					

EXPERIENCE   Management: yrs.   Training/teaching: yrs.   Sales: yrs.

Figure 7-3

Net Worth Evaluation Sheet

ASSETS

Cash in bank account(s):	_____
Stocks and bonds:	_____
Real estate:	_____
Motor vehicles:	_____
Boat/recreational vehicle:	_____
Household goods:	_____
Other (describe): _____	_____
Total Assets:	_____

LIABILITIES

Mortgage balance:	_____
Unpaid loan(s):	_____
Credit card balance:	_____
Taxes payable:	_____
Other (describe):	_____
Total Liabilities:	_____

NET WORTH

Subtract Total Liabilities from Total Assets: _____

NET WORTH PLUS TOTAL LIABILITIES

As an arithmetic check, add Net Worth to Total Liabilities: _____

Figure 7-4

Franchisee Evaluation Work Sheet

1. Briefly describe your qualifications for carrying on this activity, and to own and manage a franchise:

2. Briefly describe the traits and skills which, in your opinion, characterize an effective business owner:

3. Why are you interested in owning and operating a Widget World franchise?

4. Will you exercise every reasonable effort to operate your business in accordance with the highest standards of ethical conduct?

5. What is your total budget for establishing and developing your franchise outlet?

6. How do you propose to finance the business?

7. Have you ever owned your own business before? If yes, briefly describe:

8. Are you now or have you ever been a franchisee of another franchisor?

The applicant's personal and professional references help the franchisor assess the prospective franchisee's work stability and esteem by others. Three references are commonly required, but, in some instances, as many as five to ten names may be requested.

To demonstrate financial capability or creditworthiness, the applicant must usually complete a financial questionnaire or statement of net worth. In this document, the prospective franchisee must document his or her assets, such as any equity in real estate holdings, personal property, and monies in savings and checking accounts; and liabilties, such as any outstanding loans or other debts, credit card balances, and taxes payable.

A typical franchisor will multiply the stated assets and net worth by 80 percent to determine the amount that a conventional lending institution might be willing to lend the applicant. Usually, franchisors will have the financial information verified by an independent credit or background checking service.

As a final obstacle, most franchisors require serious applicants to visit the company's headquarters for a personal interview. You can expect the visit to be conducted at your own expense. If your residence is conveniently close to franchise headquarters, the franchisor might even move the interview to a less convenient location, just to see if you're willing to overcome this important barrier.

As discussed in Chapter Eight, a franchisor is required to provide you with an offering circular, an audited financial statement, and a copy of the franchise agreement at least ten business days before you sign a contract. If you have not received these documents before your first meeting with a franchise representative, the franchisor must provide them at that time. For this reason, many franchisors will send you the legally prescribed documents about two weeks before you are scheduled to arrive at franchise headquarters.

In most cases, you will be required to sign and return a form acknowledging that you have received the documents before the interview will be scheduled. This form is necessary to prove that the franchisor has complied with the rules and regulations.

A Ride on a Roller Coaster

After making it through the lead processing labyrinth, another door will open for you. Just outside, you will find a franchise representative waiting to strap you into the franchisor's emotional roller coaster.

The moment you send in a franchise application form, you cease to be a "lead" and become a "prospect." If you fit the ideal franchisee profile, if you qualify financially, and if your desired location or territory is available, you will be invited for a personal interview.

Most likely, when you arrive at franchise headquarters, your emotional state will be highly volatile. It will help you if you remember that most prospective franchisees undergo a series of emotional peaks and valleys. At one point, you'll be highly energetic, perhaps even wildly optimistic. At another, you'll be cautious, weary, perhaps even remorseful.

The franchisor may try to control your emotions. For example, at one point, you may view a videotape or slide presentation while seated in a comfortable, overstuffed leather chair. In this instance, the music and color are designed to stimulate your subconscious reactions, causing the roller coaster to climb. Some time later, you may sit down for an exhausting interview with a panel of department managers, setting off an emotional plunge.

Next may come a tour of a "typical" franchise outlet. In most cases, the tour will be scheduled during a period of peak customer activity. Some franchisors go so far as to hire fake "customers" to mingle in the outlet while a prospective franchisee is touring the facilities. In either case, the cash register will be constantly ringing, letting your imagination run wild with images of cascading greenbacks.

This new "high" may only precede a new "low" brought on by a dry, boring contract negotiation with a legal expert. If a franchisor is trying to manipulate your emotions, the contract will be presented for your signature when your spirits are on a sharp upturn. The closing always takes place on an optimistic peak, never in a remorseful valley.

As a prospective franchisee, you must try to maintain an even keel to prevent the franchisor's marketing experts from controlling your emotions and guiding your behavior. However, you should also recognize that buyer's remorse is a natural part of every major investment decision.

Sales pressure from a franchisor's sales staff can be extremely low key. You may not be pressured to sign; in fact, you may be discouraged. Again, this discouragement may be part of a reverse-selling strategy. The real aim may be to take away the franchise so that you'll scramble hurriedly to grab it back.

To make an intelligent decision, the best strategy is not to sign any agreement or to make any payment at the franchisor's place of business. Wait until you're in your own territory. Give yourself plenty of time to reflect, to review what you've heard, seen, and read. Share the information with your attorney, accountant, and family.

If you can afford to, take your attorney with you when you visit the franchisor's headquarters. It might also pay to hire a franchise consultant for an insider's opinion on the merits of the franchise.

Be sure you've completed your homework and know exactly what facts, if any, lie hidden behind and between the lines of the franchisor's offering circular. You'll learn how to evaluate a franchise offering circular in Chapter Nine.

Meanwhile, as you prepare to emerge from the lead processing labyrinth for a franchise roller-coaster ride, the following self-test will help you compare your specific needs with the information you have gathered.

Specifying Your Needs: A Self-Test

1. Which of the following is the most important reason you are considering a franchise investment?
   a. I want to be independent.
   b. I want to increase my earnings substantially and improve my personal prestige in the community.
   c. I enjoy giving orders.
2. How do you feel about your relationships with coworkers?
   a. I usually prefer working alone.

b. I am a good organizer, but I need help from others to get things done.

c. I prefer to work as part of a team.

3. How do you feel about job responsibilities?

a. To do a job properly, I have to do it myself.

b. I am willing to listen to advice, but I prefer to assume most of the responsibility.

c. The best results are produced by the combined contributions of different people working together.

4. How do you prefer to approach a job and carry it out?

a. I am a self-starter who prefers to work without supervision.

b. I prefer to receive broad instructions or general objectives and then carry out the details myself.

c. I prefer detailed instructions that leave no room for misinterpretation or doubt.

Scoring

Give yourself one point for answering "A", three points for answering "B", and five points for answering "C". Then interpret your needs based on the following scale:

4–7: You will probably be happiest in a business of your own with no long-term ties to a franchisor. You have a burning desire to be your own boss, but you are probably too independent-minded to be successful in a franchise. The chances are good that the franchise agreement and the franchisor's quality and performance standards will be too restrictive to suit you. You might consider a trade name or product franchise rather than a buiness format franchise, or some other type of business opportunity with minimal "control and assistance." However, be aware that you will be assuming the maximum amount of personal and financial risk by going it on your own.

8–12: You are a good candidate to own a franchise business. You have a pronounced desire to be independent, yet you also interact well with others. You might even find the element of risk exciting. Although you are capable of working with a team, you are also capable of working with minimal supervision. Compare value by contrasting the initial investment and royalties with the benefits of each franchise. You might be willing to assume a higher degree of risk for greater value — for instance, by going with a start-up program or a chain that is not dominant in its field.

13–20: Focus your search on large, successful organizations that are well established in their field. You want to be independent, but you also have a need for personal assurance and security. Look for a "cookie-cutter" franchisor that offers the maximum amount of control and assistance. The initial fee and royalties will be a little higher, but, over the long run, you'll be happier with the franchise and, therefore, more successful at running it.

Chapter Eight

Full and Accurate Disclosure

The Rules of Franchising

Although Irwin Meyer had a comfortable job managing a chain of cafeterias, he invested his life savings in a franchise for three fast-food restaurants under a contract with Pot O' Gold Franchise Corporation (a fictitious name). Irwin took over two fully developed restaurants, lock, stock, and deep-fat fryer. Pot O' Gold had operated the locations as company-owned outlets for several years. Consequently, Irwin felt he was purchasing a business with a track record, backed by a major chain with a national reputation.

What he got was not the elevator to success but only the shaft.

Since Pot O' Gold offered the restaurants as part of a franchise package, Irwin paid the company's then-current franchise fee for each location. In addition, he shoveled out close to $300,000 for the buildings, fixtures, and goodwill and agreed to assume the leases on both properties. To swing the deal, he mortgaged his home, used his savings, and took out a $175,000 small business loan.

As it turned out, the package price included an exorbitant amount for the restaurants' used furnishings and equipment — more, in fact, than the price of new equipment from any restaurant supply dealer. To make matters worse, Irwin's contract obligated him to buy food, napkins, and other supplies from specified vendors; for many items, the prices he paid were higher than the cost from independent suppliers.

Unknown to Irwin, Pot O' Gold Franchise Corporation received a percentage of the value of every order he placed.

The reason the franchisor sold the outlets in the first place? They had never turned a profit.

Four hard years later, Irwin missed a rent payment. Like a vulture perched on a light tower, the franchisor swooped in to repossess the restaurants. In less than a week, Irwin's investment, livelihood, and great American dream went up in smoke like a scorched double cheeseburger on an unattended grill.

Irwin Meyer is a fictitious name, but his story is only too true. Franchising is often called a silver lining in an economic cloud, but it is sometimes more like a dark thunderhead. Cases like Irwin's prompted various states to enact laws protecting investors against potential abuses by unscrupulous franchisors. Eventually, the federal government also entered the regulatory picture.

Federal Franchise Regulations

At the federal level, the offer and sale of franchise opportunities fall under the jurisdiction of the Federal Trade Commission (FTC). The FTC was created when the Federal Trade Commission Act became law on September 26, 1914. The new commission absorbed and superseded the federal Bureau of Corporations. Its mission was to prevent monopolies and preserve competition in commerce.

President Woodrow Wilson hailed the new law as an important safeguard of the free enterprise system, a means "to make men in a small way of business as free to succeed as men in a big way" and to "kill monopoly in the seed."

Section 5 of the act begins:

> Unfair methods of competition in commerce, and
> unfair or deceptive acts or practices in commerce,
> are declared unlawful.

The law provides the FTC with the power to make regulations and issue rules that have the full impact and enforcement of federal law. The FTC is further empowered to bring legal proceedings against any person or company that transgresses an FTC regulation or rule.

On December 21, 1978, the commission drafted an amendment to Title 16 of the Code of Federal Regulations, which deals with commerce and trade. The amendment was aimed at regulating the sale of franchises and business opportunity ventures. The new rules went into effect on October 21, 1979, requiring franchisors to disclose certain pertinent information to prospective franchisees before any sale is made.

FTC Rule 436.1 declares:

> . . . it is an unfair or deceptive act or practice within the meaning of Section 5 of the Federal Trade Commission Act for any franchisor or franchise broker: (a) to fail to furnish any prospective franchisee with the following information accurately, clearly, and concisely stated, in a legible, written document at the earlier of the "time for making of disclosures" or the first "personal meeting" . . .

In this rule, the phrase "the following information" refers to a document disclosing twenty points of information about the franchisor, the franchise business, and the franchise agreement. The rule defines the "time for making of disclosures" as ten business days before a franchise sale is made.

The FTC's franchise rule also affects the manner in which franchisors may make any claims regarding actual or potential sales or earnings of a prospective franchisee.

Information regarding FTC rules and regulations affecting franchise offerings can be obtained from the Federal Trade Commission, 6th and Pennsylvania Avenue NW, Washington, DC 20580. Telephone inquiries may be directed to 202-376-2805. The Federal Trade Commission also publishes an informative pamphlet, "Franchise Business Risks" (Consumer Bulletin no. 4), advising prospective franchisees about potential pitfalls. The publication is available for a nominal charge from the Superintendent of Documents, U.S. Government Printing Office, Washington, DC 20402.

Although the FTC rule requires the material facts of the franchise offering to be disclosed in writing, it does not require franchisors to register or file the offering with the FTC or any other federal agency.

Disclosure Requirements

The disclosure document required by the FTC is modeled after the Uniform Franchise Offering Circular, or UFOC, designed to comply with individual state franchise investment laws. The terms *UFOC, offering circular,* and *disclosure document* are used interchangeably to refer to the written disclosures required by the FTC rule and the laws of individually regulated states.

The disclosure document is required to contain information on the following subjects:

1. identifying information about the franchisor
2. business experience of the franchisor's directors and key executives
3. the franchisor's business experience
4. litigation history of the franchisor and its directors and key executives
5. bankruptcy history of the franchisor and its directors and key executives
6. description of the franchise
7. money required to be paid by the franchisee to obtain or commence the franchise operation
8. continuing expenses to the franchisee in operating the franchise business that are payable in whole or in part to the franchisor
9. a list of persons, who are either the franchisor or any of its affiliates, with whom the franchisee is required or advised to do business
10. real estate, property, or services that the franchisee is required to purchase, lease, or rent and a list of any persons from whom such transactions must be made
11. description of consideration paid (such as royalties, commissions, etc.) by third parties to the franchisor or any of its affiliates as a result of a franchisee's purchase from such third parties
12. description of any franchisor assistance in financing the purchase of a franchise

13. restrictions placed on a franchisee's conduct of its business
14. required personal participation by the franchisee
15. termination, cancelation, and renewal of the franchise
16. statistical information about the number of franchises and their rate of termination
17. franchisor's right to select or approve a site for the franchise
18. training programs for the franchisee
19. celebrity involvement with the franchise
20. financial information about the franchisor

The Franchise Rule prohibits franchisors from claiming, without reasonable proof, that franchisees can attain any actual or potential sales or earnings levels. If earnings claims are made, they must be presented in a prescribed format and accompanied by a footnote cautioning prospective franchisees.

All of the required disclosures must be made in a single document, which may not include any other information not prescribed by the Rule. Whenever a material change occurs in the information required to be disclosed, a quarterly revision must be prepared.

The Time for the Making of Disclosures

The FTC rules define the "time for making of disclosures" as follows:

> ten (10) business days prior to the earlier of (1) the execution by a prospective franchisee of any franchise agreement or any other agreement imposing a binding legal obligation on such prospective franchisee . . . or (2) the payment by a prospective franchisee . . . of any consideration in connection with the sale or proposed sale of a franchise.

Simply stated, the disclosure document must be provided to the franchisee at least ten business days before the sale is made. No franchise agreement or related contract may be executed, or any payment accepted by the franchisor, until the ten-day waiting period has elapsed.

Note the phrase "any consideration in connection" with the franchise. Remember it well when you enter the franchisor's conference room to sit down at the negotiating table.

Unless you have had at least ten business days to study the UFOC and the franchise agreement, no franchisor may ask, coerce, or encourage you to make any kind of payment. That includes any deposit, down payment, or purchase of inventory relating to the franchise.

Every professional salesperson knows well the meaning of the term *false urgency*. A franchise salesperson may create false urgency by telling you that several potential franchisees are waiting in line for the same territory. However, if that salesperson asks for a deposit to "hold" the franchise before the waiting period has elapsed, he or she is violating the FTC rule.

The First Personal Meeting

The FTC franchise rule also demands that the franchisor give every prospective franchisee a copy of the UFOC. In the event of a "personal meeting," the document must be handed over at that time. A personal meeting is defined as

> a face to face meeting between a franchisor or franchise broker (or any agent, representative, or employee thereof) and a prospective franchisee which is held for the purpose of discussing the sale or possible sale of a franchise.

Does that mean franchisors have to give out a UFOC to every "tire-kicker" who walks into a store and inquires about a franchise? Not really. The important words are "for the purpose of discussing the sale or possible sale of a franchise." So if you happen to run into a franchise salesperson at a barbecue or while tailgating at the ballpark, don't expect that person to be carrying a tote-bag full of UFOCs.

Penalties for Violation

The Federal Trade Commission Act declares unlawful any "unfair methods of competition in commerce, and unfair or deceptive acts or practices in commerce." The Franchise Rule cites this law and further declares that "it is an unfair or deceptive act or practice" for a franchisor to fail to abide by the prescribed disclosure requirements. Specifically, it is a federal crime

- to fail to furnish the prescribed disclosure document to any prospective franchisee within the time frames established by the Rule
- to make any representations about actual or potential sales, income, or profits of existing or prospective franchises except in the manner prescribed by the Rule
- to make any oral or advertised claim or representation that is inconsistent with the information in the offering circular
- to fail to furnish a copy of the franchise agreement to any prospective franchisee within the time frames established by the Rule
- to fail to return any refundable deposits or down payments to prospective franchisees

A franchisor that violates the FTC rules may be subject to civil penalties of up to $10,000 per violation. Moreover, an investor who sustains losses as a result of a violation of the federal rules can usually recover monetary damages.

The Right of Rescission

What if a franchisor pressures you into signing an agreement before the required waiting period has elapsed? Or what if a franchise salesperson fails to give you a UFOC on the day of your first personal meeting? Should you call the police? The FBI?

Though it's a federal crime to violate an FTC rule, it's not very likely a guilty franchisor will be led off in chains. If a franchisor, franchise salesperson, or broker fails to abide by the regulations, the franchisee may have the right to rescind any agreement. In addition, the franchisee will normally be entitled to full compensation for the total amount of her or his investment plus any damages she or he can prove.

The UFOC and the FTC Rules

Although the terms *UFOC* and *disclosure document* are generally used interchangeably, there are slight differences in the form of disclosure required by the FTC franchise rule and the UFOC adopted by individually regulated states.

The UFOC generally fulfills the requirements of the states that have laws requiring franchise registration and disclosure. The UFOC format is not identical to the disclosure format prescribed by the federal rule. Besides minor differences in language, the state-mandated UFOC requires more disclosure on some subjects than the FTC rules. However, the two formats are quite similar and designed to achieve the same result, regardless of the minor variations. Thus, the FTC considers that the UFOC fulfills the disclosure requirements of the Franchise Rule, provided that the franchisor complies with the prescribed time frames.

However, complying with the federal rules does not relieve the franchisor of the obligation to comply with any applicable state franchise investment laws. In instances where the state law is more severe than the FTC rules, the state law takes priority.

Exemptions from the FTC Rule

Franchises and other continuing commercial relationships that do not fall into the two categories defined by the FTC rule are exempt from the disclosure requirements. They are not, however, exempt from other aspects of the Federal Trade Commission Act, which forbids "unfair and deceptive business practices."

For example, a franchise that does not cost the franchisee anything or incurs less than $500 in costs during the first six months of operation is not covered by the FTC rule.

A second type of exemption is granted to fractional franchises (ones that account for less than 20 percent of the franchisee's total dollar volume). To qualify as a fractional franchise, the franchisee's directors or executive officers must have at least two years' experience in the type of business in which the franchise is engaged.

Exemption from the federal rules has no affect on a franchisor's obligations under any applicable state franchise investment laws.

State Regulations

In 1971, California became the first state to enact a franchise investment law requiring registration by franchisors. The law requires that, before offering franchises in the state, a franchisor must file an application with the Department of Corporations and await approval.

Section 31114 of that law declares:

> The application for registration shall be accompanied by a proposed offering prospectus, which shall contain the material information set forth in the application.

The referenced "offering prospectus" was later adopted by a consortium of midwestern securities commissioners as the Uniform Franchise Offering Circular, a standardized document designed to fulfill the requirements of various state franchise investment laws.

In brief, the prospectus discloses pertinent information about the franchisor, the franchise business, and the franchise agreement. Franchisors are specifically required to emphasize any areas that might have a negative impact on franchisees.

Fourteen other states, commonly called the registration states, have since enacted similar laws calling for the registration of franchise offerings and the filing of disclosures.

The application for registration of a franchise in a regulated state consists of four basic parts: (1) a facing page, (2) a supplemental information page, (3) a salesperson disclosure form, and (4) a copy of the proposed offering circular (UFOC). Figure 8-1 shows a typical application for registration.

Some states, including California, also require franchisors to submit copies of any proposed advertising materials that will be used to promote franchise opportunities. In most instances, both the registration and the advertisements must be approved by the regulatory agency before the franchisor may proceed. The state franchise investment laws also stipulate a waiting period, usually ten business days, after the UFOC is furnished to a prospective franchisee and before a sale is made.

Failure to register can result in criminal as well as civil penalties. In 1988, an Illinois court ruled that the executives of a franchise organization can be held personally liable for registration and disclosure violations under that state's Franchise Disclosure Act.

It is important to remember that approval of a registration by a state agency does not in any way constitute approval or endorsement of a franchisor's offering.

Table 8-1 lists the states that currently regulate franchising. In many of these states, the regulations are considerably more strict than those of the FTC.

Franchise Registration

A franchisor must apply to a government authority before offering franchises in a registration state. The application must be approved before any franchises may be offered or sold.

How does that affect you as a prospective franchisee?

Let's say you live in New York, a registration state. Any franchise company based in New York must register with the state before it may begin offering franchises. But what about an out-of-state franchisor? No matter where the company's headquarters are located, in order to offer you a franchise, the franchisor must register in New York. Even if the company is based in Nevada — a state that does not require

Figure 8-1

UNIFORM FRANCHISE REGISTRATION APPLICATION

FILE NO.

(Insert file number of previous filings of Applicant, if any)

FEE: _____
(To be enclosed by Applicant at time application is initially filed)

Date of Application: _____

APPLICATION FOR (Check only one)

___ REGISTRATION OF AN OFFER OR SALE OF FRANCHISES

___ REGISTRATION RENEWAL STATEMENT OR ANNUAL REPORT

___ POST-EFFECTIVE

___ PRE-EFFECTIVE

AMENDMENT NUMBER ___ TO APPLICATION

FILED UNDER SECTION _____

DATED_____

1. Name of Franchisor.

   Name under which Franchisor is doing or intends to do business.

2. Franchisor's principal business address.

   Name and address of Franchisor's agent in California authorized to receive process.

3. Name, address, and telephone number of subfranchisors, if any, for this state.

   NONE

4. Name, address, and telephone number of person to whom communications regarding this application should be directed.

SUPPLEMENTAL INFORMATION

1.

    A. States in which this proposed registration is effective.

    B. States in which this proposed registration is or will be shortly on file.

    C. The states, if any, which have refused, by order or otherwise, to register these franchises.

    D. The states, if any, which have revoked or suspended the right to offer these franchises.

    E. The states, if any, in which the proposed registration of these franchises has been withdrawn.

2. Following sets forth in budget form the total projected financing required by franchisor to fulfill the franchisor's obligations to provide real estate, improvement, equipment, inventory, training, and all other items included in the offering, Show separately the sources of all of the required funds includng any proposed loans or contributions to capital.

I certify under penalty of law that I have read this application and the exhibits attached hereto and incorporated herein by reference, and know the contents thereof and that the statements therein are true and correct.

Executed at _____ , _____ , 19___

_____
(Signature(s) of Franchisor and/or Subfranchisor)

(SEAL)

By _____

Title _____

STATE OF _____)
)ss.
COUNTY OF _____)

    Personally appeared before me this _____ day of

_____ 19_____ the above-named

_____ (and) _____

to me known to be the person(s) who executedthe foregoing

application (as _____ and _____

_____ respectively, of the above-named applicant) and

(each), being first duly sworn, stated upon oath that said

application, and all exhibits submitted herewith, are true and

correct.

(Notary's Seal)

_____
_____
(Notary)

```
                    CORPORATE ACKNOWLEDGEMENT

STATE OF              )
                      )ss.
COUNTY OF             )

    On this _____ day of _____ 19__, before me,

_____the undersigned officer, personally
        (Notary)
to me to be the President and Secretary, respectively, of the

above named corporation, and that they, as such officers, being

authorized to do so, executed the foregoing instrument for the

purposed therein contained, by signing the name of the

corporation by themselves as such officers.

    IN WITNESS WHEREOF, I have hereunto set my hand and official

seal.



                              _____
                              Notary Public

                              My Commission expires: _____
```

Table 8-1

State Agencies Regulating Franchisors

California	Department of Corporations 600 S. Commonwealth Ave. Los Angeles, CA 90005
Connecticut	Securities Division State Office Building Hartford, CT 06115
Illinois	Attorney General 500 S. Second St. Springfield, IL 62706
Indiana	Securities Commissioner 102 State House Indianapolis, IN 46204
Maryland	Division of Securities 26 S. Calvart St., Rm. 602 Baltimore, MD 21202
Michigan	Department of Commerce 6546 Mercantile Way Lansing, MI 48823
Minnesota	Department of Commerce Seventh & Roberts Sts. St. Paul, MN 55101
New York	Department of Law World Trade Center, Rm. 4874 New York, NY 10047
North Dakota	Securities Commission Capital Building, 3rd Floor Bismarck, ND 58505

Rhode Island	Department of Business Regulation 100 N. Maine St. Providence, RI 02903
South Dakota	Division of Securities State Capital Building Pierre, SD 57501
Virginia	Division of Securities 11 S. 12th St. Richmond, VA 23219
Washington	Securities Division P. O. Box 648 Olympia, WA 98504
Wisconsin	Securities Commission P. O. Box 1768 Madison, WI 53701

registration — the company must still register in New York before offering franchises to New York residents.

But what if the outlet will be located in a different state? If you are a resident of a registration state, the franchisor must still comply with your state's laws even though you may be planning on opening the outlet out of state. If the outlet will be located in a different registration state, the franchisor must register in that state, as well.

Fee Impoundment

If the state authorities do not find the franchisor's financial statement to be strong enough to fulfill all the promises and obligations created by the franchise agreement, they may impound franchise fees. Under an impoundment order, the franchisor must place the initial fee collected from a franchisee in an escrow account. The funds are released to the franchisor on a state order only after the franchisee signs a statement affirming that the franchisor has fulfilled all his promises and obligations.

So, if you purchase a franchise from a franchisor in a regulated state, and if the franchisor's financial statements do not show a seven-figure net worth, you may find youself writing out a check to an impoundment account.

Don't panic. It's just your state's method of assuring that you are satisfied with the franchisor's performance before committing your funds to his keeping. A franchise impoundment account is a type of escrow and, as such, may produce interest on any deposited funds. The terms of the impoundment stipulate that the monies will not be released to the franchisor until you, the franchisee, avow in writing that the franchisor has fulfilled all its promises and obligations to your personal satisfaction.

Authorization to Advertise

In many registration states, a franchisor may not place an advertisement to sell or promote a franchise until the state regulatory agency has reviewed and approved the ad. The law requires a franchisor to submit advertising materials, including brochures as well as newspaper or magazine ads, to a regulator, then wait five days for clearance. If no restraining order results, the franchisor may proceed with the ad campaign.

Periodic Updates

Franchisors approved by a regulated state must periodically update their applications in the form of biannual amendments. Even if no changes have occurred during the last six months, an update must normally be filed in order to maintain the franchisor registration. Whenever a franchisor sells a franchise, changes a contract provision, or is involved in court activity, the UFOC must be amended.

Whenever a franchisor sells a franchise, changes a contract provision, or is involved in court activity, the UFOC must be amended.

Besides state and federal regulations, the courts also influence the rights of franchisees when they rule on disputes. These decisions affect not only how a franchisor may offer and sell the franchise but also the ground rules for purchasing, pricing, and involuntary termination. We'll examine these important issues in Chapter Seventeen, when we explore the franchisor-franchisee relationship.

Meanwhile, the following questions will help you be certain whether or not a prospective franchisor is complying with the rules of franchising:

Franchising by the Rules: Were They Followed?

Has the franchisor provided you with an offering circular?

Was the circular complete and accurate?

Was the circular accompanied by a copy of the franchisor's most recent audited financial statement?

Did a copy of the franchise agreement accompany the offering circular?

Were you pressured into signing the agreement before ten business days had elapsed from the time you received the offering circular?

Were you pressured into signing any related agreement, such as a deposit or purchase agreement, before the prescribed waiting period had transpired?

Did the franchisor make any verbal promises that were not consistent with the offering circular?

Did the franchisor make any promises of earnings or profits?

If you reside in a regulated state, is the franchisor registered or otherwise cleared to offer or sell franchises in your state?

If you reside in a state that is not regulated but the franchise will be located in a regulated state, is the franchisor registered with the state where you plan to open the franchise?

Chapter Nine

Great Revelations

Inside the Uniform Franchise Offering Circular

Secure in his knowledge that Big Brother was looking out for his interests, Paul S. studied his franchisor's Uniform Franchise Offering Circular (UFOC) and duly noted the background and experience of the principals (officers, directors, executives, etc.). They seemed honest enough: apparently none had been sued or indicted, nor had they been involved with any bankrupt or fraudulent businesses. In fact, their records looked "squeaky clean" — just what you'd expect from those you're entrusting with your livelihood and savings.

Unknown to Paul, the president of the franchise corporation had been convicted of shoplifting and child molestation, had once been committed to a mental institution, and was sued for fraud on four different occasions. Moreover, the company's marketing director had gone bankrupt in a previous business.

How was it that none of these astonishing details showed up in the franchise offering circular? Although "full and accurate disclosure" is a requirement of franchisors operating in every state, there are certain limitations on the types of information that must be disclosed. In California, for instance, a criminal record must not be included in a franchise disclosure. In many states, franchisors do not have to divulge unsavory episodes that occurred prior to fifteen years from the date on which the circular was drafted.

Although the UFOC informs prospective franchisees about the proposed investment, it does not completely shield them from potential fraud. The burden of verifying a franchisor's credentials and credibility remains with the franchisee. So don't rely on the UFOC alone; if any gaps appear in the disclosures, ask for a *complete* resume of each of the principals, covering their *entire* business history. The Federal Trade Commission requires all U.S. franchisors to disclose certain information to the public. In cases where the local law or regulation is more severe than the FTC rule, the local restrictions take precedence. As we saw in Chapter Eight, the state rules apply whenever one of the following is true:

a.   the franchisor is headquartered in the regulated state,
b.   the franchisor plans to offer or sell franchises in the regulated state,
c.   a franchise outlet will be opened in the regulated state,
d.   a person who purchases a franchise is a resident of the regulated state, even though the outlet may be opened in another state.

But what about franchisors headquartered in one of the states that do not require registration? When they offer or sell franchises to people who live in unregulated states, the important requirements are preparing a UFOC and complying with the FTC's mandated waiting period.

The Disclosure Document

The UFOC is sometimes referred to as the *disclosure document*, because its purpose is to disclose vital information about a franchise opportunity. It presents highlights of the franchise agreement and describes the backgrounds of the franchisor and his associates.

But often, what is said in an offering circular is not as important as what is *not* said. An omission of a pertinent fact is a form of inaccuracy and a violation of the full-and-accurate-disclosure requirement. Nevertheless, omissions do occur, and it is usually difficult to prove in a court of law that they were made with an intent to defraud. Moreover, a UFOC is not policed with the same rigor as, say, a securities prospectus.

To see how to evaluate a disclosure document and how to search between the lines for disguised or hidden meanings, let's examine each section of the UFOC separately.

1. The Franchisor and Any Predecessors

The first section is devoted to the franchisor's personal and business names, address, organization, background, and financial history. Any predecessors of the franchising company must also be listed. A "predecessor" means a previous business operated by the franchisor which has a direct relationship to the franchise.

Consider, as an example, a franchisor who once owned a taxicab company before starting a successful toy store. After a few years, he decides to package a franchise program based on his retail toy operation. So, he founds a new company to sell toy store franchises.

In his UFOC, the franchisor must disclose that he owned the original toy store, because that business was a predecessor to the franchising company. But he does not have to disclose his involvement in the taxicab business, since that operation has no relation to the toy store franchise.

Most franchising companies are operated as separate business entities from their original operations. Assume, for example, that an entrepreneur owns a successful health-food restaurant, and he decides to begin selling franchises. He starts a new business whose only activity will be franchising. As a result, he now owns two separate businesses — a health-food restaurant and a franchising company.

The reason a franchisor creates a separate franchising company is to limit his risks. If the franchising business runs into trouble, the original operation may not fail or even be liable for the losses or damages incurred by the franchising operation.

The issue of predecessor companies raises several important questions:

- How long has the franchisor operated a business similar to the proposed franchise outlet?
- What kind of success did the franchisor experience in the business?
- Can that success be duplicated in your locality?
- Were any of the principals involved in an enterprise that might suggest ethical impropriety, poor judgment, or just plain bad management?

If a franchisor has nothing to hide, he will most likely list all the companies he founded or owned prior to developing the franchise.

In addition to his predecessor companies, the franchisor must describe the business of the franchise, the types of customers for this type of product or service, and the competition.

2. Persons Affiliated with the Franchisor

The identity and business experience of the directors, trustees, partners, principals, and other managers of the franchising company must be disclosed in this section. A short biography of each person states name, position, and experience for the last five years.

Note that the rules require a background disclosure for only the five years previous to the effective date of the offering circular. For bankruptcies, the period of disclosure is fifteen years. For example, let's say the vice president of a franchising company was hired three years ago. For the prior three years, he was an executive with a large corporation in the same industry. But before that, he ran a side show for a traveling carnival. Under the franchise rules, only the officer's business background for the past five years has to be disclosed. So, the UFOC would have to list only his positions as vice president of the franchising company and as a corporate executive in the industry. Because his carnival-show period took place more than five years ago, this entire episode may lawfully be omitted from the UFOC. Yet, that fact, if disclosed, might very well influence your final decision whether or not to purchase a franchise from this company.

Naturally, most franchisors disclose only as much information as is legally required. Moreover, the rules actually exempt certain kinds of lawsuits or indictments from having to be disclosed. For example, if your franchisor was sued for not paying his bills, but not for fraud or fraudulent conversion, the incident most likely would not have to be disclosed in the offering circular. Even a suit for fraud, if it occurred more than fifteen years ago, does not have to be disclosed.

Moreover, *California law actually forbids the disclosure of any criminal arrest or conviction*. So, it's possible even for a convicted rapist or a bank robber to appear flawless on a franchise offering circular.

Franchisors who really are squeaky clean are more likely to publish a full declaration of each principal's criminal, financial, and business background in the UFOC, above and beyond the legal time limits for disclosure. If a franchisor's disclosures stick closely to the limits, it's wise not to rely on the UFOC alone to assess such information.

Ask the franchise representative for the complete resumes of all the individuals listed in the offering circular. Bluntly inquire if any of them have *ever* been sued or declared bankrupt. Your franchisor may decline to answer, but it's against the law for him — or any of his representatives or brokers — to lie to you about this, or any other matter related to the franchise. If you don't get the information you ask for, and you feel it's important, you can always break off negotiations and look for a different franchise.

3. Litigation

In this section of the offering circular, the franchisor must describe any criminal or civil actions involving any violation of a franchise law, fraud, embezzlement, or unfair business practices. But any lawsuit which did not specifically involve one of these violations does not have to be disclosed in the UFOC. Since California law forbids the disclosure of a criminal record, in that state only civil actions will appear in a UFOC.

When a criminal or civil action is disclosed, the UFOC must reveal the title and parties of the action, the court, the nature of the claim, and the relationship between the litigating parties. If there is no pending litigation, that, too, should be stated.

In an age of widespread and often casual litigation, the question arises: just how extensive must these disclosures be? Can they be limited to those cases that are pertinent to the franchise business? For example, assume you're the vice president of a franchise corporation and you sell your house to relocate. Several months after escrow closes, the buyer discovers a leak in the roof. Disgruntled, he sues you for fraud, claiming you knew the roof leaked all along. You, of course, claim you had no prior knowledge of the leak. But until the matter is settled, the litigation remains on the books. Does this case have to be disclosed in your company's franchise offering circular?

The rules are clear on this issue. For the franchisor or any director, trustee, partner, officer, financial, marketing, training, or service executive, the offering circular must disclose any *pending* administrative, criminal or material civil action

> . . . alleging a violation of any franchise law, fraud, embezzlement, fraudulent conversion, misappropriation of property or comparable allegations.

Note the rule says "alleging." Even while the case is in dispute, the particulars have to be disclosed. In addition, the UFOC must describe any felony conviction or court injunction relating to the franchise in the last ten years.

4. Bankruptcy

In this section, the franchisor must reveal whether he, any predecessor in the business, or any of his partners or officers have been declared bankrupt in the last fifteen years. Specifically, he must tell whether any of the foregoing have been

> ". . . adjudicated bankrupt or reorganized due to insolvency . . ."

If an individual was an officer or partner in a company that went bankrupt, that, too, must be disclosed. Because personal bankruptcies are so prevalent under present law, it is not uncommon for a franchisor to have at least one principal or executive who has undergone the process of insolvency. For example, the franchise sales director for a well-known franchisor in the transportation field once owned a small shoe store which fell on hard times during the nationwide recession of the late 1970s. But that bankruptcy had no bearing whatsoever on his performance as a sales director for his current employer. So, even though the incident was recorded in the company's UFOC, it was not likely to influence a prospective franchisee's decision.

You should realize that just because a franchisor has in his employ an executive who once declared bankruptcy does not *per se* doom the franchise to failure. But beware of the franchisor who attempts to disguise a past bankruptcy rather than openly disclose it.

5. The Initial Fee or Other Payment

This section of the UFOC states the amount of the franchise fee. The disclosure should also describe the franchisor's provisions for refunds, and state whether the fee is payable in a lump sum or in installments.

For example, some franchise agreements do not allow for the initial fee to be refunded under any conditions. Others provide for fifty percent of the fee to be refunded if the franchisee fails to pass the franchisor's training program. Whereas some franchisors demand the entire initial fee be paid in a single lump sum when the franchise agreement is signed, others will accept or defer partial payments.

The franchisor must also state where the initial fee will end up; usually, it is deposited in the "general funds" of the franchising company. It's common for an offering circular to say that the initial fee is "fully earned by the franchisor." Simply stated, that means when you sign the franchise agreement and pay the initial fee, you agree that you are not entitled to a refund if you decide to back out later.

6. Other Fees

Any other fees or payments, such as the ongoing royalty or advertising fund, must be disclosed in this section of the UFOC. If, after signing a franchise agreement, you end up having to pay special charges or fees not specifically disclosed in the UFOC, there's a possibility your franchisor may have violated the law.

For example, let's say you are considering a franchise for a family-style restaurant. Recognizing that location is important to success in this line of business, the franchisor agrees to select the site for your outlet. Two weeks after you sign the franchise agreement, a representative arrives in your hometown to scout out the trading area. Aided by local real estate consultants, the franchise representative finally picks the "perfect" site for your new restaurant. He even stays around long enough to help you negotiate the lease. Two weeks later, you receive a bill for the representative's air fare, lodging, food, and a "site selection fee."

In cases like this example, the site selection fee and all related charges must be listed in the UFOC for you to inspect before you sign the agreement. Likewise, any similar charges for consultation services, accounting, marketing, or other assistance should be fully and accurately disclosed.

7. *Initial Investment*

This section of the offering circular breaks down your total initial investment. The breakdown must say exactly who receives each payment item and when it is due. For example, the initial fee is payable to the franchisor, and it is usually due "on signing" the franchise agreement. But a lease deposit for your store or office is paid to your lessor, due "as agreed" by you and the lessor. If the lessor of the site happens to be your franchisor, that fact will appear in this section of the UFOC.

When the initial investment is likely to vary — e.g., due to local economic conditions — a high-low estimate is often made. The high estimate includes the highest initial fee charged by the franchisor, as well as maximum amounts for such items as real estate, equipment, and supplies. The low estimate reflects the lowest investment for which a franchisee could conceivably get into the business. However, the low investment breakdown is usually based on costs found only in certain areas of the country, i.e., the most economically depressed markets.

The breakdown may include the cost of real estate, equipment, fixtures, inventory, deposits, or other payments. Figure 5-3 shows an example of a franchisor's estimated initial investment breakdown. The illustration gives an amount for working capital; this figure represents the estimated cash required to sustain the business until it begins to turn a profit. Franchisors are not specifically required to include working capital as part of the initial investment breakdown. If you are considering a franchise and the estimated investment does not include working capital requirements, be sure to ask the franchisor for a low-high estimate.

By omitting working capital, the franchisor produces a seemingly lower cost of getting into the franchise; but it is impossible to start a business without an amount set aside for working capital.

8. *Obligations of Franchisee to Purchase or Lease from Designated Sources*

In this section of the UFOC, franchisors must disclose whether you will be required to buy any products, equipment, or services either from the franchisor or from a specified source. For example, if you obtain a franchise to open a muffler shop, will you have to purchase and sell only mufflers offered by your franchisor? If you don't have to buy them from your franchisor, will be you forced to buy them from a particular supplier? If so, what is the supplier's connection (if any) with your franchisor?

It is difficult, but not impossible, for a franchisor to force franchisees to purchase equipment, supplies, or inventory from a designated source. In the past, the courts have frowned on such sole-source purchasing obligations, unless it can be proved that the product is so unique it cannot be obtained from any other supplier.

For instance, let's say you're considering a franchise to open a photography studio. The franchisor cannot usually force you to purchase film from either the franchisor or the franchisor's designated supplier. But he can force you to comply with his specifications for film type and quality. You're free to purchase that film from any supplier. But the chances are good that your franchisor — or his designated source — will offer the best combination of availability and pricing. Most franchisors encourage their franchisees to purchase from a designated source by offering discount pricing or other benefits.

9. *Obligations of Franchisee to Purchase or Lease in Accordance with Specifications or from Approved Suppliers*

This section of the UFOC must disclose whether, as a franchisee, you will be required to buy any products or supplies based on the franchisor's specifications or prior approval. For instance, assume you are considering a franchise to start a computer store, and the franchisor requires that you sell only computers that appear on his "approved product" list. That requirement must be disclosed before you sign the franchise agreement, not after you begin setting up your showroom.

Purchasing standards are usually designed to encourage franchisees to buy particular brands or to use a particular supplier. For example, if you own a video store franchise, your franchisor cannot force you to carry only a certain brand of video cassette recorder. What he *can* do is stipulate a set of specifications that conform to a particular make or model. You have the choice of carrying the product line which conveniently meets the franchisor's specifications, or, as an alternative, investing a few million dollars to manufacture your own version. Now, which option is more attractive?

10. Financing

This section of the UFOC is used to describe any financing arrangements offered by the franchisor or another party associated with the franchise. Many franchisors offer financial assistance to franchisees. Some will finance all or part of your investment, others only the initial fee.

A franchising company that does not offer its own financing arrangement often has ties with a local bank or investment company. For example, let's say you want to buy a franchise, but you'll need a bank loan to swing the deal. The franchisor you have in mind doesn't offer financing, but during your visit to franchise headquarters, you are introduced to an officer of a nearby bank. To your surprise, the banker has already transferred all your financial data from the franchise application onto a loan application. "All you have to do," the loan officer assures you, "is sign."

Sound easy? Maybe *too* easy, you might think. The bank in this example probably handles all the franchisor's banking business. The franchisor may even have agreed to co-sign for the loan. In some cases, the franchisor receives a commission or "finder's fee" for sending the bank new business.

No matter what the arrangement, the details must be disclosed in the UFOC.

11. Obligations of the Franchisor

Under this heading, the franchisor describes the service he promises to provide you after you sign the franchise agreement. The list of services is broken down as follows:

a. services provided prior to opening;
b. other supervision or assistance;
c. services provided while you are open for business;
d. assistance in selecting the site for your outlet.

Also in this section, the franchisor discloses the location and length of the training program, and states exactly who must pay for the travel and living expenses. It may surprise you to learn that most franchisees must pay for their own airline tickets, hotel rooms, and meals while they are attending franchise training school. If that's the case, your obligation must be clearly stated in the UFOC.

A typical franchise training program lasts from one to three weeks. Unless you live in the franchisor's hometown, the cost of travel, lodging, and meals is likely to be considerable. Yet, this cost is almost always excluded from the initial investment breakdown in Section 6 of the UFOC. If you are required to pay for your own transportation and lodging to attend the training program, the UFOC should state a reasonable estimate of the *per diem*, or daily cost.

The following example is extracted from Section 11 of an actual UFOC:

> Franchisee is required to pay his own costs in connection with attending the training program. The cost *per diem*, including lodging and meals, is likely to be ninety dollars ($90) per day.

Like the low estimate in the initial investment breakdown, the cost *per diem* is usually based on budget lodging and inexpensive restaurants. Although you may actually be able to contain your travel costs within this estimate, chances are you won't find the accommodations satisfactory or the meals appetizing. As a general rule, it's a good idea to multiply the franchisor's estimate for lodging and meals by one and a half.

12. Exclusive Territory

In this section of the UFOC, the franchisor must state whether or not you will receive a protected territory as part of your franchise. Will you receive an exclusive territory? Does the franchisor promise not to sell any other franchises in your territory? Can the franchisor sell the same products to customers in your territory by mail order or through any other means?

Territories don't always come with a franchise. When they do, their boundaries may be subject to change. For instance, if you have a franchise to sell cosmetics in a designated part of the city, you might be obligated to maintain a certain sales volume. If you fail to meet the quota, you may find your territory shrinking in size. On the other hand, if you happen to exceed the sales quota, your franchisor might see fit to expand your territorial boundaries.

The concept of an exclusive franchise territory is widely misunderstood. When a franchisor grants you a territory, he is simply agreeing not to compete with you by selling other franchises or placing company sales representatives in your territory. He does not, and cannot, assure you that other franchisees will not sell to customers in your territory. As independent business owners, franchisees are free to sell to any customers anywhere they like, including customers situated in another franchisee's territory. That freedom applies equally to you as well as to your neighboring franchisees.

13. Trademarks and Symbols

In this section of the UFOC, the franchisor must disclose what steps he has taken to protect the use of the franchise name, trademarks, and symbols. The most obvious step is to register the name or mark with the federal government.

The franchisor must list and describe all logos, slogans, or other commercial symbols associated with the franchise. If there is art work involved in the registered logo or trademark, it should be reproduced in the UFOC.

You should note that franchisors do not always own the exclusive rights to their own trade marks. For example, the trade mark may simply be "applied for," not registered. In that instance, you may run the risk of losing the right to use the trade mark if for some reason the registration should be denied.

On the other hand, there is a lengthy period during which every trade mark is only "applied for," before registration is finally granted. This status is by no means a cause for discounting a franchise opportunity. But a fully registered trade mark is clearly more valuable than one that is still under application. Until the registration has been approved by the U.S. Registrar of Trade Marks, there remains a risk, no matter how small, that the name or mark will not be protected.

Be sure the trade name or trade mark has been registered with the federal government, not just with a city or state agency. Protection of a trade name in the franchisor's home town is useless in your area unless it is backed by federal registration.

14. Patents and Copyrights

Under this heading, the franchisor must list any special patents or copyrights that are "material" to the value of the franchise. If a franchise is supposed to be based on a unique patent or design, look in this section of the UFOC to find the patent number, date, and description. If this information is missing, you might ask yourself whether the product or design is really "unique."

15. Obligation of Franchisee to Participate in the Conduct of the Business

In this section of the disclosure document, the franchisor must state whether the person who buys the franchise must run the business himself, or whether he may hire someone else to manage it for him. Many franchisors sell to "absentee" owners who do not actively participate in the management of the business. If you are investing in a franchise as a "silent" partner, be sure you know whether the franchisor permits absentee partnership. If you intend to hire someone else to manage the business, check to see that the offering circular specifically discloses the franchisor's permission to do so.

16. Restrictions on Goods and Services

It must be disclosed in this section if the franchisee will be limited as to the type of products and services he may sell. For instance, if you are buying a franchise to sell exercise equipment door-to-door, can the franchisor prevent you from selling encyclopedias at the same time? Or if you plan to open a computer store franchise, will you be able to sell copy machines and office furniture as well?

On the surface, this issue may not seem important. But if you already own a convenience store franchise and you're considering a second franchise to sell hot dogs or flavored ice on the premises, you had better be certain the franchises are compatible under the provisions of both franchise agreements.

17. Renewal, Termination, Repurchase, and Assignment

This section of the UFOC spells out the provisions of the franchise agreement dealing with your right to renew the franchise when the contract expires; how the agreement can be involuntarily terminated by either party; whether the franchisor has the right of first refusal to repurchase the franchise; and any restrictions governing assignment of the contract to someone other than the person who originally bought the franchise.

We'll take a closer look at these important issues in Chapter Twelve, when we translate a franchise agreement into plain English.

18. Arrangements with Public Figures

In this section, the franchisor must disclose all the details behind any arrangement to use the name and reputation of a public figure. For instance, let's say you are considering a franchise to start a fast food restaurant with the name of someone called Granny Opry on the sign. Just exactly how is Granny associated with the business? How much is the franchisor paying her to use her name? Unless these facts were disclosed, you might think Granny actually owns the franchising company.

Franchisors sometimes pay famous sports figures, singers, or movie stars to put their names on a franchise offering. Some of these public figures own stock in the franchising corporation, but others have no ownership participation at all.

19. Projected Earnings

This section of the offering circular is used to predict how much you can expect to make in the business. The prediction must be accompanied by the formula used to calculate the projected profits or earnings. No matter how the projections are made, the franchisor must inform you that there is no assurance that you can actually attain such sales levels or earnings.

An earnings projection can only be safely made when the franchisor actually has a large number of outlets that have been open for many years. Even then, the projections should be considered hypothetical, since economic conditions vary greatly from one geographic area to the next.

A far more reliable projection is your own forecast of the economic potential of the business, based partly on information contained in the UFOC, but also on accurate estimates of costs and expenses in your locality. A step-by-step guide to projecting the franchise's potential profits is described in Chapter Eleven.

20. Information Regarding Franchises of the Franchisor

This section is used to list the number of franchises currently sold and open, their names and addresses, and an estimate of the total number to be granted in the forthcoming year in each state. If a franchisor has problems with franchise terminations, lawsuits, or other disputes, these must be disclosed here.

A new franchisor with no outlets can simply estimate the number to be sold in each state within the twelve months after the effective date of the offering circular.

Before you make a final decision to purchase a franchise, it's wise to contact some of the franchisor's established franchisees. Ask them if, given the opportunity to do it over again, they would make the same decision.

21. Financial Statements

A copy of the franchisor's current, audited financial statement *must* be attached to the circular. The rules do not allow any franchisor to substitute an un-audited financial statement of any kind. The financial statement must be audited by a certified public accountant whose official stamp appears on the document, and must be current within six months of the effective date of the offering circular.

22. Contracts

A copy of the franchise agreement should be attached to the UFOC. If there are any other related agreements, such as a purchase contract or lease agreement, each of these should be included, as well.

A sample Uniform Franchise Offering Circular based on the specific language prescribed by the FTC appears in Appendix C.

Reading Between the Lines

Although the UFOC is intended to shield you, the prospective investor, against fraudulent business practices, no official regulatory body checks the accuracy of the information. Even in states with strict regulations, the franchise authorities have neither the staff nor the budget to verify the contents of the thousands of UFOCs which cross their desks each year.

In the next chapter, you'll find a list of questions to ask when you evaluate a franchisor's disclosure document.

Chapter Ten

How to Evaluate an Offering Circular

In the last chapter, we examined each section of the Uniform Franchise Offering Circular, or UFOC, and saw what kind of information you can expect to find there. Technically, it's illegal for a franchisor to omit any relevant information, distort or misrepresent some unsavory episode in his past, or disguise a disagreeable aspect of the franchise agreement. But in reality, most UFOCs are prepared by experts who are highly skilled in portraying the franchisor in the most favorable light possible, without stretching or breaching the rules.

It's worth repeating here that nobody but the franchisor actually checks every paragraph of the UFOC to be sure it is accurate or that no vital piece of information has been omitted.

So, to help you sort out the facts, this chapter contains an exhaustive list of questions related to the offering circular. Some of the answers may be found in the franchisor's UFOC; others can only be provided by the franchisor, at your request.

Each set of questions is keyed to one of the sections in the UFOC.

What You Must Know about the Franchisor

1. Franchisor and Any Predecessor

- What other business(es) has the franchisor been associated with in the past?

- How long has the franchisor operated a business similar to the proposed franchise outlet?
- What kind of success did the franchisor have in the business?
- What happened to the "predecessor" businesses? Did the franchisor sell them? If so, to whom?

2. *Persons Affiliated With the Franchisor*

- The UFOC discloses the identity and experience of the principals for the last five years. What are their business backgrounds prior to five years ago?
- Does each principal have the kind of background that justifies his or her present role in the franchise company? For instance, does the finance director have extensive banking or financial experience, and does the training director have solid educational credentials?
- Are the disclosures current and accurate? Are there any major omissions or misrepresentations?

3. *Litigation*

- The UFOC discloses any relevant criminal or civil actions taken against any of the principals (except in California, where criminal actions are omitted by law). Are the disclosures current and accurate? Have any lawsuits been omitted or misrepresented?
- Only cases involving a franchise law, fraud, embezzlement, or unfair business practices must be disclosed. Are there any other types of litigation pending or in the franchisor's past? If so, what are the nature of the cases?

4. *Bankruptcy*

- Have any of the principals been involved in a bankruptcy that, for some reason, may have been omitted from the UFOC? If so, what are the particulars? Does the business in question have any bearing on the proposed franchise?
- If a bankruptcy is disclosed, is it largely irrelevant to the franchise business or the principal's qualifications?

5. Initial Fee or Other Payment

- Is the franchise fee payable in a lump sum, or may it be paid in installments?
- Where will the initial fee be deposited? In an impoundment or escrow account? In the "general funds" of the franchise company? In the account of a subsidiary or affiliated business?
- Is the initial fee "fully earned" as soon as you pay it? Will you be entitled to a refund if, for some reason, you are unable to open the franchise? If so, how much will be refunded?

6. Other Fees

- Are there any other fees, charges, or royalties besides the franchise royalty? If so, what are they, and how are they payable?
- Does the franchisor charge for site selection assistance? If so, how much is the charge and when must it be paid?
- Does the franchisor charge for marketing consultation or other special assistance? If so, what is the rate and how is it incurred?
- Is there a charge for the training program? If so, how much is it? Will you have to pay for your own travel and living expenses to attend the program?
- Are you required to purchase an opening inventory from the franchisor? If so, what is the wholesale value?

7. Initial Investment

- What is the total amount of all fees, charges, and initial purchases payable to the franchisor?
- What expense items are payable as a lump sum?
- What items may be paid for as they are incurred? To whom must they be paid?
- What is your estimated investment in leases or real estate? In equipment, fixtures, and improvements? In opening inventory purchases? In deposits? In working capital required to sustain the business until it begins to turn a profit?

Use the following form to document the expense items that should be included in the estimated initial investment. If the UFOC omits any of the expense items, ask your franchise sales representative to supply educated estimates *in writing*.

Initial Investment Work Sheet

Item	How Paid	Franchisor's Estimate	Actual Estimate	When Due
Initial Franchise Fee				
Lease				
Fixtures and Improve- ments				
Insurance				
Equipment and Vehicles				
Initial Inventory				
Business Supplies				
Working Capital				
TOTAL		$_____	$_____	

8. *Obligations of Franchisee to Purchase or Lease from Designated Sources*

- Will you be obligated to purchase any equipment, supplies, fixtures, or inventory items from a designated supplier? If so, for what reason?

- Are the prices offered by a designated supplier comparable or lower than those offered by any other supplier carrying the same or comparable goods?

- What other benefits are provided by the designated supplier(s)? Availability? Repair-or-replacement warranty?

9. *Obligations of Franchisee to Purchase or Lease in Accordance with Specifications or from Approved Suppliers*

- Will you be obligated to purchase equipment, supplies, fixtures, or inventory based on minimum technical specifications defined by the franchisor? If so, are the specifications reasonable?

- Are the specifications written in such a manner as to include a number of alternative brands or makes available from a wide range of suppliers? Or are they written so as to limit the type and source?

10. *Financing*

- Does the franchisor offer any financial assistance? If so, how much of your investment will he finance? At what interest rate?

- Is financing available for any part of your investment, or only for the physical inventory and fixtures?

- Does the franchisor receive any fee or other consideration from the financial source?

- Will the franchisor finance the entire investment over the term of the franchise, and allow you a set income until the loan is fully repaid? In other words, are you really buying a job, rather than a business?

153

11. Obligations of Franchisor

- Specifically what services does the franchisor promise to provide as a normal part of the franchise arrangement (i.e., without additional charge)?
- What services will be provided prior to opening the business? Site selection assistance? Help with negotiating the lease? Help with designing and procuring signage?
- What services will be provided after the business is open? Marketing assistance? Accounting help or advice? Purchasing assistance?

12. Exclusive Territory

- Will you receive a protected territory? Will the franchisor be allowed to sell other franchises or market products within your territory?
- How is the territory defined? Are the geographic boundaries spelled out in detail?
- Is the territory or its size tied to a sales quota or other measure of performance?

13. Trademarks and Symbols

- What steps has the franchisor taken to protect the use of the franchise logo or other trademark?
- Is the logo or trade mark registered with the federal government? Or is it merely registered with some local city, county, or state agency?
- Has the registration been granted, or is it still merely "applied for"?
- Are there any pending conflicts or disputes that might affect your right to use the franchise name, logo, or trade mark in your trading area?

14. Patents and Copyrights

- Are the franchisor's so-called trade secrets protected by patents or copyrights?

- What is the value of any disclosed patents or copyrights to the proposed business?

15. Obligation of Franchisee to Participate in the Conduct of the Business

- Do you have the right to hire someone else to actively manage the business?
- Are you contemplating a partnership? If so, does your partner meet all the franchisor's qualifications?
- If the agreement prohibits absentee ownership, what happens if you become permanently disabled during the term of the franchise? Will you lose your investment?

16. Restrictions on Goods and Services

- What kinds of business activities, if any, are prohibited by the franchisor? Are the prohibitions reasonable?
- Will you be allowed to own, operate, or participate as an investor in any other type of business besides the franchise? Will you have to sell or discontinue any other businesses you currently own?
- Will entering into the franchise agreement bar you from owning stock in any particular corporation of your choosing? Will you have to sell any stock that you currently own?

17. Renewal, Termination, Repurchase, and Assignment

- Will the franchisor have the right to terminate the agreement against your will? If so, on what grounds? Are the stated grounds legal, justifiable, or reasonable?
- On what grounds will you be able to cancel or terminate the agreement?
- Are there restrictions governing your right to sell or otherwise assign the franchise to someone else? If so, are the restrictions legal and reasonable?
- Will the franchisor have the right of first refusal to repurchase the franchise if you decide to sell? If so, on what terms and conditions?

18. Arrangements with Public Figures

- Is a well-known public figure a prominent factor in the likelihood of your success?
- Is the public figure a principal in the business, or tied to a long-term contract?
- If the public figure should back out of the business, how will it affect your business? Is the main value of the franchise derived from the figure's presence?
- Exactly how does the public figure benefit from his or her association with the franchise company?

19. Projected Earnings

- If the franchisor makes any statement regarding projected earnings of the proposed business, what formula was used to calculate the projections?
- Has the franchisor advised you that there is no assurance that you can actually attain the sales or earnings levels disclosed in the UFOC?
- How many outlets were used by the franchisor to produce the projections? Where are they located? How long have they been in business? How long did it take them to begin yielding the sales or earnings used in the projections?
- Are the projections based on average sales or earnings of actual outlets, or are they largely hypothetical (e.g., based on a predicted "trend" or linear regression)?

20. Information Regarding Franchises of the Franchisor

- The names and addresses of established franchisees must be disclosed in the UFOC. Is the list current and accurate?
- When you contacted the franchisees in the list, were they satisfied with their investments? Did they speak favorably about the franchisor? Are their sales or earnings commensurate with the franchisor's statement of projected sales or earnings?
- Do any of the franchisees on the list receive a fee or other consideration for endorsing the franchise operation or otherwise aiding the franchisor to sell new franchises?

21. *Financial Statements*

- Are the franchisor's audited financial statements current, within the last six months?
- What proportion of the franchisor's assets is represented by cash? Are any of the assets intangible?
- If the franchisor is lean on cash, what arrangements exist for backing the company's promises? An approved credit line or letter of credit? An impoundment or escrow fund? Stocks, bonds, or other convertible securities?

Chapter Eleven

Grand Designs

How Much Can I Make?

Any sound venture begins with a sound plan. When you sign a franchise agreement, one of the first things your franchisor will do for you is to help you create a business plan. But the most important time to have a financial forecast at your fingertips is before you sign the contract.

Franchisors are prohibited by law from making wild claims of projected sales or earnings. Any projections you do receive are probably unreliable. It's up to you to create a financial forecast for the proposed business, based not on what other franchisees earn in other trading areas, but on what you can realistically do in your own back yard.

One of the important things you can do before making a franchise decision is to construct a business plan to forecast your potential earnings.

The franchise business has many traits in common with a conventional business plan: it predicts revenue from sales, subtracts the cost of goods, budgets expenses, and forecasts cash flow. But as a prospective franchise owner, your forecast will contain at least one extra direct cost: a continuous outgoing flow of franchise royalties.

Before we examine the components of a franchise business plan, let's look at a case history. A bookkeeper, whom I'll call Maxine, decides to open her own accounting service. After researching the franchise market, she settles on a company that, for the sake of illustration, we'll call Book Works, Inc. To determine the viability of the business in her trading area, Maxine conducts a survey of local companies. In a sampling of a hundred business owners in her city, eighteen say they would sign up for Maxine's bookkeeping service.

Encouraged by these results, she sets out to determine just how profitable the franchise might become. Maxine plans to start the business as a sole proprietorship, then incorporate after six months. She estimates that the average revenue she will derive from each client will be $250 per month.

Before she forecasts sales, Maxine talks to the managers of several bookkeeping businesses in her trading area. She discovers that the average monthly enrollment is forty-eight. Maxine divides this number in half to estimate her own first month's sales. In addition, she sets the following sales goals: a five percent increase in sales in each of the first six months after the Grand Opening; a two percent per month increase through the first two years; and a one percent per month increase through the end of the first three years. The following table summarizes Maxine's marketing assumptions:

Average revenue per customer:	$250
First month sales:	24
Sales increase in Months 2-6:	5% per mo.
Sales increase in Months 7-24:	2% per mo.
Sales increase in Months 25-36:	1% per mo.

From the Book Works, Inc. franchise salesman, Maxine learns that, in addition to herself, she will need one employee in the first year, and a second employee hired in the thirteenth month. From the start, she will need a commissioned salesperson to cultivate new business. After checking with other bookkeeping services in the area, Maxine decides to pay each full-time employee a salary of $900 per month. She figures payroll taxes and benefits at twenty percent of salaries. Maxine also decides to pay fifteen percent of gross sales to her commissioned sales representative.

With a little research, she is able to provide accurate estimates for commercial space, supplies, insurance, freight, advertising, and communications in his trading area. In addition to all these expenses, Maxine will have to pay five percent of the gross revenues of the business to her franchisor.

Figure 11-1 shows Maxine's first-year projection. According to this forecast, Maxine's franchise would lose money through the first three months of operation. But in the fourth month, she would begin to recoup her losses and build a profit.

Figure 11-1

Year One

	Month						
	1	2	3	4	5	6	7
Customers	24	25	26	28	29	31	31
Revenues	$6000	6300	6615	6946	7293	7658	7811
Expenses:							
Salaries	2900	2900	2900	2900	2900	2900	2900
Taxes/Ben.	580	580	580	580	580	580	580
Commiss.	900	945	992	1042	1094	1149	1172
Lease	900	900	900	900	900	900	900
Telephone	60	60	60	60	60	60	60
Insurance	300						
Suppl. (.02)	120	126	132	139	146	153	156
Adver. (.12)	720	756	794	833	875	919	937
Janitorial	40	40	40	40	40	40	40
Prof. Svc.	200						200
Misc. (.01)	60	63	66	69	73	77	78
Tot. Exp.	6780	6370	6465	6564	6668	6777	7023
Fran. Royalty	300	315	331	347	365	383	391
Net Profits	$-1080	-385	-180	35	260	497	397

	Month					
	8	9	10	11	12	Totals
Customers	32	33	33	34	34	
Revenues	$7967	8126	8289	8455	8624	90083
Expenses:						
Salaries	2900	2900	2900	2900	2900	34800
Taxes/Ben.	580	580	580	580	580	6960
Commiss.	1195	1219	1243	1268	1294	13512
Lease	900	900	900	900	900	10800
Telephone	60	60	60	60	60	720
Insurance						300
Suppl. (.02)	159	163	166	169	172	1802
Adver. (.12)	956	975	995	1015	1035	10810
Janitorial	40	40	40	40	40	480
Prof. Svc.						400
Misc. (.01)	80	81	83	85	86	901
Tot. Exp.	6870	6918	6967	7016	7067	81485
Fran. Royalty	398	406	414	423	431	4504
Net Profits	$699	802	908	1016	1125	$4094

What does this forecast tell Maxine about the Book Works, Inc. franchise? For one thing, she must be prepared to sustain the business with working capital for at least three months after the Grand Opening. In addition to the costs of equipping and supplying the business prior to opening, she'll need at least another $20,000 to safely weather the difficult startup period before the business begins to turn a profit. For another, she can expect her first-year profits (in addition to the salary she pays herself) to be no greater than about $4000. However, when Maxine extends the forecast for six years, she'll find her total earnings potential in this franchise to be as high $60,000 per year.

This example points out three vital pieces of information that a business plan will tell you: how much working capital you need to start the business, whether or not the franchise can succeed in your market, and how much you can realistically expect to earn.

The Franchise Business Plan

Every franchise business plan has three primary components:

- a prediction of revenues;
- an estimate of expenses;
- a calculation of royalties.

Technically, the franchise royalty is a type of expense. But, because it is directly related to gross revenues and is significantly different from such cost items as lease payments, telephone charges, salaries, etc., it's logical to consider your monthly royalty payment(s) in a separate category.

Since your franchise is largely hypothetical at this point, you'll have to use realistic estimates for most items. A good place to start is by using statistics from other businesses in the same field. If you have an accountant or investment counselor, he or she should be able to provide you with some meaningful averages for income and expenses in the franchise's line of business. You can estimate most of your future expenses yourself simply by doing a little research. To predict revenues, you may need help from your franchisor, or one of his existing franchisees.

Estimating Revenues

Ask your prospective franchisor for sales data of a typical or average outlet. If, for some reason, this data is not available to you, contact one or more of the franchisor's existing franchisees. Consult the list of franchise owners in Section 20 of the UFOC. Find out their average monthly revenues or, if that information is proprietary, the average number of products they sell each month in different price categories. For instance, if you are thinking about a franchise to start a computer store, how many computers does a typical franchisee sell each month? How many printers? How many software programs? What's the average price of an item in each category?

Also find out from an accountant or business broker how much a comparable business in your market sells in an average month. In the example above, what are the average gross monthly sales of a store already established in your city? Do sales fluctuate from one season to another, or do they remain relatively static? What factors seem to affect the sales picture: interest rates, holiday spending?

To estimate your own revenues, start by predicting the number of customers you believe you will have in each month of the year. Be conservative at the start, using a modest figure for starting sales. In Maxine's example, she took a competitor's average monthly sales and divided that figure in half to estimate her starting sales. Each month thereafter, increase the monthly sales figure by a set percentage. For example, you might show a ten percent increase from one month to another, over the first year.

Let's look at an example. Assume you are considering a franchise to rent videotape movies. If it takes you sixty days to procure a site and outfit the store, you can expect to receive no revenues at all in the first two months. But, let's assume that when you open the store in the third month of the fiscal year, you can conservatively expect to rent tapes to 600 customers. If you use a ten percent monthly sales increase, the projection of your first year's revenues would look like the following:

Sales:

			Month			
	1	2	3	4	5	6
Videotape Rentals	$0	0	600	660	726	799

Create a complete monthly sales forecast for the first six years of your proposed franchise. Once you have finished the sales forecast, it's a simple matter to estimate your future revenues. Multiply the number of units you expect to sell in each month by the average selling price.

For instance, let's say that, in your hypothetical video business, the average price of a tape rental will be four dollars. According to your sales prediction, your revenue picture over the first six months would appear as follows:

Revenues:

	Month					
	1	2	3	4	5	6
Videotape Rentals	$0	0	2400	2640	2904	3196

Use your sales prediction to project revenues for all six years of your business plan.

How do you estimate sales if you will have many different products in varying price ranges? The easiest thing to do is to categorize your inventory into three or four manageable ranges. Then compute the average price for a product in each range. Construct a separate sales prediction for each product category and use the average price to project revenues. Add the monthly revenues derived from each category to calculate your total monthly revenue forecast.

For example, let's say that, besides tape rentals, your video business will also rent video cassette recorders, or VCRs. Assume that you expect to rent one VCR for every 20 tapes you rent. Your sales estimate for VCR rentals in the first six months would look like the following:

Sales:

	Month					
	1	2	3	4	5	6
VCR Rentals	$0	0	30	33	36	40

Let's say your price for a VCR rental will be ten dollars. Your total six-month revenue picture would appear as follows:

Revenues:

			Month			
	1	2	3	4	5	6
Videotape Rentals	$0	0	2400	2640	2904	3196
VCR Rentals	$0	0	300	330	360	400
Total Revenues	$0	0	2700	2970	3264	3596

Include a projection for all your primary product categories, using an average price to compute monthly revenues. Be sure to extend the forecast for six years into the future.

Estimating Expenses

The second component of the business plan is expenses. The franchisor's initial investment breakdown in the UFOC lists some of your initial expenses, e.g., opening inventory, fixtures, etc.

But you must determine expenses like monthly lease payments, telephone costs, and salaries firsthand.

● *Wages and Salaries*

Specify a monthly salary amount for yourself as the manager of the business. Then set salaries for any other employees you plan to hire. Compute the total amount you will have to pay out each month for wages and salaries.

For example, let's say you set aside $2,000 per month as your own salary. This figure will allow you to survive during the initial period before the business begins to turn a profit. Let's also assume you plan on hiring two store assistants, each of whom will receive an average of $900 per month in wages. Your total monthly budget for wages and salaries is thus calculated as follows:

Owner/manager	$2000
Assistant #1	900
Assistant #2	900
Total Wages/Sal.	$3800

● *Taxes and Benefits*

To compute employee taxes and benefits, multiply the total figure for wages and salaries by twenty percent. In practice, this amount may be slightly lower or higher, but for planning purposes, twenty percent is usually a reasonable figure.

In the example, you would estimate your taxes and benefits as follows:

$$\text{Taxes/Ben.} = \$3800 \times .20 = \$760$$

● *Monthly Lease Payment*

To estimate your monthly lease payment, pretend you have already purchased the franchise, and conduct a search for the perfect site. Consult the classified section of your daily newspaper, or call a commercial real estate agent to get a realistic figure for leasing your prospective site.

If you intend to purchase or build your own site, find out how much your mortgage payments will be at the prevailing interest rate.

Let's assume you decide to lease commercial space for your video store. The site you have in mind is 1800 square feet. If the lessor charges fifty cents per square foot, your monthly lease payment would be computed as follows:

$$\text{Lease Pyt.} = \$1800 \times .50 = \$900$$

● *Utility Bill*

Contact your local utilities company, and ask them what the average monthly utility bill is for the actual or potential site you selected.

Let's say the power company informs you that in the last year, the previous occupant paid a total of $480 in utility bills. Your monthly utility expenses would be calculated as follows:

$$\text{Utilities} = \$480/12 = \$40$$

● *Telephone Charges*

Use your local phone company's actual monthly charges as an estimate of your telephone bill. Multiply the basic rate by two, to

166

account for long-distance calls with your franchisor and suppliers.

For instance, let's say that in your area, the phone company's basic charge for a commercial establishment is $30 per month. You would estimate your monthly telephone bill as follows:

$$\text{Telephone} = \$30 \times 2 = \$60$$

● *Advertising Expenses*

Most businesses budget advertising costs as a percentage of sales. For example, a typical retail business might budget twelve percent of its revenues for advertising. Your franchisor should be able to provide you with realistic guidelines for his line of business. Otherwise, contact your accountant or investment counselor to obtain a general average of what comparable businesses spend on promotion.

First, multiply the percentage by the total predicted revenues for the year; then, divide by twelve to calculate the monthly average.

For example, assume a typical franchise spends an average of eight percent of its gross sales on advertising. If you predict $120,000 in total revenues for the year, your monthly advertising expenses would be estimated as follows:

$$\text{Adver.} = (\$120,000 \times .08)/12 = \$800$$

● *Professional Services*

Don't forget to include a budget for your accounting or bookkeeping service and your attorney. Use the actual monthly fee quoted by your accountant, and figure the cost of two conferences with your attorney per year.

Assume, for instance, your accountant will charge you $125 per month to maintain your books. Let's say a typical visit to your attorney's office costs you $50. In ten months of each year, your professional services budget will be $125, but in the two months in which you include a conference with your lawyer, the budget will be:

$$\text{Prof. Svcs.} = \$125 + \$50 = \$175$$

● *Commission Expenses*

If your business will use commissioned sales representatives to sell its products or services, estimate your total commission expense by multiplying your figures for sales revenues times the percentage commission.

If all of your sales will be handled by commissioned sales agents, multiply the commission times your total monthly revenues. For example, if you predict $10,000 in sales in a particular month, and your sales representatives earn a five percent commission, you would calculate your commission expenses as follows:

$$\text{Commissions} = \$10,000 \times .05 = \$500$$

If you expect only half of your monthly revenues to be derived from the efforts of commissioned salespeople, your commission expense would be calculated as follows:

$$\text{Commissions} = (\$10,000/2) \times .05 = \$250$$

• Insurance Premiums

Contact your insurance agent to find out what your business liability and comprehensive fire/damage insurance premiums will be. Be sure to consult the UFOC or franchise agreement to determine the exact type and amount of coverage you will require.

It is common to make two semi-annual premium payments, so show half of the annual premium paid out in two different months. For example, let's say your business insurance will cost you $300 per year. In the first and seventh months of each year, you would show the following estimated insurance payments:

$$\text{Insurance} = \$300/2 = \$150$$

• Cost of Supplies

The cost of supplies, like advertising, can be expressed as a percentage of revenues. In a typical retail business, supplies run from one to two percent of revenues.

Assume, for example, your total predicted revenues for the year will be $120,000. First, multiply that figure by the percentage amount; then, divide by twelve to determine the monthly estimate. If your budget for supplies is two percent, the monthly cost of supplies would be calculated as follows:

$$\text{Supplies} = (\$120,000 \times .02)/12 = \$200$$

● *Other Expenses*

Be sure to include any other expense categories that pertain to the proposed business. For instance, if you will be buying and selling products, include the cost of goods and other items, such as freight, delivery, or postage. These costs are normally computed as a percentage of revenues.

The following table illustrates some of the important expense items that might be included in your franchise business plan:

Cost of Goods Sold
Wages/Salaries
Employee Taxes/Benefits
Commissions
Insurance Premiums
Freight/Shipping
Advertising and Promotion
Professional Services
Telephone Charges
Janitorial Service
Supplies
Taxes
Bank Charges
Travel Expenses

Estimating Royalties

The third component of the franchise business plan is the total amount you must send to your franchisor at the end of each month. In most cases, that amount will include both a standard franchise royalty and a co-op advertising royalty.

Franchise royalties are usually determined from gross revenues, not net profits. In other words, the royalty comes off the top, before expenses are deducted.

For example, let's say that in a given month your franchise will generate $10,000 in gross revenues. If your franchise royalty is six percent, your royalty payment would be estimated as follows:

$$Royalty = \$10,000 \times .06 = \$600$$

If your co-op advertising royalty is two percent, this payment would be computed as follows:

Co-op Adv. = $10,000 x .02 = $200

Thus, your total estimated royalty payment for the month would be determined as follows:

Franchise Royalty	$600
Co-op Adv. Royalty	$200
Total Royalty Pyt.	$800

The Profit Forecast

To determine your projected profits from the business, subtract your projected total expenses and royalties from the projected total revenues. In our example of a videotape rental franchise, the profit picture for the first months might appear as follows:

Net Profits

	Month					
	1	2	3	4	5	6
Total Revenues	0	0	2700	2970	3264	3596
Total Expenses	32400	3650	3720	3425	3600	3220
Total Royalties	0	0	135	147	163	180
Net Profits	-32400	-3650	-1155	-602	-499	196

In this example, the business begins to make a profit in the sixth month (four months after the doors have opened for business). From this prediction, you would know that you must be able to sustain the business with working capital for at least five months.

Forecasting Cash Flow

Besides projecting your profits or losses at the end of each month, it would be useful to know the business's true cash position at any point. The term "cash position" means how much cash you will actually have on hand at the end of each month. "Cash flow" is a measurement of the positive and negative trends in the cash position of a business.

To project cash flow, add the profit for each month to the profit for the previous month. The business's cash flow is the running total of monthly profits. Express a loss as a negative profit.

In our example of the videotape franchise, the cash flow for the first six months would look like this:

Cash Flow

	Month					
	1	2	3	4	5	6
Net Profits	-32400	-3650	-1155	-602	-499	196
Cash Flow	-32400	-36050	-37205	-37807	-38306	-38110

In this example, cash flow is negative (i.e., a minus figure). The situation gets steadily worse until the sixth month, when the business finally starts to realize a small profit. From here on, the deficit is gradually reduced. If you continued this forecast, you would eventually see the cash flow turn positive, indicating a surplus of cash on hand.

What does this analysis tell you? For one thing, the maximum amount of negative cash flow is $38,306, occurring in the fifth month. After that, the picture starts to improve. In this instance, you would figure your working capital requirement at around $39,000 — enough to keep the business going until it begins to turn a profit.

Figure 10-2 illustrates a three-year forecast for a typical franchise business.

Figure 11-2

Year One

	Month						
	1	2	3	4	5	6	7
Revenues	$36000	39600	43560	47916	52708	57978	63776
Expenses							
Cost of Goods	21600	23760	26136	28750	31625	34787	38266
Salaries	4500	4500	4500	4500	4500	4500	4500
Taxes/Ben.	900	900	900	900	900	900	900
Commiss.	3600	3960	4356	4792	5271	5798	6378
Lease	900	900	900	900	900	900	900
Telephone	60	60	60	60	60	60	60
Insurance	300						
Suppl. (.02)	720	792	871	958	1054	1160	1276
Adver. (.12)	4320	4752	5227	5750	6325	6957	7653
Janitorial	120	120	120	120	120	120	120
Prof. Svc.	250	125	125	125	125	125	250
Misc. (.01)	360	396	436	479	527	580	638
Tot. Exp.	37630	40265	43631	47334	51406	55887	60940
Fran. Royalty	1800	1980	2178	2396	2635	2899	3189
Co-op Adv.	720	792	871	958	1054	1160	1276
Net Profits	-4150	-3437	-3120	-2772	-2388	-1628	1967
Cash Flow	$-4150	-7587	-10707	-13479	-15867	-19462	-17834

	Month					
	8	9	10	11	12	Totals
Revenues	$70154	77169	84886	93375	102712	769834
Expenses:						
Cost of Goods	42092	46302	50932	56025	61627	461901
Salaries	4500	4500	4500	4500	4500	54000
Taxes/Ben.	900	900	900	900	900	10800
Commiss.	7015	7717	8489	9337	10271	76983
Lease	900	900	900	900	900	10800
Telephone	60	60	60	60	60	720
Insurance						300
Suppl. (.02)	1403	1543	1698	1867	2054	15397
Adver. (.12)	8418	9260	10186	11205	12325	92380
Janitorial	120	120	120	120	120	1440
Prof. Svc.	125	125	125	125	125	1750
Misc. (.01)	702	772	849	934	1027	7698
Tot. Exp.	66236	72199	78758	85974	93910	734169
Fran. Royalty	3508	3858	4244	4669	5136	
Co-op Adv.	1403	1543	1698	1867	2054	15397
Net Profits	-993	-431	186	865	1612	-18223

Year Two

	Month						
	13	14	15	16	17	18	19
Revenues	$107848	113240	118902	124847	131089	137644	144526
Expenses:							
Cost of Goods	64709	67944	71341	74908	78654	82586	86716
Salaries	4500	4500	4500	4500	4500	4500	4500
Taxes/Ben.	900	900	900	900	900	900	900
Commiss.	10785	11324	11890	12485	13109	13764	14453
Lease	900	900	900	900	900	900	900
Telephone	60	60	60	60	60	60	60
Insurance	300						
Suppl. (.02)	2157	2265	2378	2497	2622	2753	2891
Adver. (.12)	12942	13589	14268	14982	15731	16517	17343
Janitorial	120	120	120	120	120	120	120
Prof. Svc.	250	125	125	125	125	125	250
Misc. (.01)	1078	1132	1189	1248	1311	1376	1445
Tot. Exp.	98700	102859	107672	112725	118031	123602	129577
Fran. Royalty	5392	5662	5945	6242	6554	6882	7226
Co-op Adv.	2157	2265	2378	2497	2622	2753	2891
Net Profits	1598	2454	2907	3383	3882	4407	4832
Cash Flow	$-16625	-14171	-11264	-7881	-3999	408	5240

	Month					
	20	21	22	23	24	Totals
Revenues	$151752	159340	167307	175672	184456	1716624
Expenses:						
Cost of Goods	91051	95604	100384	105403	110674	1029974
Salaries	4500	4500	4500	4500	4500	54000
Taxes/Ben.	900	900	900	900	900	10800
Commiss.	15175	15934	16731	17567	18446	171662
Lease	900	900	900	900	900	10800
Telephone	60	60	60	60	60	720
Insurance						300
Suppl. (.02)	3035	3187	3346	3513	3689	34332
Adver. (.12)	18210	19121	20077	21081	22135	205995
Janitorial	120	120	120	120	120	1440
Prof. Svc.	125	125	125	125	125	1750
Misc. (.01)	1518	1593	1673	1757	1845	17166
Tot. Exp.	135595	142044	148816	155927	163393	1538940
Fran. Royalty	7588	7967	8365	8784	9223	85831
Co-op Adv.	3035	3187	3346	3513	3689	34332
Net Profits	5535	6142	6780	7449	8151	57520
Cash Flow	$10775	16917	23697	31145	39297	39297

Year Three

	Month						
	25	26	27	28	29	30	31
Revenues	$184456	184456	184456	184456	184456	184456	184456
Expenses:							
Cost of Goods	110674	110674	110674	110674	110674	110674	110674
Salaries	4500	4500	4500	4500	4500	4500	4500
Taxes/Ben.	900	900	900	900	900	900	900
Commiss.	18446	18446	18446	18446	18446	18446	18446
Lease	900	900	900	900	900	900	900
Telephone	60	60	60	60	60	60	60
Insurance	300						
Suppl. (.02)	3689	3689	3689	3689	3689	3689	3689
Adver. (.12)	22135	22135	22135	22135	22135	22135	22135
Janitorial	120	120	120	120	120	120	120
Prof. Svc.	250	125	125	125	125	125	250
Misc. (.01)	1845	1845	1845	1845	1845	1845	1845
Tot. Exp.	163818	163393	163393	163393	163393	163393	163518
Fran. Royalty	9223	9223	9223	9223	9223	9223	9223
Co-op Adv.	3689	3689	3689	3689	3689	3689	3689
Net Profits	7726	8151	8151	8151	8151	8151	8026
Cash Flow	$47023	55175	63326	71478	79629	87781	95807

	Month					
	32	33	34	35	36	Totals
Revenues	$184456	184456	184456	184456	184456	2213472
Expenses:						
Cost of Goods	110674	110674	110674	110674	110674	1328083
Salaries	4500	4500	4500	4500	4500	54000
Taxes/Ben.	900	900	900	900	900	10800
Commiss.	18446	18446	18446	18446	18446	221347
Lease	900	900	900	900	900	10800
Telephone	60	60	60	60	60	720
Insurance						300
Suppl. (.02)	3689	3689	3689	3689	3689	44269
Adver. (.12)	22135	22135	22135	22135	22135	265617
Janitorial	120	120	120	120	120	1440
Prof. Svc.	125	125	125	125	125	1750
Misc. (.01)	1845	1845	1845	1845	1845	22135
Tot. Exp.	163393	163393	163393	163393	163393	1961261
Fran. Royalty	9223	9223	9223	9223	9223	110674
Co-op Adv.	3689	3689	3689	3689	3689	44269
Net Profits	8151	8151	8151	8151	8151	97268
Cash Flow	$103959	112110	120262	128413	136565	136565

Interpreting the Forecast

After you have projected your proposed franchise's future profits and cash flows, you will be in possession of some very useful information. For one thing, you will have a realistic snapshot of how well this type of business can do in your own market. For another, you will have a clear view of how much you can expect to earn. You'll also know how much working capital you will need to keep the business going until it becomes profitable. Finally, the franchise business plan will provide you with a basis for obtaining financial assistance when and if you need it.

The work sheets on the following pages will help you organize information about revenues and expenses, and construct a meaningful financial forecast for any franchise you are considering. Before you start, make a separate photocopy of each work sheet for every year of your forecast. Use the first sheet to record your estimates for the first six months of each fiscal year, and the second sheet for months seven through twelve. The last sheet is used to record the annual totals.

Year						
Month	1	2	3	4	5	6
Net Sales	___	___	___	___	___	___
Cost of Goods	___	___	___	___	___	___
Total Revenues	___	___	___	___	___	___
Salaries	___	___	___	___	___	___
Taxes/Ben.	___	___	___	___	___	___
Commissions	___	___	___	___	___	___
Space Lease	___	___	___	___	___	___
Supplies	___	___	___	___	___	___
Equipment	___	___	___	___	___	___
Insurance	___	___	___	___	___	___
Advertising	___	___	___	___	___	___
Legal/Acct.	___	___	___	___	___	___
Communications	___	___	___	___	___	___
___	___	___	___	___	___	___
___	___	___	___	___	___	___
___	___	___	___	___	___	___
Royalty Pyt.	___	___	___	___	___	___
Co-op Ad Fund	___	___	___	___	___	___
___	___	___	___	___	___	___
Tot. Oper. Exp.	___	___	___	___	___	___
Pre-tax Profit	___	___	___	___	___	___
Income Taxes	___	___	___	___	___	___
Net Income	___	___	___	___	___	___

Year						
Month	7	8	9	10	11	12
Net Sales	___	___	___	___	___	___
Cost of Goods	___	___	___	___	___	___
Total Revenues	___	___	___	___	___	___
Salaries	___	___	___	___	___	___
Taxes/Ben.	___	___	___	___	___	___
Commissions	___	___	___	___	___	___
Space Lease	___	___	___	___	___	___
Supplies	___	___	___	___	___	___
Equipment	___	___	___	___	___	___
Insurance	___	___	___	___	___	___
Advertising	___	___	___	___	___	___
Legal/Acct.	___	___	___	___	___	___
Communications	___	___	___	___	___	___
_____	___	___	___	___	___	___
_____	___	___	___	___	___	___
_____	___	___	___	___	___	___
_____	___	___	___	___	___	___
Royalty Pyt.	___	___	___	___	___	___
Co-op Ad Fund	___	___	___	___	___	___
_____	___	___	___	___	___	___
Tot. Oper. Exp.	___	___	___	___	___	___
Pre-tax Profit	___	___	___	___	___	___
Income Taxes	___	___	___	___	___	___
Net Income	___	___	___	___	___	___

Annual Totals

Year _____

	Total	%
Net Sales	____	1.00
Cost of Goods	____	.___
Total Revenues	____	.___
Salaries	____	.___
Taxes/Ben.	____	.___
Commissions	____	.___
Space Lease	____	.___
Supplies	____	.___
Equipment	____	.___
Insurance	____	.___
Advertising	____	.___
Legal/Acct.	____	.___
Communications	____	.___
_____	____	.___
_____	____	.___
_____	____	.___
_____	____	.___
Royalty Pyt.	____	.___
Co-op Ad Fund	____	.___
Tot. Oper. Exp.	____	.___
Pre-tax Profit	____	
Income Taxes	____	
Net Income	____	

Chapter Twelve

A Meeting of Minds

The Franchise Agreement

When Michael R. visited the franchise headquarters of Golden Future Computer Centers, he was so dazzled by what he saw that he insisted on signing a contract on the spot. The franchisor's legal department had sent Michael a copy of the UFOC and franchise agreement two weeks before he arrived, fulfilling the company's obligation to place the disclosures in the hands of the prospective franchisee at least ten business days prior to signing. Michael had read the documents and shared them with his attorney, who, knowing little about franchising, browsed through them in two hours and rendered his general approval.

Neither Michael nor his attorney paid much attention to two seemingly minor points in the contract. The first was a statement to the effect that Michael, as the franchisee, had read the agreement in its entirety and understood and accepted all its terms, conditions, and covenants as being "reasonable and necessary." The second was a provision that in the event of Michael's disability or death, no heirs or successors could acquire any rights or interests in the franchise. In other words, if Michael should become permanently disabled or die, his wife, children, or any other heirs would lose all ownership in the business.

179

Clearly, this was not what Michael intended when he set out to start his own business. Yet, when he suffered a heart attack seven years later, the company moved in quickly and took over the business.

Later in court, Michael's attorneys contended that the franchisor's sales representatives had not adequately explained this provision to Michael prior to his signing the agreement. But when Michael executed the franchise contract, he was also signing an acknowledgment that he fully understood and agreed with every word.

What his franchisor had described as a "simple formality" ended up costing Michael and his heirs his life's work and legacy. You should remember that a franchisor's attorneys are usually experts in drafting franchise agreements, most of which are designed to produce maximum leverage for the franchisor. In contrast, your legal counsel is more likely to be an independent attorney with little experience in franchise contracts or disputes.

Knowing how a franchise contract is drafted and what ramifications may result from each provision is one of the most valuable assets you can bring to the bargaining table.

There are almost as many different franchise agreements as there are franchise businesses, but there are many elements common to all good franchise contracts. The basic agreement has fifteen parts. Each defines one of the important relationships between franchisor and franchisee.

1. *Grant of Franchise*

You might find this part of the contract in the "preambles." The preamble section summarizes the reason for the contract and states the mutual objectives of the parties signing it. However, it may also contain some legal language that may have an enormous bearing on your rights as a franchisee.

For example, the contract may contain a statement that you have read the Uniform Franchise Offering Circular and franchise agreement in their entirety, and accept all the terms, provisions, and covenants as being "reasonable and necessary." If you were the franchisor, you would certainly want this acknowledgment clearly stated and agreed to in writing. A franchisee involved in a legal dispute often claims that the franchisor failed to adequately explain all the details of the franchise contract. But as a prospective franchisee, be sure you really have read every word of the agreement, and understand what each sentence means.

When you sign the franchise agreement, you may also be signing an oath that could let your franchisor off the hook in the event of a future dispute over some aspect of the agreement.

The grant of franchise may also include a precisely defined territory. For example, the contract might state, "FRANCHISOR agrees that it will not compete with FRANCHISEE in the designated territory, nor establish another franchise therein."

In other words, the franchisor will not sell products to customers in your territory, or sell a franchise to someone else inside your territory. If a franchisor grants you a protected territory, he cannot restrain you from selling to customers outside its boundaries. The territory constrains the franchisor, not the franchisee.

2. Trademarks and Identity

This section of the agreement states who owns the trade name, trademarks, and logos associated with the franchise, and gives you a license to use them. The owner is usually the franchisor himself, or, possibly, a public figure affiliated with the franchisor. The agreement also obligates you to protect the franchisor's trademarks against infringement by others. In addition, you agree to use the trademarks only in a manner approved by the franchisor.

In plain English, that means the franchisor controls the business name and logo. For instance, he may let you order pens with the business name imprinted on the side, but he might want to forbid you from printing up girlie calendars featuring the company logo.

If you come across any unauthorized use of the trademarks by someone else, you are bound to notify the franchisor at once. For example, let's say you buy a franchise which uses the trade name "Go-Video." One day, you come across a competitor using the name "Go-Go Video." It's your duty to call the franchisor and report this obvious infringement. A registered trademark has no value unless its exclusivity is protected by those who are licensed to use it.

The agreement also usually obligates you to discontinue using the trademarks if the franchisor loses his own rights to them.

Simply acquiring the rights to a trademark through a franchise agreement may not give you the right to use it in your area. A franchisor secures federal registration of a trade name or mark by being the first one to implement it in interstate commerce. But someone else might already have the right to use the same name or trademark in a city, county, or state where the franchisor has not previously done business. As a result, you could actually end up buying a franchise and not being able to use the franchise name in your area.

Even though you obtain a license to use the franchisor's trademarks, you must obtain a business name permit (often called a DBA, for "doing business as") before you can use the name in your own business. A state, county, or city agency is usually responsible for dispensing these permits. The idea is to assure that competing businesses don't use the same name in the same trading area. If someone else has already acquired a permit to use the same or a similar name as your franchise, the trademark license may be a hollow commodity. Thus, investigate your right to use the franchise trademarks in your area *before* you sign the franchise agreement.

Assume, for example, that you buy a franchise which uses the trade name "Rocket Messenger." When you go to City Hall to take out a business name permit, you discover to your chagrin that another company in town already has the rights to that name. As a result, the permit is denied. Unfortunately, your franchisor's co-op advertising will be of very little value to you if you can't use the advertised name. You might be able to convince the other business to change its name, but not without compensation.

3. Relationships of the Parties

A franchisee is an independent business owner who contracts with a franchisor for the services and benefits specified in the agreement. As such, neither party may incur debts on the other's behalf. The franchise agreement does not make either party a subsidiary or affiliate of the other. Each is liable for his own taxes, debts, and contracts.

In plain English, your franchisor is not liable for your behavior. For example, if a customer trips on a freshly waxed floor and cracks a vertebra, you — not your franchisor — will be held liable. Likewise, if you cheat on your tax returns, it's your problem, not your franchisor's.

4. Fees and Payments

In this section, you agree to pay the initial franchise fee. The fee may be due on signing the agreement, or it may be payable in installments. As a franchisee, you also agree to pay the specified royalty, and to make sure it is paid on time each month. If your royalty payments are late, the agreement may stipulate interest or penalties.

If your franchisor has a co-op advertising fund, your monthly advertising royalty should also be stated in this section of the agreement.

If your franchisor will also be one of your vendors, e.g., a product distributor or equipment supplier, the agreement may give the franchisor the right to apply your royalty payments against any other amounts you may owe. For example, the contract may state something like, "FRANCHISOR shall have sole discretion to apply any payments by FRANCHISEE to any past-due indebtedness of FRANCHISEE to FRANCHISOR."

Let's say you buy a franchise to open a restaurant, and your franchisor happens to sell restaurant fixtures and supplies. Assume you buy these items from the franchisor on credit. Later on, when your restaurant opens, you mail in your first royalty check. To your consternation, the franchisor applies the royalty payment against the amount you owe for fixtures and supplies. As a result, your royalty remains unpaid and begins to accrue penalties.

If a provision like this appears in a franchise agreement, be sure your franchisor gives you a full and clear explanation before you sign. Ask for examples of how the provision might apply in your case.

5. Training and Guidance

In most franchise agreements, the franchisor agrees to provide a training program of a set length, e.g., two weeks. The agreement may require you to pay for your own travel and living costs to attend the training program. In addition, there may be a surcharge for additional attendees, such as a partner or manager. If these points are unclear in the agreement, ask the franchisor to clarify them.

The franchisor may also agree to provide other guidance and services, such as ongoing advice and consultation, a franchise manual, or assistance in selecting a site for your business.

Most franchise agreements state that the operating manual is loaned, not given or sold, to the franchisee. The logic is that the manual contains the franchisor's success secrets and, therefore, is accessible to you only during the term of your franchise. When your franchise expires, so does your access to the trade secrets. Hence, you usually must agree to return the manual and all updates, bulletins, and revisions to the franchisor if and when you and your franchisor part ways.

6. Operating System

In this section, you agree to abide by the franchisor's operating policies and performance standards. The agreement may also obligate you to help keep them secret.

You might also find one or more of the following provisions:

a. As a franchisee, you will be prevented from using the franchise business system in any other business.

b. You must keep every aspect of the business secret.

c. Neither you nor your employees may copy the franchise manual or any other written communication from the company.

d. Employees of your franchise must sign oaths of confidentiality.

In other words, you can't buy the franchise, learn all its success secrets, and then sell those secrets to someone else. Nor can you start another business under a different name using the methods and techniques you learned from the franchisor.

These are reasonable precautions designed to protect the value of the franchise. They work in your favor, as well as your franchisor's. Your franchisor's secrets, methods, and techniques are your competitive edge; the moment they fail to remain secret, your franchise instantly loses value.

7. Development and Improvement

The franchise agreement usually requires you to lease and develop your outlet within a specified period, e.g., ninety days. You also agree to purchase the equipment, fixtures, signs, and inventory you need to open the business. The franchisor may agree to help out with Grand Opening activities, or to send a field representative to assist you in developing the outlet.

Often, a franchise agreement is struck before there is even a site for the proposed outlet. If that's the case, be sure the deadline for opening the business gives you enough time to evaluate potential sites, negotiate a lease, and secure financing. In addition, you'll have to obtain business licenses, signs, and inventory. Negotiate for more time, if you think you really need it. Providing your request is reasonable, the franchisor should be moderately flexible on this issue.

For example, let's say you are considering a franchise to open a car rental agency, and the franchise agreement calls for you to open for business within sixty days. You will need a business loan to finance the outlet. You know a bank that will lend you the money, but it will take ninety days to process the loan application. Considering all the other things you must accomplish before opening — obtaining a site, ordering vehicles, hiring employees, etc. — you ask your franchisor to extend the deadline to 120 days. If you are serious about buying the franchise, the franchisor will probably amend the agreement to give you the time you need. But if you ask for nine months or a year, most likely the negotiations will fall apart.

From the franchisor's point of view, the deadline for developing the outlet encourages rapid market penetration in a new area. He doesn't want the territory sitting idle once he has awarded a franchise. But as a prospective franchisee, you want the deadline to be realistic in the light of business conditions in your locality.

Besides placing a deadline on opening the outlet, the franchise agreement should state exactly who selects the site. Will the franchisor determine the best location for your business? Or will he merely offer advice? Will you be responsible for picking the site? Or will a third party, such as a property developer or realtor, decide where the business will be located?

As a franchisee, you want the benefit of the franchisor's experience in the business. He knows the right customer demographics, traffic flow, and environment for the outlet. On the other hand, you might have a better grasp of the local economic conditions.

Some franchisors who say they will select a site actually contract with a commercial realtor or property manager to recommend an appropriate site. Indeed, a realtor has ready access to suitable properties. But does he have your best interests at heart? Will he focus on sites offering the highest commission or on some other self-serving benefit?

These issues may seem minor at the time, but they can easily become major problems after the franchise agreement is signed. For example, let's say you select your own site for the outlet. A few months later, the business falls into adverse financial straits. You blame your franchisor for failing to provide ongoing assistance, as promised. But, to your aggravation, the franchisor argues that your business is failing only because you selected the wrong site.

Now consider the opposite side of that coin. Let's assume you're the franchisor. As part of your program, you select the site for your franchisee's outlet. Despite your best efforts, one of your franchises fails, plagued by mismanagement and neglect. But in court, the franchisee's attorneys claim the problem was that you picked a bad location.

The solution is to make sure there's a meeting of minds before any site is selected. Both franchisor and franchisee should approve the site in writing before a lease is signed.

8. Image and Conduct

This section of the agreement spells out your obligations to maintain the franchisor's presumably high standards of image and conduct. For example, you might be obligated to keep the outlet clean and orderly, comply with certain merchandising standards, maintain adequate insurance coverage, and obey all laws and ordinances which apply to the business.

On the surface, these guidelines seem innocuous enough. After all, uniformity *is* the primary component in franchise success, and without the ability to enforce uniform standards, the whole idea of franchising dissipates. Ironically, these very contract provisions relating to quality, cleanliness, and appearance are the classic parents of franchise dispute, disorder, and distress.

Why? Because a franchisor's attorney sometimes devises these conditions as a "safety valve" for ridding the organization of an unruly franchisee. The list of standards may be so inclusive that practically any outlet could be found in violation at any given time.

A crooked poster, a wrinkled menu, a smudged uniform, or an unemptied ashtray could technically put you in default of the franchise agreement. In the past, some franchisors have used tiny spots on window panes, gum wrappers on restroom floors, and salt granules on table tops as excuses for forcefully terminating a franchise.

Over the last several decades, hundreds of franchise disputes have centered on this volatile issue, prompting several states to pass legislation granting additional rights to franchisees. Today, a franchisor must allow a franchisee a reasonable opportunity to correct the default. In some states, the law prohibits *any* involuntary termination of a franchise for a default in the franchisor's standards of image and cleanliness.

Besides mandatory standards, the agreement may also spell out how much insurance you must carry. Be certain your insurance carrier or agent understands your obligations and can comply exactly. Many carriers simply do not insure franchises at all. The agreement usually requires the franchisor to be named as an additional insured party on your business liability policy.

9. Advertising and Marketing

Most franchise agreements require you to use only advertising materials and media which were developed or approved by the franchisor. As a result, you will probably be limited as to the type of advertising programs you may conduct. For instance, the agreement may give the franchisor the right to prohibit you from using such items as pens, paper weights, or calendars with naked ladies to promote your franchise.

You might find this restriction vaguely cloaked in such generalized language as "materials which the franchisor, in its sole discretion, may deem unsuitable." Ask the franchisor exactly what kinds of advertising materials he considers "unsuitable." Besides the ones he *doesn't* want you to use, what advertising media *are* approved for promoting your business? Are those media readily available in your locality? Are they as effective in your market as in others? Are they as affordable?

For example, let's say you are considering a franchise to operate a financial counseling business. Based on his past success, the franchisor requires you to spend most of your advertising budget on radio and television ads. But what if those media are two or three times more costly in your market than in most others? Does the franchisor have an alternative advertising plan?

10. Reports and Audits

The typical franchise agreement requires you to maintain all the books and records required to document your tax liability and determine your royalty payments. In addition, you may have to prepare periodic financial statements and submit copies to your franchisor.

The agreement may also give the franchisor the right to audit your records at any time. From his point of view, it's important to be able to verify the accuracy of royalty payments. The right to conduct an audit is an integral and necessary safeguard against cheating.

As a prospective franchisee, you should ask: Who pays for the audit? It's one thing to demand an accounting, another to make you

187

bear the cost. An audit by a public accounting firm is expensive. A good compromise is for the franchisor to pay the cost unless the audit uncovers a significant discrepancy or problem. The amount of the discrepancy should be stated in the franchise agreement. Here's an example:

> If as a result of the audit a discrepancy in excess of three and one half percent (3½%) is found to exist, then FRANCHISEE shall pay all costs incurred in connection with the audit.

This kind of arrangement protects both parties. It protects the franchisor against the possibility of cheating by franchisees, and it protects you against frivolous and costly audits.

11. Assignment of the Franchise

Most franchise agreements will restrict your ability to sell your franchise to someone else. If for some reason you decide to sell the business, the buyer may have to meet with the franchisor's approval. The term most often used in a franchise agreement is "assignment" of the franchise. Assignment means any change in ownership, whether by sale or transfer. When you sell, or otherwise transfer ownership of the business, the new owner is thus the "assignee."

Who are the potential assignees of your franchise? Besides someone who buys the business, your heirs or beneficiaries might also become assignees, in the event of your death or disability. So, when a franchisor says your franchise may not be assigned without his approval, the right of your heirs to inherit the business may be at stake.

The franchisor may also reserve the "right of first refusal" to buy your franchise. This means that if you decide to sell the business, or if you should pass away while you own it, the franchisor is first in line to purchase the franchise. But he also has the right to refuse, clearing the way for a sale to someone else.

If your franchisor has the right of first refusal, you must offer it for sale to him before anyone else. He will have the right to buy the business for the same price and on the same conditions as any other buyer. For example, let's say you already own a franchise, and someone offers you $300,000 for your business. Before you can accept the offer, you must give the franchisor an opportunity to buy the franchise at the same price. If the franchisor accepts, you have no choice but to sell the business to him for $300,000. If he declines, you may proceed with the sale to the original buyer — assuming, of course, he meets your franchisor's approval.

It's not difficult to understand why a franchisor wants to have control over the sale of one of its franchises. Primarily, he wants to protect the franchise from falling into the hands of an unqualified party. After all, his company invests a great deal of time, effort, and money to recruit, train, and establish a suitable franchisee. He can hardly afford to have the business end up in the possession of someone who does not meet the standard qualifications of other franchisees.

Be sure you understand your franchisor's rights regarding assignment of the franchise. Those rights invariably restrict yours. For example, if you become disabled, the agreement may require you to sell or transfer the business to someone else. If you fail to assign the franchise within a designated period, your franchisor may have the right to take it from you without your permission.

The provisions for assignment also affect franchises operated as a corporation. A franchisor grants franchises to individuals, based on their personal traits — not to business entities such as corporations. When you incorporate, technically you are assigning the franchise to another party.

The agreement may place certain restrictions on your ability to assign your franchise to a corporation:

a. As the franchisee, you must remain in control of the business, i.e., as the majority stockholder and chief executive of the corporation.

b. You must disclose the names of all directors, stockholders, and officers to the franchisor.

c. The franchisor may have the right to approve any sale or transfer of the stock.

12. Renewal

Most, but not all, franchises have a definite term. In other words, they expire after a certain period of time, and must be renewed. Five percent of the franchise agreements currently in force do not have a definite term, meaning that the franchisee's rights never expire. About half of all franchise agreements in use today have a term of ten years.

The agreement usually gives you the right to renew the franchise for another term as the end of the first term approaches. However, to renew the franchise you must usually sign a new agreement. That agreement may not be the same as the one you originally signed. In this way, franchisors can periodically "update" their franchise programs, by changing the terms and conditions of the franchise agreements as they come up for renewal.

The shorter the term, the more flexibility the franchisor has to make changes in its organization. On the other hand, as a prospective franchisee making a substantial investment in the franchise, you deserve the opportunity to reap just rewards. It may take a business as long as three years to begin turning a profit. If the franchise term is only five years, you hardly have enough time to realize a decent return.

13. Termination

This section of the agreement spells out the rights of both parties to terminate the contract. For example, if you abandon the business, or are convicted of a felony, the franchisor may have the right to take the franchise from you. On the other hand, you may have the right to terminate the contract if the franchisor fails to fulfill his obligations.

Many franchise agreements say that a franchisor can terminate the franchise unilaterally if you declare bankruptcy. However, you should be aware that, under the Federal Bankruptcy Law, bankruptcy alone may not be used as an excuse to repossess your franchise. But if you fail to keep the doors open for business, you risk losing your investment for "abandoning the franchise."

State laws vary regarding the franchisor's right to terminate a franchise agreement. *No matter what your franchise agreement says, the local statute or ordinance is binding on your franchisor*. For example, the California Franchise Investment Protection Law forbids franchisors from terminating an agreement without "good cause." Good cause is defined as a failure to provide due notice regarding a dispute or default, or a failure to allow the franchisee ample opportunity to correct such a dispute or default. If you live in Mississippi, and a franchisor terminates the agreement, he must be prepared to repurchase your inventory of goods.

For example, let's say you buy a franchise to sell a product which is exclusively distributed by your franchisor. You order a large opening inventory of products. When the shipment arrives, your franchisor can't suddenly cancel the agreement and stick you with a warehouse full of goods. This law helps to assure that franchisors are genuinely interested in your personal success, not merely in taking advantage of you as a captive customer.

14. Obligations Upon Termination or Expiration

If, for any reason, you and your franchisor should part ways, this section of the agreement spells out your obligations. For example, you may be required to return the franchise manual and cease using any of the franchisor's trademarks. You might also have to give up your business phone number.

Most agreements contain a "covenant not to compete." In the covenant, you pledge not to compete with the franchisor in the same business after the agreement expires or is terminated. You should be aware that such covenants are not valid in some states, including California, the largest franchise market.

15. Enforcement and Construction

Every good agreement has a morass of perplexing legal terminology dealing with issues like "severability," "substitution," "governing law," and "binding effect."

The "severability" clause assures that the contract remains in force though part of the agreement may happen to be struck down in court. For example, let's say you sign a franchise agreement which contains a covenant not to compete. Later, a court rules that all such covenants are unenforceable in your state. Even though this part of your franchise agreement may be unenforceable, the rest of the agreement remains in full force and effect.

A "substitution" clause simply means that if the local law is different from any provision in the agreement, that law is automatically substituted for the offending provision. Assume, for instance, that you sign a franchise agreement which states that to renew the contract, you must notify the franchisor at least one year before the expiration date. However, the law in your state allows you to wait sixty days before the contract expires to make up your mind. In this case, the sixty-day requirement mandated by law is automatically substituted for the one-year requirement in the agreement.

The "governing law" clause stipulates which state's laws will be used to interpret the agreement in the event of a dispute. Almost invariably, this is the state in which the franchisor is headquartered.

The basic parts of a franchise agreement are illustrated in the sample franchise agreement in Appendix D. As you evaluate an agreement, you should seek the assistance of an attorney with ample franchise experience. If your own attorney doesn't have the appropriate background, ask him or her to recommend a lawyer or firm that has more experience handling franchise cases.

Remember that the franchisor's lawyers draft the contract to provide maximum advantage for the franchisor, but cloaked in innocent-sounding verbiage. An agreement between a franchisor and franchisee falls under special rules and interpretations that are different from other types of contracts.

In the next chapter, you'll find a list to help you interpret, understand, and evaluate a franchise agreement.

Chapter Thirteen

How to Evaluate
a Franchise Agreement

In the last chapter, we examined the important sections of a franchise agreement and learned how its provisions affect your rights as a franchisee. This chapter contains an exhaustive checklist for evaluating a franchise agreement.

Each set of questions is keyed to one of the main sections of a typical franchise agreement. There are many different forms of agreements, and you may find some sections ordered differently, or combined with other sections.

As you study the agreement, try to answer the questions that apply in this checklist. If you can't find the answer in the agreement, or if the answer isn't clear, circle the question on the checklist. When you sit down at the negotiating table prior to signing the agreement, ask the franchisor or his representative to answer or clarify each question you circled.

1. Grant of Franchise

- Have you read the agreement in its entirety?
- Do you understand and accept all the terms, provisions, and covenants?
- Do you consider them reasonable and necessary to the success of the business?

- Does the agreement provide you with a specified territory?
- Is the territory precisely defined according to generally accepted geographic boundaries?
- Does your franchisor agree not to compete within the specified territory?
- Does the agreement stipulate that no other franchisor will sell any franchises to others in your territory?
- Does the agreement attempt to restrict you from selling your goods or services to customers outside your territory?
- Are your rights to the territory, or its size, tied to your fiscal performance or a sales quota?
- What sub-franchising rights, if any, will you have within the territory?
- Is the term of the franchise at least ten years, or enough time to allow you to realize a decent return after enduring the difficult startup years?

2. *Trademarks and Identity*

- Does the franchisor own the trademarks associated with the franchise business?
- Are the trademarks owned by or associated with a public figure? If the answer to the previous question is "yes," is the public figure a principal in the franchising company, or merely a promotional spokesperson?
- Does the franchisor agree to protect the use of the trademarks against unlawful infringement by others?
- Is the trademark or logo registered with the federal government, or merely with some local state, county, or municipal agency?
- Is the trademark or logo registered, or is it merely "applied for"?
- Are there any trade names or marks in use by others in your trading area similar to the franchise trademark, or likely to cause confusion with the franchise trademark?
- Does any one else in your local jurisdiction have the prior right to use the same trademark as the franchise through a fictitious name permit or "dba"?

3. *Relationship of the Parties*

- Does the franchise agreement recognize that you are an independent contractor, not an agent, employee, or subsidiary of the franchisor?
- Does the agreement acknowledge that you are liable for your own debts, liabilities, and taxes, and that you are not liable for any debts, liabilities, or taxes incurred by the franchisor?
- If your franchisor should happen to be sued for some act or policy for which it is solely responsible, will you be indemnified and held free of blame?

4. *Fees and Payments*

- Is the amount of the franchise fee clearly stipulated, to the exact penny?
- Is the time at which the franchise fee is due clearly stated?
- Is the franchise royalty clearly stipulated to the exact percentage point or fraction of a percent?
- Is the day of the month on which the royalty is due clearly stated?
- Is the amount of any co-op advertising contribution clearly stated?
- Does the agreement provide for the royalty or co-op ad contribution to be increased unilaterally by the franchisor in the future?
- Does the franchisor have the right to apply your royalty payments to other accounts, such as amounts you owe for fixtures, supplies, or inventory?

5. *Training and Guidance*

- Does the franchisor provide a training program?
- What is the length of the program?
- Where is the program held?
- Are you obligated to pay for your own travel and living expenses while attending the training program?
- Will the franchisor provide you with a franchise manual?

- What type of ongoing assistance is your franchisor obligated to provide?
- Does the agreement stipulate the number and frequency of visits by a representative of the franchise company?
- Will you have the right to seek guidance from the franchisor any time you need it, or only when a representative makes one of his periodic visits?

6. Operating Systems

- What steps are you obligated to take to protect the franchisor's trade secrets?
- Does the agreement require you to make your employees sign a contract containing an oath of secrecy and a covenant not to compete?
- Will you be prohibited from conducting any other business activity while you own the franchise?
- What other kinds of businesses or activities are permitted?

7. Development and Improvement

- Are you required to lease a site within a certain period? If so, is the length reasonable, in light of local business, real estate, and regulatory conditions?
- Are you required to complete all improvements and inventory purchases within a specified period?
- What are the penalties if you fail to meet the time restrictions?
- Will your franchisor provide assistance in selecting the best site for the business?
- If so, can the franchisor delegate this obligation to a local realtor or leasing agent without your permission?
- Will a representative of the franchise company personally assist you in obtaining a site, or will the company simply hand you a site selection kit?
- If you must select a site on your own, what kind of reference materials, demographics, or other tools will the franchisor provide?
- Will the franchisor help you negotiate a favorable lease?

- Does the agreement stipulate the length of the lease, or any other terms or conditions?
- If, for some reason, you fail to meet your obligations to open the outlet within a specified period, and the franchisor has the right to cancel, will at least half of your franchise fee be refunded?

8. *Image and Conduct*

- Are the franchisor's mandatory operating standards reasonable and necessary?
- Will the franchisor have the right to terminate the agreement unilaterally, in the event of a default?
- Has the franchisor provided you with a written list containing examples of specific defaults?
- Does your state have laws giving you additional rights as a franchisee?
- If so, has the franchisor informed you that the portions of the agreement relating to defaults in operating standards may be invalid?
- What is the penalty for a default?
- How long will you have to cure an alleged default after receiving a notice from the franchisor?
- Is the length of time reasonable?
- Does the agreement stipulate the type and amount of business liability or other insurance you must carry?
- Is the stipulated insurance available in your area?
- If the answer is "yes," will you be able to afford the premiums?

9. *Advertising and Marketing*

- Does the agreement provide for a co-op ad fund?
- Is the amount of your advertising royalty clearly defined as either a set amount or percentage?
- Can the amount of your advertising royalty be increased by the franchisor without your consent?
- Does the agreement limit you as to the type of advertising media you may use to promote the business?

- What advertising assistance will the franchisor provide in your local area?
- Does the agreement obligate the franchisor to conduct a certain number or type of advertising efforts?
- Will the franchisor provide Grand Opening assistance?

10. *Reports and Audits*

- Does the agreement permit the franchisor to audit your books and records at any time without notice?
- Does the agreement clearly define the types of reports you must submit periodically?
- Are the franchisor's books available for your inspection at the principal business address?
- If the franchisor conducts an audit of your records, will you be obligated to pay all the costs?
- If there is a dispute or discrepancy as a result of an audit, will you have the right to contest the auditor's report?

11. *Assignment of the Franchise*

- What are the conditions under which you may assign the franchise to someone else?
- Does the agreement permit you to sell the franchise to someone who meets all the usual qualifications for a franchisee of the company?
- Will the franchisor have the right of first refusal to purchase the franchise if you decide to sell?
- If you should become disabled or die, will your heirs or successors lose all ownership rights to the business?
- If your successors should fail to assign the franchise to someone else within a certain time period, will the franchisor have the right to confiscate the business?
- If the franchisor, for any reason, should confiscate the franchise, what formula will be used to adequately compensate you, your heirs, or successors?
- What are the conditions for operating the franchise as a corporation?

- If the business will be a corporation, does the agreement mandate how much stock you must personally own?
- Will any transfer of stock have to be approved by the franchisor?

12. *Renewal*

- Will you have the right to renew the franchise agreement when it expires?
- If you do renew the franchise, will you re-execute the same agreement, or will a different agreement be substituted?
- What are the conditions for renewing the agreement?
- Is there a specified period before the expiration date during which you must notify the franchisor of your desire to renew?
- Does the specified period give you enough time to make a decision and comply with the conditions?

13. *Termination*

- Does the franchisor reserve the right to terminate the agreement unilaterally for any reason?
- Are the stipulated reasons justifiable and appropriate?
- Does your state have laws preventing a franchisor from unilaterally terminating an agreement, no matter what the reason?
- If so, has the franchisor informed you that your state law takes precedence over any provision in the agreement?
- Does the agreement state that your franchise may be terminated in the event of bankruptcy or reorganization due to insolvency?
- Has the franchisor informed you that the Federal Bankruptcy Law prohibits franchisors from terminating an agreement by reason of the franchisee's bankruptcy?
- If the franchisor has the right to terminate the agreement for a default on your part, will you be compensated for your investment?
- If the franchisor should terminate the agreement, will it repurchase any inventory sold to you as part of the franchise arrangement?

14. *Obligations Upon Termination or Expiration*

- What are your obligations upon termination or expiration of the agreement?
- What are your franchisor's obligations?
- If you choose not to renew when the agreement expires, will you have to give up the business?
- Will you have to vacate the premises?
- Will you have to change your business phone number?
- Does the agreement prohibit you from operating a similar business, or one which might be deemed to be in competition, after termination or expiration?
- How long will this covenant not to compete remain in effect?
- Is the time period reasonable, in light of your experience, skills, and ability to maintain a livelihood?

15. *Enforcement and Construction*

- Has an attorney adequately explained the clauses of the agreement relating to severability, substitution, and governing law?
- In the event that a provision of the agreement should be held illegal or unenforceable, will the entire agreement become invalid?
- If a dispute should arise, in which state will it be settled — yours or your franchisor's?

Chapter Fourteen

Dealer's Choice

How to Evaluate a Franchisor

As you probably realize by now, a famous name and a host of locations are no assurance of success in the franchise business. It's true that a franchisor's public exposure and number of outlets add to the benefits of the program, but there are other, often more subtle qualities that may have an even greater influence on your survival.

The Advantages and Risks of Thinking Big

There are trade-offs when you deal with a big franchisor. A large, easily recognized organization is more likely to be well capitalized. Experience shows in a mature franchisor. Many, if not most, of his support staff emerged from the field. Moreover, it's impossible to open five hundred or a thousand outlets and handle their day-to-day headaches without acquiring some very useful know-how.

A major franchise operation has the best public exposure and offers the most potent cooperative benefits to franchisees, particularly advertising reach and purchasing power.

On the opposite side of the coin, a big-time operator is more apt to evolve into a "hot shot" with an inflated self-image and overbearing authority. The best franchisor is the one who guides, not coerces . . . counsels, not commands. There is a natural tendency among franchisors to grow militaristic as their networks swell to nearly unmanageable proportions.

In government, "power corrupts," but in a franchise organization, "power corrodes." Over time, a large franchisor often forgets that his success was borne on the shoulders of numerous franchisees. As a result, he grows more distant from the industry and becomes less and less tuned to the marketplace.

A second risk of selecting a large, rapidly proliferating franchisor is the peril of getting lost in the shuffle. Any company that expands too quickly soon finds itself with more people who have questions than those who have answers. The support staff become diluted with too many priorities. Eventually, the franchisee mortality rate may equal or exceed the recruitment rate.

Consider the case of a famous hairstyling salon that sprang up in 1979 and expanded meteorically to more than 3,000 outlets by the end of 1980. Normally, one would consider such a performance to be a sterling testimonial to entrepreneurial success. Unfortunately, the overextended company declared bankruptcy in 1983 and disappeared from the franchise scene even as the founder's glistening smile adorned the cover of a national business magazine.

The Advantages and Risks of Thinking Small

Simply because a franchisor is small — or just starting to sell franchises — is no reason to discard his offering altogether. However, when there's little history to rely on, your research must be extremely thorough.

It's worth repeating that when people buy franchises, they are looking to replicate the franchisor's own personal success. Nowhere is this quality more pronounced than in the case of the small-time or first-time franchisor. All franchisors started out small, and many insist on staying that way.

An entrepreneur with a successful small business is often goaded into franchising by demand. People walk into the restaurant or store, and ask how they can get into the business themselves. Few, if any, franchisors invest the considerable effort and funds it takes to put together a franchise program without first conducting a painstaking feasibility study. Consequently, although a small franchisor poses somewhat higher risks than a prolific one, the odds are not insurmountable. In fact, a modest organization often provides better one-on-one support.

Experts consider the "ideal" ratio to be one field representative for every twelve franchisees. Beyond that, the level of personal support begins to erode. A small franchisor is often better equipped to handle his franchisee's day-to-day problems. Moreover, he invariably has greater sensitivity toward and rapport with the people in the organization. As a franchisee, you may even have access to the company founder — a benefit essentially unheard of in a large franchise organization.

The main drawbacks to a diminutive franchise chain are less advertising power, which results in higher marketing overhead, and fewer cooperative benefits. You will generally pay higher wholesale prices and invest a greater percentage of your income in advertising. If the franchisor is not well capitalized, you run the risk that the entire program will collapse in an economic downswing or industry slowdown.

Just because a "prototype" business may be successful is no assurance that its success can be replicated elsewhere by others. Often, that success revolves around the genius or skill of its owner, and not on its concept, recognition, or product. Besides that, prototypes don't pay franchise royalties. Deduct from five to fifteen percent from the gross revenues of any business, no matter how successful, and see how much profit it produces (if any). Too many businesses based on concepts that "can't miss" have failed to produce workable franchises. Better to rely on a franchisor with a track record — one who has proved his success can actually be cloned — than one with nothing but a "revolutionary" idea or a "phenomenal" prototype.

The Final Decision

To a franchise marketing director, your decision is just one more sale. But to you, the franchise represents your livelihood and quality

203

of life. Whether or not to franchise — and which franchise to purchase — will be one of the most important decisions you will ever make. Don't make it lightly.

When you evaluate a franchise opportunity, peer behind the glossy color photographs, the meticulously groomed flagship, and the affable smile of the franchisor's representative. Look for signposts from the past telling you about the future.

Just as a franchisor evaluates the qualifications of many franchisees before selecting the right candidate, you should evaluate prospective franchisors according to their "qualifications." Here are some of the important traits to evaluate.

Background Traits

• *Length of time in business*

The longer a franchisor has been in business, the more experience he has to share with you. He knows what works in his line of business. But his "negative" experience is as important as his successes. He knows what *not* to do to be successful: how to avoid the innumerable mistakes, large and small, that characterize a small business when it first starts out.

• *Length of time in franchising*

The longer a franchisor has been involved in franchising, the more capable he is to lead, guide, and motivate the franchise organization. He know what makes franchisees "tick": their ambitions, drives, hopes, and dreams. He knows how to handle problems and stave off crises.

• *Prior litigation or other legal problems*

The fewer lawsuits and legal entanglements a franchisor has had, the more ethical he is likely to be. Favor the franchisor who conscientiously walks the "straight and narrow." Some franchisors have the attitude that a large number of lawsuits is inevitable in the franchise business. But, among other things, legal fees burden the entire franchise organization, eating up funds that might otherwise be spent to the benefit of franchisees.

● *Civil actions/expulsions from securities associations*

A history of civil actions involving fraud or the violation of a franchise law is a red flag for concern. It's true that unscrupulous operators sometimes reform, but unethical business conduct is often part of a lifelong behavior pattern. A slogan heard too often in franchise circles is "anything's legal as long as you get away with it."

Don't take chances. If you have the poor sense to buy a franchise from a convicted felon, or someone who was once expelled from a securities association, you probably deserve whatever consequences befall you.

Industry Know-How

● *Length of time in the industry*

Some franchisors have spent a great deal of time in business, but only a relatively small portion of that time in their current industries. For instance, a franchisor in the electronics industry sold shoes for ten years — twice as long as he has been involved with electronics. Real know-how is derived from real experience.

Give added weight to franchisors who were successful in their own industries *before* they started to franchise.

● *Credentials of the franchise staff*

As you evaluate the backgrounds of the franchisor's staff, compare their credentials to your needs as a franchisee. Are the officers and managers well qualified for their jobs? Is their experience appropriate for the business of the franchise? For example, a franchise sales director might simply be a good sales professional, but the field representative should have abundant experience in the business.

205

• *Market share or influence*

The greater a franchisor's influence in the marketplace, the greater the cooperative benefits to his franchisees. If a company is dominant in its industry, your franchise may well dominate your local market.

If, for instance, you buy a Hertz car rental franchise, you can be assured the franchisor's market influence will automatically bring you many customers. But if you buy a franchise with little or no share of the national market, you really have no indication of how well the business will do in your area.

• *Advertising reach*

Favor the franchisor that has already conducted national or regional advertising programs that reach customers in your area. When your franchise opens, the public will already know who you are, what you're selling, and why they should patronize your business.

Some franchisors don't conduct advertising campaigns on behalf of their franchisees. If that's the case, you'll end up shouldering the advertising burden yourself. That burden will take a healthy chunk out of your monthly revenues, making it all the more difficult for you to grow.

• *Number of outlets*

Decide whether you'd rather be part of a large franchise chain or a small one. If you're a sharp business person who doesn't need a lot of personal guidance, favor the large organization. Sheer strength in numbers creates powerful cooperative benefits, including national advertising and discount purchasing. If you need or desire personal attention, though, a smaller but established franchisor may be better for you.

• *Net worth*

Give added weight to the franchisor who is well capitalized. In an economic crisis, he is the one who will lead you through the economic waters. As you evaluate the franchisor's net worth, look for the answers to these questions: How much of the asset value of the company represents tangible assets, such as equipment, buildings, and cash on hand?

How much represents intangible assets, such as the value of a trademark or goodwill?

In other words, how much is real, and how much is "fluff"?

• *Past financial stability*

A company that has maintained an even keel through times of economic hardship has extra know-how that may help *you* survive, as well. Give preference to a franchisor whose company has led a life of economic stability, without undergoing numerous re-organizations, mergers, and acquisitions.

• *Cash reserves for handling a crisis*

Study the franchisor's audited financial statement. How much cash does he have on hand? If the amount is not impressive, how many of his assets are convertible — i.e., can be easily liquidated in a crisis?

Give added weight to a franchisor who is prepared to handle cash emergencies if the economy or industry takes an unexpected turn for the worse.

Other Qualifications

• *Quality of training program*

Ask the franchisor for an outline of his training curriculum. Does it touch all the bases? Does it have real substance and value? Think of your initial fee as your tuition to attend the franchise training school, and consider whether the curriculum is worth the price.

• *Franchise operating manual*

Ask to see the operating manual, or, if the franchisor considers it "too secret" to let you browse through, ask to inspect the table of contents. Is the manual comprehensive? Does it provide a complete how-to "bible" for running the business?

● *Level of franchisee satisfaction*

Give preference to franchisors who have the happiest franchisees. Be sure to contact at least three franchisees listed in the franchisor's UFOC. Ask them the questions shown in Chapter Nine of this book under the heading *20. Information Regarding Franchises of the Franchisor.*

● *Management style*

Ultimately, the ideal franchisor is one whose management style and personality blend well with yours. We'll discuss franchisor's management styles in detail in Chapter Fifteen.

The Franchisor Evaluation Worksheet

Once you've considered all these qualifications, you're prepared to evaluate a prospective franchisor's strengths and weaknesses. At this end of this chapter, you'll find a Franchisor Evaluation Worksheet with which to rate each franchisor under your consideration.

This worksheet lists each of the key traits discussed in this chapter. Rate each factor on a scale of 1 to 10 — 1 signifying the lowest rating, 10 the highest. Then multiply your rating by the corresponding weight factor on the right. The result is the "index" for that trait. When you have rated the franchisor on all the traits in the worksheet, add the numbers in the index column. The sum is the franchisor's final "score."

With this evaluation worksheet, there's no set "passing" grade. The worksheet is designed to help you compare the strengths and weaknesses of different franchisors. Before you make a franchise decision, evaluate their scores to find out how each franchisor rates against the others.

Franchisor Evaluation Worksheet

Factor	Weight	Rating	Index
Background			
Length of time in business	.10	X _____	= _____
Length of time in franchising	.05	X _____	= _____
Litigation	.05	X _____	= _____
Civil actions	.05	X _____	= _____
Industry Know-How			
Length of time in the industry	.05	X _____	= _____
Staff credentials	.05	X _____	= _____
Market share	.05	X _____	= _____
Advertising reach	.05	X _____	= _____
Number of outlets	.05	X _____	= _____
Financial			
Net worth	.15	X _____	= _____
Past stability	.05	X _____	= _____
Cash reserves	.05	X _____	= _____
Other			
Training program	.06	X _____	= _____
Operations manual	.05	X _____	= _____
Franchisee satisfaction	.06	X _____	= _____
Management style	.08	X _____	= _____

Final Score _____

Part 3

Franchising in Action

Chapter Fifteen

Capital Ideas

How to Finance a Franchise

Many, if not most, franchises are started with financial assistance from a third party, such as a bank, savings and loan, investment firm, leasing company, financial partner, or venture capitalist. In addition, over one-half of all franchisors offer some form of direct or indirect financial assistance to franchisees.

Start-up capital is an investment in a new business for which a business plan and management team are already in place. This type of financing is used for such purposes as real estate purchases, building construction, equipment, fixtures, and opening inventory.

Working capital is money applied to keeping an established business afloat. This type of financing is used to pay wages and salaries, make lease payments, and replenish inventory and supplies.

Expansion capital is an investment in a merger, acquisition, diversification, or market expansion program. This type of financing is used to expand a business beyond its present markets and territories.

A prospective franchisee seeking financing to open a franchise outlet is usually looking for start-up capital — money to swing the initial investment. Six sources of start-up financing are commonly used by franchisees:

- conventional lenders
- the Small Business Administration and other federal agencies

- Small Business Investment Companies and Minority Enterprise Small Business Investment Companies
- finance, credit, and leasing companies
- franchisors that offer financial assistance
- private investors

Conventional Lenders

A common source of start-up capital for small businesses such as new franchise outlets is a conventional lending institution, such as a bank, savings and loan, or credit union. Commercial loans are generally available at prevailing interest rates, subject to the creditworthiness of the borrower and current economic conditions. To guarantee the loan, the borrower must usually put up personal property, such as equity in a home or the assets of the business, as collateral. In addition, you will need a good business plan and a detailed account of your personal finances.

One advantage of obtaining financing from a conventional lender is the availability of funds at prevailing interest rates. However, tightened banking regulations and the crisis in the savings and loan industry of the late 1980s and early 1990s have made bank financing somewhat more difficult to obtain. Still, lenders are more likely to lend money to open a franchise outlet than to an independent business, providing that the franchisor has an established track record.

If you do not have a large amount of liquid assets or substantial property to pledge as collateral, you will have difficulty securing a conventional loan. Moreover, it will probably take you fifteen to thirty years to repay the loan, saddling your business with a lengthy debt service.

To qualify for a conventional loan, you will need collateral that will hold its value throughout the duration of the loan. Equipment and real estate are good ways to secure a long-term loan. Also, you will probably be required to guarantee the loan personally and maintain a large financial interest in the business. If the franchise business will have partners or stockholders, you should have a controlling interest — no less than 51 percent of the voting stock. To swing a real estate loan, you will probably have to come up with a 30 percent down payment.

Your creditworthiness will also be important in securing a conventional business loan. The lender will verify whether you pay your bills on time, both personally and in business. Nothing will derail a loan application faster than a poor credit history. It will also help if you have a high personal net worth outside the business and a large bank balance.

Loan officers are interested in four things, known in banking circles as the "four Cs:"

- Character and credit. Do you have the reputation and good credit history to ensure repayment of the loan?
- Capital. Do you have a sufficient amount of equity in the business?
- Capacity. Do you have the management skills to run a profitable business?
- Collateral. Do you have enough personal property to pledge as collateral?

At times, banks run out of money to lend, or their reserves become low. Before you waste your time applying for a loan, find out whether the bank has money available for business loans.

The Small Business Administration

The Small Business Administration (SBA) is a federal agency established by law in 1951 to assist small businesses by distributing information and arranging financial assistance. The SBA has long been regarded by many Americans as an "economic equalizer," helping to preserve the entrepreneurial spirit.

The SBA is best known for offering financial assistance in the form of direct loans, grants, and guaranteed third-party loans to small business owners. Franchise businesses qualify for SBA assistance under the agency's guidelines and, in fact, are often preferred over independent businesses.

The Loan Guarantee Program provides loan guarantees to small businesses that do not qualify for conventional bank loans. According to the agency, the SBA program includes about 1,000 private lenders who offer business loans to borrowers who might otherwise not qualify. The loan is arranged through an institution such as a bank, savings and loan, or finance company, but the SBA guarantees to fulfill the borrower's obligations.

Two types of guaranteed loan programs are available — the 7(a) program and the 504 program. The 7(a) program, which is the broadest and largest of all the SBA loan programs, is also the most flexible. Under this plan, a loan of $50,000 to $1 million can be obtained from a lending institution approved by the SBA. Money can be borrowed to provide working capital or to finance the purchase of equipment or real estate. Under the 7(a) program, the SBA guarantees to repay the loan if the borrower defaults, but the loan is extended by an independent lending institution.

In the 504 program, the SBA puts up part of the loan money in conjunction with a lending institution. These loans are available for the purchase of real estate and heavy equipment up to $3 million in value.

Direct loans are available from the SBA for special situations — for example, to help victims of a natural disaster or for a business owned by a physically challenged individual.

To qualify for a typical SBA-guaranteed loan, you must first be turned down by at least three conventional lenders. The SBA interest rates are usually lower than commercial loan rates. In addition, an SBA program may get you more money than a private lender would be willing to lend you. You can usually borrow up to four dollars for every dollar you put into the business yourself.

SBA-guaranteed loans tend to be quite flexible. An SBA program can get you a seven-year working capital loan, a ten-year equipment loan, or a twenty-five-year real estate loan. A real estate loan requires only a 10 percent down payment. You may also be able to put up such property as jewelry, paintings, antiques, or classic cars as collateral.

Because the SBA is funded by Congress, funding is not always available to underwrite or guarantee small business loans. SBA offices are located throughout the country. Look in the telephone book under "United States Federal Government" or contact

> Small Business Administration
> 1441 L Street NW
> Washington, DC 20416
> Telephone: 800-368-5855

In addition to financial assistance, the SBA also distributes information to help small business owners make intelligent planning and financial decisions. Two publications, *Franchise Index/Profile* and *Are You Ready for Franchising?* may be of interest to prospective franchisees.

The SBA has provided numerous franchisees with start-up capital over the last four decades. An advantage to SBA-guaranteed financing is that franchises are favored over independent businesses because of their higher success rate. A drawback is the lengthy application process, which may take from six to twelve months. Most franchisees are required to open the business three to four months after signing a franchise agreement. The SBA will also impose certain restrictions on how you run your business. The lending institution will closely monitor how much you spend and how you spend it.

Office of Small and Disadvantaged Business Utilization

Besides the SBA, other federal agencies may also be able to help you finance a franchise, depending on your economic or ethnic status. The Office of Small and Disadvantaged Business Utilization provides funding for businesses that are owned or controlled by a socially or economically disadvantaged person. Women, African Americans, Hispanics, Asians, and Native Americans all qualify as disadvantaged entrepreneurs under this program. For information about this agency, contact

> Office of Small and Disadvantaged Business
>   Utilization
> 400 7th Street SW, Room 9410
> Washington, DC 20590
> Telephone: 202-366-5335

Minority Business Development Agency

Another federal agency that helps disadvantaged business owners is the Minority Business Development Agency. This agency is part of the Department of Commerce and offers a wide variety of programs, ranging from export development to rural assistance. The Franchise Assistance Program and the Minority Business Opportunity Committee Program are of particular interest to prospective franchisees. For information about this agency, contact

> Minority Business Development Agency
> U.S. Department of Commerce
> 14th Street Between Constitution and E Streets NW
> Washington, DC 20230
> Telephone: 202-377-1936

Small Business Investment Companies

Small Business Investment Companies (SBICs) are privately owned venture capital firms that are licensed and partially financed by the SBA. Some SBICs specialize in franchise outlets. Many such firms limit their investments to a particular industry or trade, such as lodging, fast food, or electronics.

A Minority Enterprise Small Business Investment Company (MESBIC) invests in only minority-owned businesses. SBICs often have more than one type of funding available. They may make SBA-type loans, based on competitive rates, or they may invest in a business by purchasing a percentage of its ownership.

The money comes from the investment company's membership, usually private investors pooling their money to make a profit. However, the group is usually interested in a diversity of investments, including stocks, treasury bills, commodities, and money market funds.

As a result, a typical SBIC may confine its lending activity to a few select businesses. To receive funding, your business plan will have to compete favorably with other proposals vying for the SBIC's limited loan dollars, but if you have a franchise granted by a particularly successful franchisor in a dynamic growth industry, the SBIC might be interested in a direct investment in your business.

Whereas a lending institution extends loans to creditworthy franchisees at prevailing interest rates, an SBIC or a MESBIC may make a direct investment in the business. The investment company may purchase from 5 to 50 percent of the ownership but is prohibited from taking control of the business. Such firms may also lend start-up, working, or expansion capital to business owners who might not otherwise qualify for commercial loans, but usually at relatively high rates.

A big advantage to SBIC and MESBIC funding is that these sources expressly favor franchises. This attitude is based on the high survival rate of franchise outlets as well as the training and assistance provided by franchisors. A minority business owner with a franchise is in an excellent position to receive financial aid from a licensed MESBIC.

Finance Companies

Finance companies, leasing firms, and property management businesses that arrange for partial funding of the franchisee's investment are also potential sources of financing. Finance companies, such as ITT Small Business Finance Corporation or Allied Capital Corporation, extend start-up loans to franchisees. Credit companies, such as General Electric Credit Corporation or Westinghouse Credit Corporation, may provide financing for inventory, equipment, or fixtures. A

219

leasing company, such as Phoenix Leasing, Inc., based in San Rafael, California, may purchase equipment or real estate to lease back to the franchisee. Property management firms may invest in real property required by the franchisee, either through conventional financing or through a leaseback program.

Financial Assistance from a Franchisor

Each year, hundreds of franchise outlets are opened with the benefit of direct or indirect financing from a franchisor. A small percentage of franchisors offer to finance the franchisee's entire initial investment, including working capital. Others may finance a portion of the investment or merely the initial fee. Still others provide assistance by leasing equipment or real estate or by offering credit terms for purchases of supplies and opening inventory.

Why would a franchisor put up money to put you in business for yourself? For one thing, a franchisor with numerous outlets has a demonstrable success formula. The company believes in its formula and knows how well it works. When it sells a franchise, the franchisor is more interested in finding someone with the right personality and skills than in just adding another initial fee to its coffers.

For another thing, successful franchisors have money to reinvest. Any company that enjoys extraordinary success has a unique if enviable problem: a surplus of cash. By lending money to franchisees or offering credit terms for purchases of equipment, inventory, or real estate, a franchisor realizes additional profits from the interest charged. On the financing of equipment or machinery purchases, the company also gains depreciation benefits.

Many franchisors have arrangements with third parties, such as finance companies, leasing firms, or product distributors, to finance all or part of the initial investment. A franchisor that offers any form of financial assistance to franchisees, either through itself or through a third party, must disclose the details in section 10 of the UFOC. The disclosures must include the terms, interest rates, and conditions of the financing as well as information regarding the source. Under federal regulations, franchisors must tell whether they receive "finder's fees" or kickbacks from third-party lenders who offer financing to franchisees.

Private Investors

Each year, more than 7,000 new businesses are financed by private investors. The total amount of capital represented by these investments exceeds $12 billion. Besides established venture capital groups, thousands of small, independent investors are constantly looking for small businesses to invest in.

Many small business owners obtain financial assistance from relatives and friends who are willing to extend a personal loan or purchase an ownership stake in the business. The franchisee might offer a partnership or stock in a closely held corporation. The requirements for a closely held corporation vary from state to state, but, in all instances, the number of stockholders is limited, and all the investors must be acquaintances of the person who forms the corporation. The stock cannot be advertised for sale or otherwise promoted to the public.

However, as you discovered in Chapter Twelve, most franchise agreements impose restrictions on a franchisee's freedom to incorporate the business. The franchisee is usually required to own a controlling interest and to disclose all stockholders to the franchisor. The investors must also agree to abide by the terms and conditions of the franchise agreement.

To attract start-up money from private investors, you will need a good business plan and a capable management team. Two good sources for locating investors are small business brokers and the classified section of your daily newspaper.

Advertising for a partner in a newspaper is legal in most states, but it may not be permissible simply to advertise for money. It is absolutely illegal to offer to sell securities, such as stock in your corporation. However, you can advertise for a general manager with partnership possibilities.

Weighing the Financial Decision

Each of the potential financial sources discussed in this chapter — conventional lenders, SBA loan guarantee programs, other federal agencies, SBICs or MESBICs, franchisors, and private investors — has certain advantages and drawbacks that must be evaluated with caution.

221

As you weigh the risks, benefits, advantages, and drawbacks of each funding source, the best answer for your particular situation will make itself obvious. Ask yourself the following questions before you make the final decision:

How much financing do I really need?

If the amount of funding you require is less than $100,000, venture capital groups will not be interested. The potential payout is simply not worth their bother, even at a high rate of return. Even SBA-guaranteed loans have established minimums. In most cases, a loan under $40,000 will be considered too small.

How will I spend the money? For what specific purposes?

Some lenders will finance real estate or equipment but not working capital. How you plan to allocate the capital will also influence the lender's decision to approve the loan.

What protection can I provide the lender in the event the business cannot meet its obligations?

A conventional loan requires more collateral than an SBA-guaranteed loan. A private investor may not require any protection at all. The best forms of collateral are real estate and heavy equipment, because of their ability to hold their value over a long period of time.

How long will it take to arrange financing?

The fastest way to obtain financing is usually by approaching private investors. A typical conventional bank loan takes one to three months, whereas SBA financing may take six months or longer. Typically, SBIC or MESBIC financing can be arranged within two to four months.

How long do I want to take to pay back the money?

A loan from the SBA, a participating bank, or an SBIC can typically be structured to allow fifteen to thirty years to pay back the original funds plus a reasonably low interest. With a venture capital investment, you will normally have from three to five years to pay back the initial investment.

Which source best complements my own personality and business style?

Ultimately, your favored funding source should be the one you can work with best. Even banks and government agencies have personality quirks and business styles in the personalities of their officers. In more ways than one, your financial backer will be your business partner. You should seek that delicate chemistry wherein your own personality traits, management behavior, and business objectives blend smoothly and effortlessly with your partner's.

Chapter Sixteen

Breaking Ground

Getting Started in a Franchise Business

Despite the rigors of researching, investigating, evaluating, applying for, negotiating, and financing a franchise, signing a franchise agreement is just the beginning of your adventure. Your next challenge will be to organize the business, select a location, complete the franchisor's training program, study the operating manual, develop the site, and prepare the outlet for opening. Although your franchisor may help you with some or all of the details, it will help you to have a clear picture of the myriad responsibilities that lie ahead, and in some cases, your franchisor may not tell you everything you need to know.

Many would-be entrepreneurs view a franchise as only an investment opportunity without realizing the amount of hard work it takes to develop a business and make it successful, and some franchisors are better at motivating franchisees to invest than at teaching them the ropes. This chapter will help you come to grips with the realities of starting and managing a business and organizing your time and energies effectively during the crucial start-up period.

Organizing the Business

One of the first decisions faced by a business owner is the form of organization under which to conduct the business. There are legal as well as tax considerations that must enter into this decision. A wise franchisee seeks and relies on competent counsel, such as a small business attorney, CPA, or other licensed advisor, before deciding on a particular form of organization.

Normally, a business may be conducted as one of three entities: (1) sole proprietorship, (2) partnership, or (3) corporation.

Tax Considerations

A business operated as a sole proprietorship does not pay income taxes. Instead, the sole proprietor reports profits or losses from the business on her or his own income tax return.

Profits from a corporation are usually taxed both to the corporation and again to the individual shareholders when profits are distributed as dividends. A competent attorney should be consulted to determine the legal, organizational, and tax implications of incorporation. Most franchise agreements stipulate certain conditions and actions required when a franchise business is organized as a corporation.

Following is a general discussion of the distinguishing traits, advantages, and drawbacks to each form of business organization.

Franchises Operated as Sole Proprietorships

The sole proprietorship is the simplest form of business organization. The business has no identity separate from its owner's. Its liabilities are the owner's personal liabilities. Income from a sole proprietorship is part of the owner's total gross reportable income.

The proprietor must report all income from the business on federal and state tax returns. In addition, the owner is subject to self-employment tax.

The Internal Revenue Service allows sole proprietors to deduct such expenses as advertising, bank charges, equipment depreciation, insurance, office supplies, rent, utilities, and other costs of doing business.

Franchises Operated as Partnerships

In a general partnership, each partner shares both the liabilities and the assets of the business. Each is taxed according to his or her share of the profits. As with a sole proprietor, the partner must report all income from the business on state and federal tax returns and may have to pay self-employment tax in addition to income tax.

The partnership must also submit a separate tax return disclosing the profits, draws, and advances paid out to the partners. Similarly, partners are jointly and severably liable for all liabilities of the business.

In a limited liability partnership, only the general partners have direct responsibility for the debts and liabilities of the business. The limited partners receive a share of the profits, which are then taxed as ordinary income.

Franchises Operated as Corporations

When a business is operated as a corporation, profits are taxed to the corporation. When profits are distributed in the form of dividends, these are taxed to the individual shareholders. However, the corporation itself is a separate entity — another "person" in the view of the law. In general, the corporation, not its shareholders, is responsible for the liabilities of the business. In some instances, the officers and directors of a small corporation may be held liable for debts of the business and the actions of employees.

In a subchapter S corporation, the corporation is not taxed, but shareholders must report their share of profits and losses on their gross income statements when reporting tax liabilities.

To form a corporation, all shareholders must transfer money, property, or both to the corporation in exchange for stock entitling each shareholder to a portion of the profit. As a general rule, stock should not be exchanged for services, but corporate shares may be issued in return for cancelation of indebtedness for past services.

A competent attorney experienced in small businesses and closely held corporations should be consulted in all matters pertaining to the formation of a corporation, issuance of stock, and reporting of tax liabilities.

Usually, a franchisee's election to incorporate is governed by certain provisions in the franchise agreement. A franchise is normally granted to an individual in reliance on his or her character, aptitude, business skill, management ability, and other qualities. The franchisee must assign the franchise to the newly formed corporation. The assignment usually requires the franchisor's prior approval, but approval will not be reasonably withheld.

The following stipulations are typical.

Control of Ownership

The franchisee must own and control the majority of the ownership (equity) and voting power of the corporation. This provision protects both the franchisor and the franchisee against the involuntary wrenching of control from the franchise by other shareholders.

Management Control

The franchisee must actively manage and direct the corporation. In other words, the franchisee must be the corporation's chief executive officer.

Exclusive Business

The corporation must not be engaged in any other business besides the franchise business.

Stock Legends

The stock certificates of the corporation may not bear any trademark or symbol of the franchisor, unless they are accompanied by a statement that the stock is stock in a franchise (not stock in the franchising corporation).

All stock certificates must bear a legend stating that the transfer of the stock is limited or such other legend as is required by the appropriate state or federal corporate regulatory agency for stock in a corporate franchise.

Personal Guarantee

The franchisee usually signs a personal guarantee stating that he or she will be empowered to act on behalf of the new corporation and will personally guarantee all the liabilities, debts, and obligations under the franchise agreement.

Corporate Documents

Upon organizing the corporation, the franchisee must usually submit the following items to the franchisor:

- a resolution of the board of directors stating full acknowledgment and approval of the franchise agreement
- a list of all shareholders, stating their names, addresses, and the number of shares owned by each
- a list of all officers and directors
- a copy of the articles of incorporation, corporate bylaws, and any other pertinent resolutions

Selecting a Site for Your Business

After organizing the business, the selection of a site for the outlet is usually the next decision faced by a business-format franchisee. A principal business address must be secured before certain licenses or permits required to conduct the business can be obtained. Moreover, location may have a bearing on the outlet's success or failure.

Some franchisors select the locations for their franchisees' outlets or, as an alternative, offer to perform this service for a fee. Others, though they may not actively assist with securing a site, may reserve the right to approve the franchisee's selection. In such cases, you may be required to submit three to five potential sites for the franchisor's review and approval.

The following considerations influence the selection of a site for a typical retail or commercial franchise outlet.

Zoning

As with other businesses, the outlet must comply with local zoning laws, statutes, and ordinances. Among other considerations, zoning may affect fire inspections, health inspections, business permits, and other licenses or permits relating to the site.

Security

Your business files and records are confidential. All information, correspondence, records, and customer lists dealing with the franchise business should be adequately safeguarded against potential abuse, including theft. Security from loss by fire, flood, etc. should also be a consideration, because insurance alone will not provide adequate compensation if your business records and files are destroyed.

Space Requirements

The franchisor may require the outlet to be situated in a particular type of facility, such as a shopping mall, business park, high-rise complex, strip center, or standalone retail site. As a new franchisee, you must anticipate both interior and exterior space requirements. If a long-term lease is required, future expansion needs should also be taken into consideration.

Allow for ample parking for both customers and employees. Employee parking should be situated away from the entrance to the place of business, providing maximum parking convenience for customers.

Fixtures and Improvements

As you evaluate prospective sites, seek the answers to the following questions: What are the existing provisions for lighting, heating, ventilating, air conditioning, and parking? What share of these costs will the franchisee be required to undertake?

Your outlet's exterior sign is one of a franchise's principal advertising media. Where applicable, the site should allow the outlet sign to be prominently displayed and easily visible to passing traffic in both directions. If you will operate a retail outlet, avoid sites that are located away from the main thoroughfare, e.g., in the back of a business park where the exterior sign is hidden from passing traffic.

Environment and Image

It is important in most franchise businesses to select an attractive building surrounded by other businesses that project a favorable image on the outlet as well as the franchise. Even though a franchisor may not require the outlet to be situated in the most expensive and prestigious building complex in a given locality, the franchisee is responsible for maintaining the high standard of image and quality of the franchise organization.

The site should be professional in appearance, clean, attractive, and preferably located in a well-maintained area. On a personal note, franchisees should also consider that they will be spending the majority of their waking hours in their franchise outlet. Will the location provide a comfortable environment for the business's employees? Will customers feel comfortable?

Surrounding Area

The overall image of the surroundings, the proximity to major customer groups, accessibility of major traffic arteries, and visibility all also may influence the outlet's success. The franchisee's own personal image is derived, in part, from the company he or she keeps. Similarly, the business's image will be derived, in part, from the surrounding businesses. An office in a modern shopping mall or business park projects a professional, success-oriented image. Conversely, a business located in a rundown strip center or warehouse area presents a poor image.

Proximity to Customers

In most businesses, to some extent location will determine the makeup of the outlet's primary customers. For example, a business located near upper-income residential areas is more likely to attract consumers who have ample disposable income. A business located in an industrial park or high-rise complex caters to business customers. A franchisee who selects a strip center or shopping mall for the outlet will be perceived as catering to housewives and shoppers.

Access to Thoroughfares

One important attribute of the outlet site is accessibility to major thoroughfares. Convenience is a key factor in the consumer's decision to patronize retail establishments. Access to major arteries and thoroughfares is a substantial advantage, particularly in a large metropolitan area.

Most franchisors have a profile of the ideal outlet site, with specifications for space requirements, lease provisions, visibility and access from major thoroughfares, and other considerations. Many franchisors rely on local realtors or property managers to select sites in geographical markets where the franchisors may have limited prior experience.

Because site selection is often a major factor in the success or failure of a business, the matter of who chooses the location — and how — sometimes becomes an issue in franchisor-franchisee disputes. If a franchise outlet fails, one of the first arguments the franchisee's attorney is likely to raise is that the franchisor selected or approved a poor location. However, the franchisor's know-how and experience are integral components of the franchise relationship, and, reasonably, no franchisee should be expected to assume the responsibility of site selection without some form of guidance or assistance.

The Franchise Operating Manual

The franchisor's know-how is usually documented in a series of publications collectively referred to as the franchise operating manual. The Guidelines for Preparation of a Uniform Franchise Offering Circular, issued by the Midwest Securities Commissioners Association and accepted by the Federal Trade Commission, refer to operating manuals in the instructions for completing Section XI-C of the disclosure document:

> (3) Describe any operating manual provided to the franchisee to assist the franchisee and his employees in the operation of the franchised business and whether the franchisor retains the right to change the terms of the manual and, if so, under what circumstances.

By providing an operating manual, a franchisor fulfills an important condition of the federal definition of a franchise relationship. You will recall that, under the FTC rules, a franchise is any commercial relationship involving a licensed trademark, payment of a fee, and "significant control or assistance."

Normally, an operating manual is regarded as a trade secret of the franchisor. Consequently, most franchise agreements obligate the franchisee to keep the contents confidential. A typical operating manual is loaned, not given, to the franchisee for the term of the franchise agreement. Upon expiration of the franchise, all copies of the manual in the franchisee's possession must be returned to the franchisor. Many contracts obligate the managers and employees of the franchisee's outlet to sign confidentiality oaths, preventing disclosure of any portion of the operating manual to unauthorized parties.

A typical franchise agreement gives the franchisor the right to modify the manual periodically, providing that the modifications do not alter any of the franchisee's rights. Franchisees are usually bound to adhere to any mandatory policies, procedures, specifications, and standards published in the operating manual.

Although there is no standard franchise operating manual, a good manual touches on virtually every aspect of starting, developing, staffing, managing, operating, and promoting the franchise business. The manual may be divided into a series of volumes, each devoted to a separate topic, such as marketing or daily operating procedures. It is common for managers and rank-and-file employees to have separate manuals, as well.

The sample table of contents in Figure 16-1 illustrates the organization of a typical franchise operating manual and lists representative topics. Obviously, the actual contents of any manual depend on the industry, business, type and size of the outlet, and franchise business system.

Figure 16-1

Franchise Operating Manual Contents

Preface
1.00 A Letter from Your Franchisor
1.01 Our Corporate Philosophy
1.02 Our Obligations as Your Franchisor

The Industry
1.10 Industry Overview
1.11 Our Market Position

The Organization
1.20 Our Company History
1.21 Our Future Outlook
1.22 Business Description
1.23 Facilities Description
1.24 Product Mix
1.25 Market/Customer Mix
1.26 Names and Numbers

The Franchise
1.30 Franchising: An Overview
1.31 Your Franchise Outlet
1.32 Policy Regarding Use of the Manual

Franchise Standards

Basic Standards
2.00 Your Obligations as a Franchisee
2.01 Franchise Reports
2.02 Important Dates (Reports and Payments)
2.03 Suggestions, Grievances, and Complaints

Operating Standards
2.10 Business Hours
2.11 Appearance and Maintenance of Facilities

Salesmanship and Selling

Personal Selling
5.00 Salesmanship and Selling
5.01 Personal Selling
5.02 Principles of Effective Salesmanship
5.03 Qualifying the Customer
5.04 Identifying the Key Decision Maker
5.05 Using Key Benefits Statements
5.06 Overcoming the Obstacles
5.07 Presenting the Close

Sales Style
5.10 Sales Styles
5.11 Basic Telephone Techniques
5.12 Listening Techniques
5.13 Sales Vocabulary

Marketing and Sales Promotion

Sales Administration
6.00 Introduction to Marketing
6.01 The Sales Organization
6.02 Market Planning
6.03 Market Analysis
6.04 Customer Analysis
6.05 Budgeting for Marketing

Authorized Media
6.10 Media Analysis
6.11 Metropolitan Newspapers
6.12 Television
6.13 Trade Publications and Magazines
6.14 Direct Mail
6.15 Outdoor Advertising
6.16 Radio
6.17 Competition Analysis

Advertising and Public Relations Policies
6.20 Introduction to Advertising
6.21 Budgeting Advertising Expenditures

Inventory Management
9.00 Introduction to Inventory Management
9.01 Approved Specifications
9.02 Opening Inventory
9.03 Inventory Control
9.04 Inventory Planning

Suggested Pricing Strategies
9.10 Factors That Influence Pricing
9.11 Figuring Margins and Markups
9.12 Figuring Hourly Rates

Personnel Administration

Personnel Recruitment
10.01 Principles of Personnel Recruitment
10.02 The Self-Motivated Applicant
10.03 Classified Advertising
10.04 Employment Placement Offices
10.05 Community Colleges, High Schools, and Trade Schools
10.06 Screening Applications
10.07 Interviewing Techniques
10.08 Selecting and Hiring Employees

Employment Regulations and Laws
10.10 Summary of Employment Regulations and Laws
10.11 Equal Opportunity Employment Policy
10.12 Policies Regarding Discrimination on the Basis of Sex
10.13 Policies Regarding Discrimination on the Basis of Age
10.14 Minimum Wage

Personnel Policies
10.20 The Importance of Personnel Policies
10.21 Employee Safety Policies
10.22 Employee Probationary Period
10.23 Policy Regarding Review System for Problems or Complaints
10.24 Policy Regarding Jury Duty
10.25 Policy Regarding Funeral Leave
10.26 Policy Regarding Voting in Public Elections
10.27 Policy Regarding Public Holidays
10.28 Policy Regarding Vacations

10.29 Service Awards
10.30 Policies Regarding Employee Termination

Countdown to Opening:
Things to Do Before You Open

As we mentioned previously, some franchisors provide complete start-up assistance or a fully developed "turnkey" business. However, in many cases, franchisors rely on their franchisees to exercise independence and initiative to establish the business and prepare the outlet for opening. If that is the case, the following checklist will help you cover all the bases and, if necessary, fill in the gaps between what you need to know and what you'll learn at franchise training school.

Business Organization

—corporate documents

—partnership documents

—business license

—trademark registration/trade name permit

—federal employer's ID number

—payroll tax forms

—payroll tax deposit account

—business checking account

—business license

—zoning use permit

—fire inspection

—health inspection

—safety inspection

—credit card services

—check verification services

—business liability insurance

—fire and damage insurance

___motor vehicle insurance
___employee group insurance
___life insurance
___construction permit(s)
___sign permit(s)

Site Development

___utility deposits
___telephone deposits
___telephone installation
___inventory fixtures
___storage fixtures
___wall decorations
___locks
___security/alarm system
___exterior signs
___equipment and furnishings
___vehicle lease(s)

Finance

___business plan
___loan application
___vendor contacts
___bank accounts
___computer hardware system
___software installation and training
___invoice file
___expense file
___asset file
___liability file
___travel and entertainment expense file
___employee file
___social security file

—payroll tax depository
—tax files
—banking procedures
—business checks
—business forms
—petty cash fund
—rate sheet
—credit file
—office supplies

Public Relations and Promotion

—competition analysis
—media contact list
—business forms
—Yellow Pages advertising
—handouts and fliers
—newspaper/magazine ads
—television commercials
—radio commercials
—stationery
—business cards
—grand opening plan
—grand opening invitations
—press release stationery
—grand opening press release
—personnel policy manual
—mailing labels
—ad budget
—ad calendar
—ad plan
—reception planning
—reception invitations
—grand opening

Chapter Seventeen

In All Fairness

The Rights and Obligations of Franchisees

In the 1990s, no issue in franchising is more important — or has received more publicity — than the legal, ethical, and financial relationship between franchisors and franchisees. In the 1960s and 1970s, the main problems of the industry were associated with fraud in the sale of franchises or violations of antitrust laws. The 1980s were a period of rapid expansion of franchise outlets. That expansion, combined with the economic downturn of the latter part of the decade, caused a substantial percentage of franchisees to experience financial difficulties.

In recent years, disputes between franchisors and franchisees have received widespread publicity. Most of these disagreements focused on the mutual rights and obligations of franchisors and their franchisees.

At various times, I have been asked to testify as an expert witness in court cases involving franchise disputes. In most of these cases, the main issue was the franchisor's "duty of competence" — an implied obligation to provide know-how and support to franchisees.

What makes up a franchisor's "duty of competence"? Merely by offering a franchise, a franchisor implicitly alleges that it possesses specific knowledge and skills related to its industry. By selling a franchise, the franchisor also implies that the franchisee has the appropriate personal traits and abilities to succeed in the business. If a franchisor fails to provide adequate training or ongoing assistance, it violates its implied duty to help franchisees achieve success. However, the franchisor is not always to blame if a franchisee fails.

A franchise is not a guarantee of financial success. Frankly, some investors embark on franchising without the slightest notion of the long hours of hard work that are required to make a business profitable. Many prospective franchisees who previously held "nine-to-five" jobs are unprepared, both mentally and emotionally, for the twelve-hour workdays and seven-day work weeks that lie ahead.

The International Franchise Association (IFA), which promotes the interests of franchisors, insists that reports of franchise failures and disputes are exaggerated. But the House Committee of Small Business of the U.S. Congress wants to pass new laws to regulate the relationship between franchisors and franchisees.

Various state laws already provide franchisees with special rights. For example, some states give franchisees the right to renew their franchise agreements upon expiration and protect franchisees from involuntary termination.

Most of the franchisee's rights and obligations are defined by the franchise operating manual and in other written communications, such as newsletters and bulletins.

Obligations of a Franchisee

From a franchisor's point of view, uniform standards are key aspects of a franchise. Consumers patronize a franchise outlet because of an assurance that the level of performance, quality, and service will be largely the same from one outlet to another.

To maintain uniformity among outlets, franchisors commonly require their franchisees to adhere to strict standards and specifications. Typically, a franchisee is obligated to maintain high standards of integrity and ethical business conduct and to promote a favorable image in all conduct with the public. Franchisees are required to maintain all licenses, permits, certificates, and other applicable documentation required by community and state laws. They must also promise to pay all fees and royalties due to their franchisor, as well as suppliers, promptly and accurately.

Franchisees are required to maintain their places of business in a clean and orderly condition and to keep all equipment, inventory, and supplies in proper working condition. In particular, they must maintain a clean, attractive, efficient customer area with proper safeguards and security.

Franchisees must agree to maintain fair but rigorously enforced personnel policies to promote a favorable image to the public. They must also adhere to all franchise standards and specifications for advertising, inventory, quality, service, performance, working hours, and procedures.

Franchise Reports

Besides adhering to quality standards, franchisees are required to furnish their franchisors with various types of reports. The following are typical.

Weekly summary. A summary of the outlet's sales may be required weekly.

Monthly recap. A recap of weekly sales may be required monthly.

Operating statement (profit and loss sheet). A statement of the outlet's income and expenses, showing the business's profits or losses, may be required monthly, quarterly, or annually.

Pro forma operating statement (projected profit and loss sheet). A projection of the outlet's future income and expenses, showing anticipated profits or losses, may also be required monthly, quarterly, or annually.

Federal tax return(s). Franchisees may be required to submit a true and accurate copy of their federal tax returns, or those portions relating to the franchise business, within a reasonable time after the date of filing.

Miscellaneous reports. In addition, franchisees may be required to submit any of the following occurrences in writing within a specified time after the event:

- *Changes in ownership.* If the franchise outlet is operated by a corporation, the franchisee may be required to report the names and addresses of any new shareholders or address changes of any existing shareholders.
- *Changes in management.* Franchisees may be required to promptly report any changes among the principal management of the franchise outlet.
- *Equipment failures.* Franchisees may be required to promptly report breakdowns or damage to any equipment that may be required to operate the business.
- *Trademark infringements.* The franchise agreement may obligate franchisees to assist in protecting the franchise name and trademarks by promptly reporting any apparent infringement or unauthorized use of the trademark by another business.

Outlet Maintenance

Franchisees are usually required to maintain the condition and appearance of their franchise outlets according to exact quality standards. Franchisees are usually required to pay for all routine and normal maintenance and repairs; replacement of worn-out or obsolete accessories, fixtures, equipment, signs, obsolete or unsellable inventory; and periodic refurbishing of the facilities.

Franchisors specifically prohibit their franchisees from making any material alterations to the outlet or to the business system without prior approval in writing from the franchisor. This prohibition may apply to the layout, accessories, fixtures, signs, or equipment of the outlet.

Appearance and Grooming of Employees

The franchise operating manual may include detailed standards for appearance and grooming on the job. The franchisee is responsible for ensuring that employees exhibit neatness, cleanliness, and a friendly, professional demeanor toward customers.

Inspections and Audits

To assure uniform standards of image, conduct, and performance, franchisors usually reserve the right to periodically evaluate their franchisees' outlets. In personal inspections by a field manager or other representative, franchisees may be monitored for adherence to the franchisor's standards, specifications, policies, and procedures. In addition, the outlet may be subject to an unnanounced audit of its books and records.

If the franchisor should discover a discrepancy in the reporting of franchise royalties or other fees, the franchisee may be held responsible for paying all costs associated with the audit.

Rights of a Franchisee

Although the franchise agreement and operating manual define many of the rights and obligations of a franchisee, various federal and state laws provide franchisees with specific rights. Many of these rights are derived from case law.

Case law is based on court decisions, in contrast to statutory laws enacted by legislative bodies. Most case law is determined by decisions rendered by federal and state appellate judges. Appellate courts, also called courts of appeals, are courts that hear cases appealed from lower trial courts. The decisions and opinions of the appellate judges are published in documents called "reporters."

When a case has been decided by a lower trial court, the decision may be appealed to an appellate court. For example, a case decided in a federal district court may be appealed to a federal court of appeals. The appellate court has the authority to redecide the case, based on arguments presented by the opposing parties.

After both parties to the lawsuit, or litigation, have submitted briefs and presented arguments, the judge, or in some cases a panel of judges, renders its decision to reverse or affirm the decision of the lower court. When a panel of judges votes to render a decision, the view of the judges who voted in favor of the winning decision is called the "majority opinion." Likewise, the views held by the judges who voted against the winning decision are called the "minority opinion."

The courts have helped to shape franchising practices in numerous ways. Several landmark decisions have established the ground rules for price fixing, tie-in arrangements, vicarious liability, and quality standards.

Price Fixing

In *Coors Brewery v. U.S. Federal Trade Commission* and again in *U.S. v. Parke Davis & Co.*, the courts ruled that franchisors and other contractors may not fix the prices at which franchisees sell products to the public. Any minimum, maximum, or fixed price constitutes illegal price fixing.

Tie-In Arrangements

In *Siegel v. Chicken Delight,* the Supreme Court declared that franchisors may not, without reasonable justification, force franchisees to purchase equipment and supplies from designated suppliers. However, in *Krehl v. Baskin-Robbins,* the court upheld the right of Baskin-Robbins to obligate franchisees to purchase and sell only its private brand of ice cream. The distinguishing factor, said the court, is whether a product is trademarked, unique, and not generally available from other sources.

Vicarious Liability

In 1986, a Docktor Pet franchisee was sued by a customer who had bought what he thought was a purebred Doberman pinscher. The store had misrepresented the dog's authenticity, and the franchisor was held to be vicariously liable for the conduct of its franchisee. In another landmark case, involving Avis Rent A Car, an appellate court declared that the franchisor was equally liable for an accidental death caused by one of its franchisees. However, a district court in Kansas found that a gasoline franchisor was not vicariously liable for a franchisee's racial discrimination against a customer.

Quality Standards

In *Ramada Inns v. Gadsden Motel Co.*, a federal appellate judge ruled that franchisors have the right to require their franchisees to upgrade their outlets to meet new quality standards. Ramada Inns had terminated a franchisee for deficiencies under the franchise agreement and had instructed the owner to cease using the franchisor's trademark. When the franchisee failed to comply, Ramada was awarded more than $250,000 in damages for injuries to its reputation.

Arbitrating Disputes

Arbitration is the resolution of a legal or contract dispute by a disinterested third party. Arbitration is an alternative to court action. Under arbitration, both parties in a dispute agree to be bound by the decision of an independent arbitrator.

In disputes between a franchisor and a franchisee, a third-party arbitrator, such as the American Arbitration Association, can usually render a decision much faster and at far less cost than the courts. In addition, most arbitration hearings are conducted in private, out of public view, minimizing the potential for negative publicity for either party.

Approximately one-fourth of the franchise agreements currently in force include arbitration clauses stipulating that disputes between the franchisor and franchisee are to be decided by arbitration. Under such clauses, both parties agree to submit any grievances or disputes to the designated arbitrator and to be bound by whatever decision is finally rendered.

From a franchisee's standpoint, arbitration helps to ensure fair practices by the franchisor. From a franchisor's perspective, an agreement to submit to arbitration helps control litigation costs and enhances the ethical image of the franchise industry.

The IFA encourages its members to use negotiation and arbitration wherever possible to resolve franchisor-franchisee disputes.

The Ethics of Franchising

In philosophy, ethics refers to the science that investigates right and wrong behavior. In industry, ethics refers to the code of conduct practiced by the members of a vocation or profession. In both fields, the main concerns of ethics are the behavior of people and the definition of right and wrong.

The foundation for ethical business conduct consists of the people who work for a company. Work habits and attitudes are highly influential in a close working environment. If the majority of the employees are basically honest, the largest part of the ethics battle is already won.

The ethical obligations of a franchisee are not limited to customers but also extend to the franchisor and to other franchisees. Franchisees have an obligation to report sales and pay royalties to the franchisor honestly and accurately. If a franchisee cheats his franchisor, he also cheats himself and other franchisees by undermining the very support system on which the business is based.

In a competitive field such as franchising, it is sometimes easy to overlook the fact that people — not marketing methods, royalty payments, or quality standards — are the most important factor. No matter what type of business it is engaged in, every franchisor has an obligation higher than simply distributing products, enforcing standards, and collecting royalties. All franchisors have an ethical, as well as a legal, responsibility to every franchisee they serve. Franchisees also have a responsibility to their franchisors, customers, and vendors.

According to the American Management Association, the primary objectives of management are the production of profits, the provision of meaningful employment, and the responsible exercise of power. The obligation of honest and ethical business conduct is inherent in the responsible exercise of power.

With respect to ethics, franchisors and their brokers or agents must be above suspicion. Even though a franchise salesperson's actions may, in fact, be ethical, if a client *believes* he or she has not been entirely ethical, both that salesperson and the franchisor will suffer as a result of the client's false impression.

The IFA requires its members to abide by a code of ethics. The major provisions of the code are highlighted as follows:

> 1. In the advertisement and grant of franchises . . . a member shall comply with all applicable laws and regulations. . . .
>
> 2. All matters material to the member's franchise . . . shall be contained in one or more written agreements, which shall clearly set forth the terms of the relationship and the respective rights and obligations of the parties.
>
> 3. A member shall select and accept only those franchisees . . . who, upon reasonable investigation, appear to possess the basic skills, education, experience, personal characteristics and financial resources requisite to conduct the franchised business. . . . There shall be no discrimination in the granting of franchises based solely on race, color, religion, national origin or sex.
>
> 4. A member shall provide reasonable guidance to its franchisees. . . .
>
> 5. Fairness shall characterize all dealings between a member and its franchisees. . . . A member shall make every good faith effort to resolve complaints by and disputes with its franchisees . . . through direct communication and negotiation.

At various times, instances of irresponsible behavior or fraudulent practices have damaged the reputation of the franchise industry. In the past, innocent people have been victimized by promoters that accepted franchise fees but returned few, if any, benefits to franchisees. Other franchisees have paid for equipment, products, or services that were never provided. A number of franchisees have filed complaints with the Federal Trade Commission and the Better Business Bureau, alleging that franchisors never informed them about some aspect of the franchise or failed to provide promised services.

It should be emphasized that the overwhelming majority of franchisors and franchisees are honest, but even an isolated instance of irresponsible or unethical conduct can damage the reputation of an entire industry.

It is often said that most people are neither completely honest nor completely dishonest, but are rather merely somewhat honest or somewhat dishonest, depending upon the circumstances. To ensure ethical conduct, both franchisors and franchisees must create an environment that is conducive to such conduct. The work habits, actions, and attitudes of employees and managers are the most influential factors in determining the overall ethical conduct of a business and the industry or profession to which they belong.

A Code of Ethics for Franchisees

Ethical conduct by a franchisee can be ensured by adhering to the following basic principles:

- Consider your customers' interests first in all transactions.
- Be receptive to competent counsel from your franchisor, vendors, and colleagues.
- Purchase and sell products without prejudice, seeking to obtain the maximum value for every customer.
- Seek constantly to expand your knowledge of your products, prices, and options.
- Adhere to and work for honesty and truthfulness in purchasing and selling and, if necessary, place your customer's interests above your own.

- Extend promptness and courtesy in all dealings with the public, vendors, and your franchisor.
- Counsel and assist other franchisees, as the occasion permits.
- Cooperate with all organizations and individuals engaged in activities designed to enhance the professional standing of franchising and your industry.

Chapter Eighteen

Future Tense

Tracking Franchise Trends

Not long ago, Susan Tennyson invested in a franchise to open a retail boutique specializing in infant apparel. Unfortunately, the market for infant products and services declined sharply over the next two years, and she was barely able to keep the store open. If she had taken the time to study population growth statistics, she might have realized her market area would not have enough families with children to sustain such a business over the long haul.

In the same month Susan opened her store, Max Waggoner opened a retail computer outlet across town. At the time, the computer revolution was in full swing, and consumer electronics looked to Max like a fast track to financial security. Five years later, an unexpected downturn in the personal computer industry sent his business into a tailspin.

As these cases illustrate, where franchising is concerned, reading the future is often as important as interpreting the past. Of course, it is far easier to reflect on what has already occurred than to predict what will happen next. However, no one considering a franchise investment can afford to ignore the combined influence of social, economic, and cultural trends on the business.

That doesn't mean you should consult a fortune teller or your daily horoscope before making a decision. Relying on wild, unscientific guesses about the future is as hazardous as plunging ahead blindly.

Savvy investors devote serious thought and analysis to tracking industry trends. For example, stock market investors study fluctuations in stock prices and try to determine what factors may cause a particular stock to rise or fall.

Trend Tracking

Studying the past in order to make informed predictions about the future is called *trend tracking*. A trend is an identifiable tendency of a particular market, industry, or customer group measured over time. The simplest type of trend is an average — for instance, the average increase or decrease of a particular stock price. However, in trend tracking, the most recent changes are sometimes the most important. For instance, if a stock price has increased steadily over the past three years but suddenly declined this year, the stock might actually be on a downward trend.

Most financial experts use simple logic to track trends. To illustrate, consider the logic used by a commodities trader to gauge the effect of interest rates on lumber futures. When interest rates drop, real estate sales tend to increase, creating demand in the housing market. As the supply of available homes shrinks, new home construction begins to climb. Lumber mills are generally idle except during periods of peak demand, so the existing supply of seasoned lumber is quickly exhausted. The resulting shortage drives lumber prices up.

Conversely, when interest rates rise, real estate sales drop, a housing surplus develops, new home construction declines, and lumber mills, which were active while construction was soaring, produce a new surplus, driving the price of lumber down.

To some extent, this type of reasoning can be applied to franchise investments. For example, following periods of low population growth, the market for children's and infants' products may be expected to decline. In contrast, when a baby boom is in progress, it might be a good time to invest in a diaper service, daycare center, or children's apparel store.

By paying attention to consumer habits and economic developments, it is possible to track some trends over a relatively long period of time. When fast-food sales burgeoned in the 1960s and 1970s, it was predictable that weight loss and physical fitness would become popular in the 1980s. Likewise, as fuel costs climbed in the 1970s, it might have been predicted that air transportation costs would rise and distressed carriers would launch fare wars, causing airline profits to decline.

Of course, unexpected upswings and downturns can occur in any industry. For example, few experts expected the computer industry to plummet in the mid-1980s or predicted the crisis in the savings and loan industry.

No matter how logical or scientific it may be, any prediction about industry trends is really just guesswork. Still, a franchise decision should be based not merely on a franchisor's track record but also on some sense of the future. With that objective in mind, let's examine some past, present, and future trends that may influence franchising and impact franchise businesses.

Travel and Hospitality

Every minute of every day, somewhere in North America, someone boards an airplane, checks into a hotel, rents a car, plans a cruise trip, purchases a train ticket, or makes some other type of travel arrangement. According to a study conducted in 1992 by the World Travel and Tourism Council, the travel industry is both the largest individual industry in the world and the largest contributor to global economic development.

Worldwide, the travel industsy generates more than $2.5 trillion in gross annual revenues, representing 5.5 percent of the world economy. This industry also provides jobs for more than 112 million people, or one of every fifteen employees in the world. Statistics show that the average American family spends more money on travel than on any other item except groceries.

Two factors will fuel the travel and hospitality industries into the next century — the development of a global economy and the graying of the American population. Business travelers now account for two-thirds of all travel industry revenues. From 1982 through 1992, international travel tripled. Business relations between companies in different countries will increase significantly as economic unions are developed and trade pacts are implemented.

As the most affluent Americans continue to age, the popularity of vacation travel will also increase. During the next decade, more Americans will reach retirement age than ever before. They will also have more leisure time and money to spend than any other population group in history.

What are the top franchises in the transportation and travel fields? The best opportunities may be in the hospitality, automobile rental, and travel agency industries.

The hospitality industry is made up of businesses that provide lodging, food and beverages, and related services to travelers. Hotels, motels, and resorts make up the world's seventh largest industry, generating over $36 billion in annual sales. The market for food and beverages will continue to shift from families to working people and elderly consumers. The hotel and restaurant industries both will benefit as franchising expands across Europe — especially Eastern Europe, where tourism development is a priority.

Automotive rental outlets are among the oldest franchise businesses. The traditional Big Four in the field are Hertz, Avis, National, and Budget, but relative newcomers such as American International, Thrifty, Dollar, and Alamo have had a major impact on the industry. Franchisees in this field benefit from national advertising, centralized reservations, and strong name recognition.

Travel agencies generate $86.1 billion in annual revenues, mostly from the sale of airline tickets and package vacations. A typical travel agency thrives by serving as a one-stop resource for business and vacation travelers. Hotels, tour operators, airline carriers, car rental companies, and cruise ships pay the agency a commission for business sent their way. A franchise in this field offers an opportunity to learn and rapidly penetrate the industry.

Fitness and Fashion

Franchising has long been a favorite expansion strategy of companies in the personal services industry. Hairstyling and beauty salons first became popular haunts of American housewives in the 1950s. The casual fashion trend of the 1960s led to the rise of unisex haircutting establishments. Hair care today is a thriving $13-billion industry.

Besides being fashion conscious, Americans are also more fitness conscious than ever before. The fitness craze has revitalized the careers of aging actresses and made aerobic dancing, weight loss counseling, and sports apparel into multibillion-dollar industries. At any given time, six of every ten Americans are on some kind of health-related diet. As a nation, we spend over $50 billion annually on diets and fitness.

The baby boom of the 1970s and the two-decade-long health and fitness craze has ignited explosive growth in sports apparel franchises. The trend began with jogging in the mid-1970s and spread to aerobic dancing, weightlifting, and tennis in the 1980s. With the fashion scene shifting from nightclubs to health clubs, even people who don't exercise regularly want to look like they do. Americans spend over $3.5 billion on athletic shoes every year, from traditional tennis shoes to costly designer models. Enough fashion sportswear is sold every two years to completely clothe every man, women, and child in the United States.

The growing young adult market should also favor retailers in more traditional apparel fields. More high school proms, graduation dances, and weddings will mean higher profits for formal wear stores.

Population Trends

To some degree, virtually every retail industry will be affected by population trends. The post–World War II baby boom created what became the largest, most affluent consumer group in history. As this huge spending machine advanced in age, entire industries rose and fell. Another, smaller baby boom occurred in the 1970s, when the U.S. population increased by 3.15 million babies every year.

The "super consumers" born between 1945 and 1955 have now reached the peak age of their personal purchasing power. They are the main buyers of cars, homes, and airline tickets and control 80 percent of all the money in savings accounts. As this monied generation reaches retirement age, a huge demand will unfold for products and services that cater to the elderly.

People who were born in the 1970s are teenagers or young adults today and account for 40 percent of all retail clothing sales. As today's teens reach marital age, yet another baby boom may occur. If that happens, demand for infants' and children's products and services should remain strong into the next century.

The Future of Franchising

In the early 1990s, during the worst economic downturn since the Great Depression, franchising continued to expand. Despite sluggish U.S. retail sales and fluctuating unemployment, total franchise industry revenues and the number of outlets increased. Some economists believe that franchising is now the most important cornerstone of the retail economy.

If the 1980s were an era of increasing franchise regulation, the 1990s are becoming a period of increased ethical responsibility. Inevitably, new laws will be passed and more regulations will be adopted to secure the rights of franchisees. To soften the attitude of the U.S. Congress and state legislatures toward franchisors, the industry will emphasize voluntary self-regulation and promote high ethical standards.

The most dramatic changes will occur overseas, where franchising is still relatively new. While larger franchisors such as McDonald's and Holiday Inn are well established in Western Europe, much of the expanding global economy remains virgin territory for franchise expansion.

Still, in all the excitement about franchising and the optimism of economic forecasts, it is easy to forget that franchising is not just about industries, trends, and markets but also about people. In a franchise business, the most important person is you. No matter how successful a franchisor's track record may be or how rosy the future may seem, it will be your money, time, and hard work that make the business profitable. All other factors being equal, the ideal franchise business is the one that best matches your motives, desires, management style, and personality.

In the end, the future of franchising is *your* future.

Appendices

Appendix A

Where to Find Franchise Opportunities

Business Journals

Barron's
22 Cortland St.
New York, NY 10007

Forbes
60 Fifth Ave.
New York, NY 10011

Wall Street Journal
22 Cortland St.
New York, NY 10007

Franchise Directories

The Encyclopedia of Franchises and Franchising
Facts on File, Inc.
460 Park Avenue South
New York, NY 10016

The Rating Guide to Franchises
Facts on File, Inc.
460 Park Avenue South
New York, NY 10016

Directory of Franchising Organizations
Pilot Books
103 Cooper St.
Babylon, NY 11702

Franchise Opportunities Handbook
National Technical Information Service
5285 Port Royal Rd.
Springfield, VA 22161

The Franchise Annual
Info Press
278 Center St.
Lewiston, NY 14092

Source Book of Franchise Opportunities
Business One Irwin
1818 Ridge Rd.
Homewood, IL 60430

Worldwide Franchise Directory
Gale Research, Inc.
835 Penobscot Building
Detroit, MI 48226

Magazines

Entrepreneur
2392 Morse Ave.
Irvine, CA 92714

Venture
35 W. 45th St.
New York, NY 10036

Appendix B

Requirements for the Preparation
of a Franchise Offering Circular

The following information is condensed from the Guidelines for Preparation of the Uniform Franchise Offering Circular and Related Documents, prepared by Midwest Securities Commissioners Association, Committee on Uniform Franchise Regulation, and amended by North American Securities Administrators Association.

The Franchisor and Any Predecessor

The first item required to be disclosed is pertinent information about the franchisor and any predecessor. In the context of the UFOC, the term *predecessor* refers to any prior owner of the franchising company or its assets. The following information must be disclosed:

- the complete name of the franchisor and any predecessors to the franchisor's business
- the name under which the franchisor does business, if different from above
- the franchisor's principal address and the principal addresses of any predecessors to the franchisor's business
- the form of organization of the franchisor's business, i.e., corporation, partnership, or other form of organization
- a general description of the franchisor's business and of the business in which franchisees are engaged, including the market for the goods and services to be sold by the franchisee and a general description of the businesses with which the franchisee will have to compete
- the prior business experience of the franchisor and any predecessors to the franchisor's business, including

    the length of time the franchisor has conducted a business of the type to be operated by the franchisee

    the length of time each predecessor conducted a business of the type to be operated by the franchisee

    the length of time the franchisor has offered franchises for such business

    the length of time each predecessor offered franchises for such business whether the franchisor has offered franchises in other lines of business and, if so, the nature, number sold, and length of time offered

whether each predecessor offered franchises in other lines of business and, if so, the nature, number sold, and length of time offered

Identity and Business Experience of Persons Affiliated with the Franchisor; Franchise Brokers

In this section, the franchisor must list by name and position the directors, trustees, general partners, principal officers (including the chief executive officer, chief operating officer, and financial, franchise marketing, training, and service officers), and other executives or subfranchisor. For each person listed, the franchisor must disclose the principal occupations, title, and employers during the five-year period prior to the effective date of the offering circular.

Litigation

In this section, the following information must be disclosed about each person named in the item above:

- whether each person has any pending administrative, criminal, or material civil action alleging a violation of any franchise law, fraud, embezzlement, fraudulent conversion, restraint of trade, unfair or deceptive practices, misappropriation of property, or comparable allegations

- during the ten-year period prior to the effective date of the offering circular, whether each person has been convicted of a felony or pleaded nolo contendere to a felony charge, or been held liable in a legal proceeding involving any of the charges named above

- whether any person is subject to any current court order relating to the franchise or under any federal, state, or Canadian franchise, securities, antitrust, trade regulation, or trade practice law

Bankruptcy

This section must disclose whether the franchisor or any predecessor, officer, or general partner has been declared bankrupt or filed for reorganization due to insolvency during the fifteen-year period prior to the effective date of the circular. If so, the pertinent details must also be disclosed.

Franchisee's Initial Franchise Fee or Other Initial Payment

The amount of the initial franchise fee is disclosed in this section of the offering circular. The following information must also be stated:

- whether the initial fee is payable as a lump sum or in installments
- the manner in which the franchisor will use or apply the payment
- whether the fee is refundable and, if so, under what circumstances

If the initial fee charged by the franchisor varies from one agreement to another, the formula for determining the actual amount must be disclosed.

Other Fees

The franchisor must describe in detail any other separate or recurring fees or payments for which the franchisee will be obligated. The following information is required to be disclosed:

- a detailed description of any fees or charges payable to the franchisor or to an affiliate or designate of the franchisor, including:

    periodic royalties or service fees

    fees for negotiating a lease for the franchisee's site

    fees or payments for construction, remodeling, decoration, or equipment

    training fees

    rent or lease payments for the premises, equipment, or fixtures of the franchisee's outlet

    fees or charges for advertising and promotion of the franchisee's outlet

    fees or charges for cooperative advertising with other franchisees

    fees for operating assistance or supervision

    fees for inspections or audits

    payments of insurance premiums

    payments for goods or supplies, in excess of actual wholesale cost

    bookkeeping, accounting, or inventory fees

    assignment or transfer fees

- whether each fee is payable to the franchisor or to an affiliate of the franchisor

- whether any fee is imposed or collected on behalf of a third party

- the date on which a recurring fee, such as an ongoing royalty, is due

273

- the formula used to compute each fee or payment
- whether each fee or payment is refundable and, if so, under what circumstances

Franchisee's Initial Investment

This section of the UFOC is used to detail the franchisee's estimated initial cash investment. If the specific amount is not known, a high-low range may be stated, based on the franchisor's experience. The following expenditures must be disclosed:

- real property, whether financed by contract, installment, purchase, or lease
- equipment, fixtures, other fixed assets, construction, remodeling, leasehold improvements, and decorating costs
- inventory required to open the business
- security deposits, other prepaid expenses, and working capital required to open the business
- any other expenditures that the franchisee will have to make in order to open the business

The franchisor must also state whether any part of the franchisee's initial investment may be financed, and, if so, the estimated loan repayments and interest must be disclosed.

The estimated initial investment breakdown must conclude with the following statement:

> There are no other direct or indirect payments in conjunction with the purchase of the franchise.

Obligations of Franchisee to Purchase or Lease from Designated Sources

In this section, the UFOC should list those items that the franchisee is obligated to purchase from designated sources, such as merchandise, services, supplies, fixtures, equipment, inventory, or real estate. This item refers to purchases or leases that are obligatory on the part of the franchisee as a condition of obtaining or retaining the franchise. Items included as part of the franchise at no additional charge to the franchisee do not have to be listed.

The following information must be disclosed:

- the general category of each article or service required to be purchased or leased from the franchisor or its designated suppliers
- whether the franchisor will or may derive income as a result of any such required purchases or leases
- the approximate percentage of the franchisee's total purchases or leases represented by the goods and services required to be purchased or leased from the franchisor

Obligations of Franchisee to Purchase or Lease in Accordance with Specifications or from Approved Suppliers

In this section, the franchisor must identify any products or services that the franchisee is required to purchase or lease in accordance with specifications prescribed by the franchisor. The following information must be disclosed:

- the categories of goods, services, supplies, fixtures, equipment, inventory, or real estate required to be so purchased
- the manner in which the franchisor formulates and modifies the specifications and standards, including the methods by which suppliers are evaluated and approved or disapproved
- whether the franchisor or an affiliate of the franchisor is one of the approved suppliers or the only approved supplier
- whether the franchisor or an affiliate will or may derive income from such purchases

Financing Arrangements

This section of the offering circular is devoted to any financing arrangements offered directly or indirectly by the franchisor. The information should include the exact terms of any lease arrangements and any financing covering:

- the initial franchise fee
- the purchase of land and the construction or remodeling of the premises
- the purchase of equipment, fixtures, opening inventory, and supplies
- the purchase of inventory and supplies
- replacement of equipment or fixtures
- any other continuing expense incurred by the franchisee

The terms of the financing must also be disclosed, including the identity of the lender, the annual interest rate charged, the term for which the financing is available, the nature of any security that must be given, requirements for a personal guarantee, any prepayment penalty, and any other material terms.

The franchisor must state whether it, its agent, or its affiliate now sells, assigns, or discounts any note, contract, lease, or other financial instrument executed by franchisees; has done so in the past; or intends to do so in the future.

Obligations of the Franchisor; Other Supervision, Assistance, or Services

This section lists the obligations to be met by the franchisor, both prior to the opening of the franchisee's outlet and during the operation of the franchisee's business. For each obligation relating to the franchise agreement, the corresponding section and page of the contract must be cited. The following information should appear in the offering circular:

Before the outlet opens, the agreement may obligate the franchisor to provide such services as selecting a site or negotiating a lease for the premises; securing licenses and permits for the business; acquiring and installing equipment, signs, and fixtures; acquiring opening inventory and supplies; hiring and training employees; or conducting a preopening advertising campaign in the franchisee's area.

Any other services to be provided by the franchisor prior to the opening of the franchisee's business must also be disclosed, even though they are not prescribed by the franchise agreement.

During the operation of the franchisee's business, the agreement may obligate the franchisor to provide ongoing assistance such as advising the franchisee about products or services to be offered by the franchisee; assisting with hiring and training of employees; conducting advertising campaigns; offering improvements and new developments; establishing administrative, bookkeeping, accounting, inventory control, and general operating procedures; and troubleshooting operating problems encountered by the franchisee. The circular should include a description of any operating manual provided to the franchisee to assist the franchisee and employees in the operation of the business.

Other ongoing supervision, assistance, or services must also be disclosed, even though they are not prescribed by the franchise agreement.

If the franchisor selects the site for the franchisee's outlet, the methods and criteria must be disclosed. The circular should describe such factors as the general location and neighborhood, traffic patterns, parking, size, layout, and other physical characteristics of the premises.

The approximate length of time between the signing of the franchise agreement and the opening of the franchisee's outlet must be disclosed.

The circular must also include a description of the franchisor's training program, including the location, duration, and content. Any charges for training or materials and transportation and living expenses incurred by attendees must also be disclosed.

Exclusive Area or Territory

This section of the circular is devoted to the exclusive area or territory, if any, granted to the franchisee. The disclosure should include a description of the boundaries or a map of the designated

277

territory. The franchisee's rights relative to the territory should be explained in detail. For example, it should be stated whether the franchisor agrees not to operate a company-owned outlet or grant a franchise to another party in the territory in competition with the franchisee's outlet. It should also be stated whether or not the franchisee or other franchisees are restricted in any manner from soliciting sales or accepting orders outside their defined territories.

Any conditions for the continuance of the franchisee's territorial rights must be disclosed in this section. For example, if the franchisee must meet a sales quota or open additional outlets in order to retain his territory, the requirements and quotas must be described in detail. Any circumstances that might allow the franchisor to modify the franchisee's territory must be clearly explained.

Trademarks, Service Marks, Trade Names, Logos, and Commercial Symbols

In this section, the franchisor must describe any trademarks, names, logos, or other commercial symbols licensed to the franchisee. A reproduction of any logo or other commercial symbol may be included as part of the disclosure. The circular should identify which, if any, of the trademarks has been registered or applied for registration with the U.S. Patent and Trademark Office. A list of state registrations and applications, if any, should also be included.

If the franchisor's trademark rights are limited in any way, the reason and circumstances must be disclosed. Any determination, petition, claim, or litigation that might affect the franchisor's right to use any trademark, name, or symbol must be listed and summarized.

The circular must state whether the franchisee is obligated to notify the franchisor of any apparent infringements on the trademarks and if the franchisor is obligated to protect the franchisee's right to use them.

Patents and Copyrights

This section is devoted to any special patents or copyrights owned by the franchisor. For each patent listed, the patent number, issue date, and title should be shown. Copyrights should be identified by registration number and date. If the franchisor has no patents or copyrights, a statement to that effect should appear in the offering circular.

If any of the franchisee's rights to use the patents or copyrights are restricted or threatened, for example, by another contract or by an infringement or challenge, the reason and circumstances must be explained.

Obligation of the Franchisee to Participate in the Actual Operation of the Franchise Business

In this section, the franchisor must disclose whether the franchisee must actively manage the outlet in person. If the franchisee is permitted to hire a manager for the outlet, the offering circular should provide the following additional information:

- whether the franchisor recommends on-premises supervision by the franchisee
- who the franchisee can or cannot hire to manage the outlet
- whether the manager must attend the franchisor's training program
- whether the franchisor must be informed of the manager's identity

Restriction on Goods and Services Offered by Franchisee

The offering circular must describe any obligations of the franchisee to sell or provide only those goods and services approved by the franchisor or to sell to only those customers stipulated by the franchisor. The restrictions and conditions must be explained in detail.

Renewal, Termination, Repurchase, Modification and Assignment of the Franchise Agreement and Related Information

In this section, the franchisor must disclose the term of the franchise and the conditions under which the franchise may be renewed, terminated, or assigned. The following information must be provided:

- the length of the initial term and whether the term is affected by any other agreement
- the conditions under which the franchisee may renew or extend the agreement
- the conditions under which the franchisor may refuse to renew or extend the agreement
- the conditions under which the franchisee may terminate the agreement
- the conditions under which the franchisor may terminate the agreement
- the obligations of the franchisee after termination or expiration of the franchise
- the franchisee's interest upon termination or expiration of the franchise
- the conditions under which the franchisor may repurchase the franchise, including any right of first refusal
- the conditions under which the franchisee may sell or assign all or any interest in the ownership of the franchise or the assets of the business
- the conditions under which the franchisor may sell or assign its rights and obligations under the franchise agreement

- the conditions under which the franchisee may modify the agreement
- the conditions under which the franchisor may modify the agreement
- the rights of the franchisee's heirs upon her or his death or disability
- the provisions of any covenant not to compete

Arrangements with Public Figures

A "public figure" is a person whose name or image is recognizable by the general public in the area where the franchise will be sold. The disclosure should include a description of the franchisee's rights to use the public figure's name to advertise the outlet and any charges for those rights. The UFOC should also explain whether the public figure is actually involved in the management or ownership of the franchising company. The total investment of the public figure in the franchise operation, if any, must be disclosed.

Actual, Average, Projected, or Forecasted Franchise Sales, Profits, or Earnings

If the franchisor makes any claim to a prospective franchisee regarding actual or average sales, profits, or earnings of franchisees, an exact copy must be included as an exhibit to the offering circular. This earnings claim must bear the following statement in capitalized boldface type:

THESE SALES, PROFITS OR EARNINGS ARE (AVERAGES) OF (A) SPECIFIC FRANCHISE(S) AND SHOULD NOT BE CONSIDERED THE ACTUAL OR POTENTIAL SALES, PROFITS,

OR EARNINGS THAT WILL BE REALIZED BY ANY OTHER FRANCHISE. THE FRANCHISOR DOES NOT REPRESENT THAT ANY FRANCHISEE CAN EXPECT TO ATTAIN THESE SALES, PROFITS, OR EARNINGS.

Where projected or forecasted franchisee sales, profits, or earnings are proposed to be used, an exact copy must be included in the offering circular, along with this statement in capitalized boldface type:

THESE PROJECTIONS (FORECASTS) OF SALES, PROFITS, OR EARNINGS ARE MERELY ESTIMATES AND SHOULD NOT BE CONSIDERED AS THE ACTUAL OR POTENTIAL SALES, PROFITS OR EARNINGS THAT WILL BE REALIZED BY ANY SPECIFIC FRANCHISEE. THE FRANCHISOR DOES NOT REPRESENT THAT ANY FRANCHISEE CAN EXPECT TO ATTAIN THESE SALES, PROFITS, OR EARNINGS.

The basis and assumptions for any earnings claim, whether actual or projected, must be disclosed in detail. Any statement of actual earnings must be based on a substantial number of franchisees during the same period of time and must be prepared in accordance with generally accepted accounting principles. The locations of the outlets used in the earnings claim must be identified by address, number of years in operation, whether substantially similar to the franchises offered, whether managed by the owner, whether they received any services not generally available to other franchises, and whether their sales, profits, or earnings have been audited.

If the franchisor chooses not to make an earnings claim, a statement to that effect should be included in the offering circular. No other information bearing upon actual or projected sales, income, profits, or earnings is allowable. In a survey of franchisors published by the FTC in January 1985, only 8 percent of the respondents included an earnings claim in their offering circulars.

Information Regarding Franchises of the Franchisor

The following information must be disclosed about the franchisor's existing franchise outlets, current to the close of the franchisor's most recent fiscal year:

- the total number of franchises, not including company-owned stores, similar to the ones offered, open and operational
- the total number of franchises sold but not yet open
- the names, addresses, and telephone numbers of all franchises under franchise agreements
- the total number of franchises to be sold or granted during the one-year period following the date of the offering circular
- the number of franchises that have been canceled, terminated, refused renewal, or repurchased by the franchisor

The circular may include individual breakdowns by state, either for an individual state or for all states in which the franchisor now has or intends to open franchises.

Financial Statements

The UFOC must contain a set of the franchisor's most recent audited financial statements, prepared in accordance with generally accepted accounting principles. Unaudited statements may be used during interim periods.

283

Agreements

A copy of all franchise and other related agreements should accompany the offering circular. In addition to the franchise agreement, a license agreement, equipment lease, lease for premises, and/or loan agreement may also be attached.

Acknowledgment of Receipt
by Prospective Franchisee

The receipt form should be a final separate page to the offering circular and should not contain any disclosure items.

Appendix C

Sample Uniform Franchise Offering Circular

INFORMATION FOR PROSPECTIVE FRANCHISEE — REQUIRED BY FEDERAL TRADE COMMISSION

To protect you, we've required your franchisor to give you this information.

We haven't checked it, and don't know if it's correct.

It should help you make up your mind. Study it carefully. While it includes some information about your contract, don't rely on it alone to understand your contract. Read all of your contract carefully.

Buying a franchise is a complicated investment. Take your time to decide. If possible, show your contract and this information to an advisor, like a lawyer or an accountant.

If you find anything you think may be wrong or anything important that's been left out, you should let us know about it. It may be against the law.

There may also be laws on franchising in your state. Ask your state agencies about them.

FEDERAL TRADE COMMISSION
Washington, D.C.

1.
The Franchisor and Any Predecessor

The Franchisor

Widget World Franchise Corporation is a California corporation incorporated on July 1, 1981. Its affiliate, Widget World, Inc., was first organized in March, 1972 as a sole proprietorship under the name California Widgets, and was incorporated on November 1, 1976. Widget World, Inc. today does business under its own name and under the name California Widgets. The franchisor maintains its principal business offices at 2001 Odyssey Street, San Francisco, California 94010.

Franchisor's Business

Widget World Franchise Corporation is a franchising company which grants franchises and trains, advises, and assists franchisees in the establishment and operation of retail outlets known as Widget World Stores. Franchisor's primary activities are education, market planning, advertising, consulting, and coordination of product distribution for its franchisees.

The franchise business is a retail business engaged in the merchandising and sale of widgets and related products and services, utilizing the franchisor's systems, procedures, and trademarks. The primary customers for the outlet are individuals purchasing widgets for recreational use and education, and business customers purchasing widgets for planning, reference, and decorative uses.

The franchisee will have to compete with independent widget dealers and company-owned outlets operated by major widget manufacturers.

Prior Business Experience of the Franchisor and Predecessors

John J. Johnson, president of Widget World Franchise Corporation and its affiliate, has operated a retail widget store similar to the business to be operated by the franchisee since March, 1972.

Neither the franchisor, its affiliate nor principals have offered any other franchises in any line of business. Widget World Franchise Corporation has been offering franchises since February, 1983.

2.
Prior Business Experience of Persons Affiliated With Franchisor: Franchise Brokers

John J. Johnson	From March, 1972 until the present, Mr.
President	Johnson has operated a retail business, as sole
Widget World	proprietor of California Widgets from 1974
Franchise Corporation	until November, 1976, and as president of
	Widget World, Inc. from November 1976

until the present. He has been president of Widget World Franchise Corporation since its formation in July, 1981.

William W. Wilhelm
Vice President
Widget World
Franchise Corporation

From 1975 until May, 1981, Mr. Wilhelm was president and general manager of GadgetCo in Sacramento, California. He joined Widget World, Inc. in May, 1981 as general manager. He has been vice president of Widget World Franchise Corporation since its formation in July, 1981.

Alice A. Allison
Vice President
Widget World
Franchise Corporation

From June, 1979 until January, 1981, Ms. Allison was the marketing director for Great American Gizmos. She joined Widget World in January, 1981 as vice president of marketing. She has been vice president of Widget World Franchise Corporation since its formation in July, 1981.

Edward E. Edwards
Secretary-Treasurer
Widget World
Franchise Corporation

From May, 1978 until the present, Mr. Edwards has been a public accountant. He has been secretary-treasurer of Widget World Franchise Corporation since its formation in July, 1981.

Martin M. Martin
Franchise Director
Widget World
Franchise Corporation

From April, 1977 until October, 1984, Mr. Martin was Franchise Marketing Director for Specialty Retailers Franchises, Inc. He joined Widget World Franchise Corporation as Franchise Director in October, 1984.

There are no franchise brokers affiliated with franchisor.

3.
Litigation

Neither the franchisor nor any other person identified in Item 2 above has any administrative or material civil action (or a significant number of civil actions irrespective of materiality) pending against them alleging a violation of any franchise law, fraud, embezzlement, fraudulent conversion, restraint of trade, unfair or deceptive business practices, misappropriation of property, or comparable allegations, other than a pending proceeding involving the arrest of such a person.

Neither the franchisor nor any person identified in Item 2 above has during the 10-year period immediately preceding the date of this offering circular been convicted of a felony or pleaded *nolo contendere* to any felony charge or been held liable in any other civil action or other legal proceeding where such felony, civil action, complaint or other legal proceeding involved violation of any franchise law, fraud, embezzlement, fraudulent conversion, restraint of trade, unfair or deceptive practices, misappropriation of property or comparable allegations.

Neither the franchisor nor any person identified in Item 2 above is subject to any currently effective injunctive or restrictive order or decree relating to the franchise or under any federal, state, or Canadian franchise, securities, antitrust, trade regulation or trade practice law as a result of a concluded or pending action or proceeding brought by a public agency; nor is subject to any currently effective order of any national securities association or national securities exchange (as defined in the Securities and Exchange Act of 1934) suspending or expelling such persons from membership in such association or exchange.

4.
Bankruptcy

During the 15-year period immediately preceding the date of the offering circular neither the franchisor nor any predecessor, current officer or general partner of the franchisor has been adjudged bankrupt or reorganized due to insolvency or been a principal officer of a company or a general partner of a partnership within one year of the time that such company or partnership was adjudged bankrupt or reorganized due to insolvency or is otherwise subject to any such pending bankruptcy or reorganization proceeding.

5.
Franchisee's Initial Franchise Fee or Other Payment

The full franchise fee is payable to franchisor upon execution of the franchise agreement. The franchise fee is placed with the other general funds of the franchisor and is non-refundable unless franchisee shall fail to successfully complete the training program required by the franchisor. In that event, the franchisor will refund 50% of the franchise fee, the balance to be retained by the franchisor to cover accounting, legal and training costs.

The initial franchise fee is $

6.
Other Fees

A royalty fee of _____% of net revenues is payable monthly by the franchisee. This amount is calculated on the basis of actual cash receipts paid by customers less sales, excise or other taxes collected, and is payable to franchisor by the 10th of each month. Franchisor offers a training program in _____ or in another location which may be centrally situated among a number of franchisees scheduled to attend the training session, if deemed advisable in the discretion of the franchisor. While there is no additional charge for the training, franchisee is required to pay the expense of transportation to and from the training program and all food and lodging expenses while attending. Costs for room and board, depending on the specific location of the training session, might be $75 per day per person.

7.
Franchisee's Initial Investment

The initial investment may vary according to franchisee's choice of site, method of business organization, inventory levels and improvements. Following is a summary of estimated initial investment requirements for a low and high investment:

Estimated Initial Investment

Item	How Paid	Low	High	When Due	Paid To
Initial Fee	Lump sum	$17,500	17,500	Signing of Agreement	Franchisor
Supplies	As ordered	2,500	3,200	As ordered	Supplier(s)
Equipment	As ordered	5,500	6,500	As ordered	Vendor(s)
Lease Deposits	As agreed	5,000	7,500	As agreed	Lessor
Fixtures	As ordered	13,300	17,900	As ordered	Vendor(s)
Utilities	As agreed	1,000	1,500	As agreed	Supplier(s)
Leasehold Improvements	As agreed	3,300	6,200	As agreed	Vendor(s)
Initial Inventory	As ordered	45,000	60,000	As ordered	Supplier(s)
Working Capital (1)	As incurred	30,000	45,000	As incurred	Various
Totals		$123,100	165,300		

(1) Working capital includes grand-opening advertising and start-up promotional expenses.

Franchisor does not offer either direct or indirect financing to franchisee for any item. Franchisee must obtain his own financing, if needed, and should be aware that the availability and terms of financing will depend on factors such as the availability of financing in general, the credit-worthiness of the franchisee, other security the franchisee may have, policies of lending institutions concerning the type of business to be operated by the franchisee, and so forth.

There are no other direct or indirect payments in conjunction with the purchase of the franchise.

8.
Obligations of Franchisee to Purchase or Lease from Designated Suppliers

Franchisee is not obligated to purchase or lease any products or services or classes of products or services from any designated source. At franchisee's option, franchisee may purchase selected inventory items from franchisor, or from franchisor's list of suppliers, but is under no obligation to purchase any item from either the franchisor or any recommended supplier.

9.
Obligations of Franchisee to Purchase or Lease in Accordance with Specifications or from Approved Suppliers

Franchisee is required to purchase all of the fixtures and initial inventory specified in franchisor's operating manual, in conformance with franchisor's specifications relating to quality, design or other similar standards.

Franchisee is required to purchase or cause to be purchased certain advertising literature for use in promotion of the franchise outlet. These items may be purchased in printed form from franchisor at a price equal to franchisor's actual printing cost plus 10%. If franchisee elects to have these materials printed by another source, the printed materials must be of equal quality to those offered by franchisor and must contain only the art, photographs and wording approved by franchisor.

Franchisee is obligated by the Franchise Agreement to purchase business liability, comprehensive and fire/damage insurance in the amount of $1,000,000 combined single limit and $3,000,000 per occurrence for business liability, and fire/damage coverage sufficient to repair or replace all equipment, tools, inventory and supplies essential to the operation of the franchise business. Neither the franchisor nor its affiliate will or may derive profits from the required purchase of equipment or supplies except for equipment or supplies made available by franchisor.

10.
Financing Arrangements

Neither the franchisor nor its affiliate offer financing directly or indirectly, or arrange or guarantee financing for franchisees. There are no payments received by franchisor or its affiliate from any person, lending institution or other source for its placement of financing with such person, lending institution or other source.

There is no past or present practice of the franchisor to sell, assign or discount to a third party any note, contract or other obligation of the franchisee in whole or in part.

11.
Obligations of the Franchisor; Other Supervision, Assistance or Services

Upon execution of the franchise agreement and prior to the opening of the franchise business, it is the obligation of the franchisor to:

1. designate an exclusive territory;

2. provide a training program at a time designated by franchisor prior to the opening of the business;

3. provide a list of specifications, standards, and suppliers for inventory, equipment and supplies;

4. provide guidance in methods, procedures, techniques and operations in the form of an operating manual and other printed materials, and

5. provide camera-ready artwork for printed materials to be used by franchisee in the conduct of the franchise business.

There is no other supervision, assistance or service to be provided by the franchisor prior to the opening of the franchise business pursuant to the franchise agreement or otherwise.

Upon commencement of the business, franchisor is obligated to:

1. protect the exclusive territory by assuring that no other franchises or company-owned outlets are granted or established therein;

2. modify the operating manual as required to improve or update the systems and procedures;

3. provide ongoing assistance and guidance by personal visits to the franchise outlet by authorized personnel of the franchisor;

4. administer a cooperative advertising fund to conduct advertising and promotions in selected media as deemed appropriate, and

5. provide on-site assistance in opening and operating the outlet for at least ten business days at the time of the grand opening.

There is no other supervision, assistance or service to be provided by the franchisor during the operation of the franchise business pursuant to the franchise agreement or otherwise.

Franchisor does not select the location of the franchisee's business, but must approve the location prior to the franchisee's commencement of the business. Franchisor, at no charge, provides guidelines for site selection. Pursuant to the franchise agreement, franchisee is obligated to complete all of the required tasks necessary to commence the franchise business within 90 days after execution of the agreement.

A training program is provided by franchisor at its principal offices, or at another location to be designated by franchisor. The training program consists of industry training, product knowledge, selling techniques, marketing strategies, competitive overview, customer knowledge, advertising techniques, business management, expansion strategies, promotional methods, inventory planning, and merchandising techniques and methods. The training program must be successfully completed prior to the opening of the franchise business. While there is no charge for the training, franchisee may be required to pay for all transportation and lodging expenses incurred by attending the training. No additional training programs are available as of the date of this offering circular. Franchisee may repeat the program if he desires to do so.

12.
Exclusive Area or Territory

Franchisor grants to franchisee during the term of the franchise an exclusive area (franchised territory). Neither the franchisor nor its parent or affiliates will establish other franchises or company-owned outlets using the franchisor's trade marks or by leasing similar products or services under a different trade mark or name, in the designated territory.

A designated territory is exclusive to the franchisee for the length of the franchise and is not altered by achievement of a certain sales volume, market penetration or other contingency. Other than the territory granted by the agreement, franchisee may obtain any other territory only by executing a separate franchise agreement. A franchisee's sub-franchising rights within the exclusive territory granted by the agreement would be subject to the following conditions:

1. franchisee meets all applicable standards and complies fully with all applicable state and federal laws, rules and regulations relating to the offer and sale of franchises and to sub-franchising;

2. franchisee will pay to franchisor the then-standard initial franchise fee for each sub-franchise sold by franchisee;

3. franchisee will pay to franchisor the then-standard royalty fee for the aggregate earnings of all sub-franchises sold by franchisee in the exclusive area;

4. all sub-franchisees of the franchisee will meet all applicable qualifications and standards for franchisees of the franchisor, and execute the franchisor's standard franchise agreement, and

5. all sub-franchisees of the franchisee must complete the franchisor's training program for franchisees prior to commencement of the sub-franchise business.

13.
Trademarks, Service Marks, Trade Names, Logotypes and Commercial Symbols

Widget World Franchise Corporation has applied for a trademark registration on the Principal Register of the U.S. Patent and Trademark Office for the following:

14.
Patents and Copyrights

Franchisor owns no special patents that pertain to the offering.

Franchisor and its principals possess proprietary know-how in the form of trade secrets, operating methods, specifications, technique, information and systems in the operation of retail map stores and in the merchandising of products and services. The know-how is disclosed in part in the copyrighted operating manual which franchisee receives solely for the purpose of developing the franchise and for the term of the agreement.

15.
Obligation of the Franchisee to Participate in the Actual Operation of the Franchise Business

Franchisee is not obligated to participate fulltime in the operation of the franchise business. However, if franchisee opts not to participate fulltime, a qualified manager must be in the employ of the franchise business and must have completed the franchisor's training program. Travel, room and board, and salary of the manager would be at the expense of franchisee.

16.
Restrictions on Goods and Services Offered by Franchisee

Pursuant to the franchise agreement, the franchisee may not offer any classes or products or services not approved by franchisor. Franchisor does not stipulate the specific brands, makes or suppliers of goods and services.

Franchisee may not own an interest in, perform any business activity on behalf of, or be in the employ of another retail widget business. Franchisee is not limited in the customers to whom he may solicit the sale of goods and services.

17.
Renewal, Termination, Repurchase, Modification and Assignment of the Franchise Agreement and Related Information

The term of the franchise agreement is ten years and is not affected by any agreement other than the franchise agreement.

Upon expiration of the initial term, if the franchisee is in compliance with all the provisions of the agreement, franchisee shall have the option to renew for an additional term by notifying the franchisor of its intention to renew six months prior to the expiration of the franchise and by executing a new franchise agreement and supportive agreements as are then customarily used by the franchisor. No fee is charged for renewal of the franchise.

If, upon expiration, the franchisee is in default of the agreement or fails to renew the franchise agreement within thirty (30) days following the expiration, the franchise will be deemed terminated.

The franchisee may terminate the franchise if franchisor does not fulfill its obligations under the agreement. Franchisee may terminate by exercising its option to sell the franchise to a fully disclosed and approved purchaser.

Franchisor may terminate the franchise if franchisee fails to open the business within 90 days following the signing of the agreement, if franchisee fails to pass or complete the training program, or if franchisee is in default of the agreement and fails to cure such default within thirty (30) days of notice. Further, the franchisor may terminate the franchise if franchisee abandons the franchise, becomes insolvent or bankrupt (to the extent permitted by the Federal Bankruptcy Law), is convicted of or pleads no contest to a felony or crime involving moral turpitude, or makes an unauthorized assignment of the franchise, discloses any trade secrets of the franchisor, or has an interest in or engages in a business activity competitive with the franchise, except to the extent permitted by the California Franchise Relations Act, if franchisee is located in California.

The California Franchise Relations Act (Business and Professional Code Sections 20000 to 20043, effective January 1, 1981) provides additional rights to California franchisees concerning termination and non-renewal. No franchise may be terminated except for good cause, and franchisee must be given a notice of default and a reasonable opportunity to cure defaults (except that for certain defaults specified in the statute, no notice or cure is required by law). The statute also requires that notice of any intention by a franchisor or sub-franchisor not to renew a franchise agreement be given at least 180 days prior to the expiration of a franchise agreement. In the event that any of the provisions of the franchise agreement conflict with this statute, the offending provisions will be considered invalid.

Upon termination or expiration, franchisee is obligated to pay franchisor within 15 days any amounts that are due and unpaid for products or services, cease to identify himself as a franchisee, return all advertising materials, forms, stationery or other printed matter bearing franchisor's trademarks, cancel all fictitious name permits, business licenses or other permits relating to the franchise, notify the telephone company and other listing agencies of the termination, honor the non-compete covenant — which may or may not be enforceable in California — and return all manuals and written communications to the franchisor. Franchisee would thereafter have no interest in or rights to the franchise business.

If franchisee notifies franchisor that it desires to sell any interest in the franchise, franchisor has the right at its sole discretion to repurchase the franchise. Further, should the franchisee obtain a bona fide written offer from a responsible and fully disclosed purchaser, franchisor would have the right at its discretion to purchase the interest for the same price and on the same terms and conditions as contained in the offer. Franchisor shall have 30 days from the receipt of notification of intent to sell to exercise its right of first refusal to repurchase the franchise.

With prior approval of franchisor, franchisee may assign its assets and liabilities to a newly formed corporation that conducts no other business than the franchise and in which franchisee owns and controls not less than 60% of the equity and voting power, and for which franchisee personally guarantees all performance, obligations and debts created by the franchise agreement.

Except as set forth in the above paragraph, none of the ownership of the franchisee may be voluntarily, involuntarily, directly or indirectly assigned, sold, subdivided, sub-franchised or otherwise transferred by franchisee without prior written approval of franchisor. In the event of an approved assignment, other than to a corporation controlled by franchisee, assignee must pay to franchisor a transfer and retaining fee equal to 50% of the initial franchise fee. The approved assignee must pass the training program and execute the then-current franchise agreement.

The agreement may not be modified or amended except by mutual consent and execution of a written instrument. Franchisor is not restricted from transferring the franchise agreement or from designating any subsidiary, affiliate or agent to perform any and all acts franchisor is obligated to perform. Franchisor has the right to modify the operating procedures and specifications of the franchise, but has no right to modify the terms of the agreement subsequent to its signing. Upon death or disability of the franchisee or the principal owner, the executor, administrator or other personal representative must assign the franchise to a fully disclosed and approved person who meets the standard qualifications for franchisees of the franchisor. If such assignment is not made within 90 days after the death or disability, the failure to transfer the interest in the franchise would constitute a breach. Notwithstanding the above, at any time subsequent to the death or disability of the franchisee or principal owner, franchisor may obtain an interim manager to run the business until such assignment is made.

Franchisee agrees by signing the franchise agreement that it will not engage in any business or activity competitive with the franchise for a period of one year from the date of termination or expiration of the franchise. However, such a covenant may or may not be enforceable in the State of California, under the laws of California.

18.
Arrangements with Public Figures

Franchisor does not give or promise any compensation or other benefit to any public figure arising in whole or in part from the use of any public figure in the name or symbol of the franchise or the endorsement or recommendation of the franchise by any public figure in advertisements.

No arrangements have been made by franchisor under which the franchisee may use a public figure. Franchisee is wholly unrestricted in its use of public figures in its advertisements and promotions, with the exception that, pursuant to the franchise agreement, printed materials, including endorsements, must be approved in advance by franchisor.

19.
Actual, Average, Projected or Forecasted Franchise Sales, Profits or Earnings

Since these are the first franchises offered, the franchisor presents no statements, oral or written, or other indications of actual, average, projected or forecasted sales, profits or earnings.

20.
Information Regarding Franchises of the Franchisor

Four franchises have been sold and are operational as of the effective date of this offering circular:

Thomas Thompson	Carla Carlson
Widget World by the Bay	Napa Widget World
520 Bay Ave.	18512 Hwy. 19
San Francisco, CA 94010	Napa, CA 93313
(415) 555-0000	(707) 555-2222

Lars Larsen
Southland Widget World
910 Straightline Blvd.
Los Angeles, CA 90010
(213) 555-6616

David Davidson
Midland Widget World
2221 Plainview Dr.
Sacramento, CA 91119
(916) 555-8828

No franchises have been cancelled, terminated, refused renewal, or re-acquired by repurchase or otherwise by franchisor.

Franchisor estimates that it will grant franchises as follows during the one-year period following the date of this offering circular:

State	Number of outlets
California	5
Florida	2
Illinois	2
Kansas	1
New York	3
Texas	3
Washington	1

21.
Franchisor's Financial Statements

Attached are the most recent audited financial statements of the franchisor.

22.
Agreements

Attached is a copy of the franchisor's franchise agreement and all related contracts and agreements.

Appendix D

Sample Franchise Agreement

Franchise Agreement

1. Grant of Franchise

A. Widget World Franchise Corporation (the "Franchisor") hereby grants to Franchisee a license to use the trade name "Widget World" and the trademarks associated therewith, and a franchise to operate a Widget World outlet (the "Outlet") in the geographical market identified in an exhibit to this agreement.

B. Franchisee shall use the trade name and marks in the sale of widgets and widget-related goods, and franchisee's place of business shall be known only as "Widget World."

C. The name of any corporation operating this franchise may include the words "Widget World" or any other trademark owned or licensed by franchisor, but only with the written consent of franchisor.

2. Exclusive Territory

Franchisor shall not, while this agreement is in force, conduct a similar operation, or grant a similar franchise to any other franchisee, within the territory defined in Exhibit ___.

3. Term

This agreement shall continue for a period of ten (10) years from the date hereof, and shall be automatically renewed for an additional ten-year term, unless at least six (6) months before the expiration of this agreement, franchisee gives to franchisor notice in writing of termination at the end of the term.

4. Development and Opening

Within ninety (90) days following the execution of this agreement, franchisee shall do or cause the following to be done:

A. Secure all financing required to develop the outlet;

B. Complete all arrangements for a site for the outlet. Franchisor shall have the right and option to approve the selected site prior to the development and opening of the outlet;

C. Execute a lease for the premises in which the outlet shall be operated, and deliver to the franchisor a true and correct copy;

D. Obtain all licenses and permits required to conduct the business;

E. Obtain all improvements, fixtures, supplies, and inventory.

5. Payments

A. Franchise Fee

Franchisee shall make payment to franchisor of _____ Dollars ($_____) upon the execution of this agreement, receipt of which is hereby acknowledged. In return for this payment, franchisee shall receive the right to do business as a licensed Widget World franchisee under the terms of this agreement, and to receive the services and assistance hereinafter set forth. The initial fee shall be fully earned by franchisor and is nonrefundable.

B. Continuing Royalty

Franchisee shall, on the tenth (10th) day of each month, pay to franchisor the sum equal to   percent (%) of the net sales of franchisee for the preceding month. As used in this agreement, the term "net sales" shall include all sales made by franchisee pursuant to this agreement, but shall not include any sums collected and paid out for any sales or excise tax imposed by any duly constituted government authority.

C. Advertising Fee

Franchisee shall pay to franchisor as an advertising fee the sum equal to   percent (%) of franchisee's monthly gross sales. The sum shall be paid on or before the tenth (10th) day of each month and shall be based on the net sales of the month preceding the date of payment. The amount of franchisee's net sales shall be determined in the same manner as that specified in subsection B of this section, above.

D. Interest Penalties

If franchisee fails to remit the payments required under subsections A through C of this section, above, all amounts which franchisee owes to franchisor shall bear interest after due date at the highest applicable legal rate.

6. Advertising

A. Franchisee agrees to use all advertising designs, materials, media, and methods of preparation prescribed by or which conform to franchisor's standards and specifications.

B. Franchisee shall refrain from using any advertising designs, materials, media, and methods of preparation which do not meet with franchisor's standards and specifications.

C. Franchisor shall make available to franchisee any assistance that may be required, based on the experience and judgment of franchisor, in the design, preparation, and placement of advertising and promotional materials for use in local advertising.

D. Franchisor shall administer the Franchisee Cooperative Advertising Fund, and direct the development of all advertising and promotional programs. The content of the advertising, as well as the media in which the advertising is to be placed and the defined advertising area, shall be at the discretion of the franchisor.

7. Trademarks

A. Franchisor shall make available to franchisee franchisor's trade names and marks. For the purpose of this agreement, "the marks" shall be defined as all symbols, logos, trade marks, and trade names owned and/or under application by franchisor.

B. Franchisee agrees that its rights to use the marks are derived solely from this agreement, and franchisee shall not derive any right, title, or interest in the marks, other than a license to use them in connection with the franchise outlet while this agreement is in force.

C. Franchisee shall use the name and service marks only in such manner as prescribed by franchisor and in no other way.

D. Franchisee shall immediately notify franchisor of any apparent infringement of the use of the marks.

E. If it becomes advisable at any time in franchisor's sole discretion to discontinue or modify the use of any mark, franchisee agrees to comply within a reasonable time after notice thereof by franchisor.

8. Products, Supplies, and Equipment

Franchisee understands and acknowledges that every detail of the franchise system is important to franchisor, to franchisee, and to other franchisees to develop and maintain high and uniform standards of quality, cleanliness, appearance, services, products, and techniques, and to protect and enhance the reputation and goodwill of the franchise system. Franchisee accordingly agrees:

(1) To use all materials, supplies, goods, uniforms, fixtures, furnishings, signs, equipment, methods of exterior and interior design and construction, and methods of production and preparation prescribed by or which conform to franchisor's standards and specifications.

(2) To refrain from using or selling any products, materials, supplies, goods, uniforms, fixtures, furnishings, signs, equipment, and

methods of production which do not meet with franchisor's standards and specifications.

(3) To offer for sale any such products as shall be expressly approved for sale in writing by franchisor, and to offer for sale all products that have been designated as approved by franchisor.

(4) To maintain at all times a sufficient supply of approved products.

(5) To purchase all products, supplies, equipment, and materials required for conduct of the franchise operation from suppliers who demonstrate, to the reasonable satisfaction of franchisor, the ability to meet all of franchisor's standards and specifications for such items; who possess adequate capacity and facilities to supply franchisee's needs in the quantities, at the times, and with the reliability requisite to an efficient operation; and who have been approved, in writing, by franchisor. Franchisee may submit to franchisor a written request for approval of a supplier not previously approved by franchisor.

9. Standards and Procedures

A. Management Standards

Franchisee agrees to comply with franchisor's standards with respect to product preparation, merchandising, employee recruitment, training, equipment, and facility maintenance.

B. Personnel Standards

Franchisee shall hire only efficient, competent, sober, and courteous employees for the conduct of the business, and shall pay their wages, commissions, and other compensation with no liability therefor on the part of the franchisor. Franchisee shall require all employees to comply with franchisor's standards for grooming and appearance.

C. Best Efforts

Franchisee agrees to devote his/her best efforts to the operation of the outlet and to the supervision of its employees. Franchisee agrees that it will not engage in any other business activity which may conflict with the obligations of this agreement or impair the operation of the outlet.

D. Insurance

Franchisee shall, at his expense, procure and maintain in full force and effect during the entire term of this agreement, comprehensive public, fire damage, product and motor vehicle liability insurance in the amount of _____ Dollars ($_____) for each person and _____ Dollars ($_____) for each occurrence for bodily and personal injury, death and property damage. Fire damage insurance shall be sufficient to cover repair or replacement of all equipment, inventory, tools, and supplies normally required to operate the outlet, as specified in franchisor's operating manual. Franchisor shall be named as an additional insured under all such insurance policies, as its interests may appear, and contain a waiver by the carrier of all subrogation rights against franchisor. Maintenance of insurance under this paragraph shall not relieve franchisee of liability under the default provisions set forth in this agreement.

10. Training and Assistance

A. Franchisor agrees to make personal training facilities available to franchisee, to furnish an operating manual, to make promotional and other recommendations, and to furnish franchisee, at franchisee's place of business, a trained supervisor for not less than three (3) days during the initial six-day period of franchisee's operation.

B. Franchisee shall, at franchisee's expense, attend franchisor's training program at a place to be designated by franchisor prior to the opening of the outlet. During the term of this agreement, franchisee may send one other designee through the same program, at franchisee's expense. Franchisee agrees to pay any travel and living expenses which may be incurred by franchisee and/or his other designee in connection with the training program.

C. Franchisor shall loan to franchisee for the term of this agreement an operating manual containing the standards, specifications, procedures, and techniques of the franchise system, and may, at its sole discretion, revise, from time to time, the contents of the manuals, incorporating new standards, specifications, procedures, and techniques.

D. Franchisor agrees to furnish franchisee with the following:

(1) guidelines and approval for the location of a suitable site for the outlet. By providing such guidelines and approval, franchisor in no way promises, warrants or otherwise represents that the site location is the optimal location for the outlet;

(2) assistance in negotiating a lease for the outlet, when appropriate;

(3) assistance in planning the layout of the outlet;

(4) assistance in the conduct of a Grand Opening promotion for the outlet.

11. Business Conduct

A. All representations made by franchisee to others shall be completely factual. Franchisee agrees to abide by all laws, regulations, and codes.

B. Franchisee agrees to protect, defend, and indemnify franchisor and to hold franchisor harmless from and against any and all costs, expenses, including attorneys' fees, court costs, losses, liabilities, damages, claims and demands of every kind or nature, arising in any way out of the occupation, use or operation of any fixtures, equipment, goods, merchandise, or products used or sold at the outlet.

C. Franchisee will not divulge any business information, whether written or oral, received from franchisor or from any meetings of other of franchisor's franchisees, until such time as disclosure to the public may be required by the nature of the information. Such information may include, but is not limited to, promotional material or plans, expansion plans, new products, marketing information, costs or other financial data.

12. Reports and Inspections

A. Franchisee agrees to furnish to franchisor, within thirty (30) days after the end of franchisee's fiscal year, a full and complete statement in writing of income and expense for the outlet during the preceding year. The statement shall be prepared in accordance with accepted accounting standards and practices by an independent accountant or auditor and certified by the accountant or auditor to be correct.

B. Franchisee agrees to open his books and records to the inspection of franchisor, provided, however, that franchisee shall have been given reasonable advance notice. Franchisee agrees to cooperate fully with representatives of the franchisor making any such inspection. In the event an understatement of net revenues for the period of any audit is determined by any such audit, franchisee shall reimburse franchisor for the cost of such audit or inspection.

13. Relationship of the Parties

A. Franchisee shall be an independent contractor, and nothing in this agreement shall be construed so as to create or imply a fiduciary relationship between the parties, nor to make either party a general or specific agent, legal representative, subsidiary, joint venturer, or servant of the other.

B. Franchisee is in no way authorized to make a contract, agreement, warranty or representation on behalf of franchisor or to create any obligation, express or implied, on behalf of franchisor.

C. Franchisee shall be responsible for his/her own taxes, including without limitation any taxes levied upon the outlet.

14. Assignment of Franchise

Franchisee's rights in the franchise may be assigned only as follows:

A. Upon franchisee's death, the rights of franchisee in the franchise may pass to franchisee's next of kin or other beneficiaries, provided that such next of kin or other beneficiaries agree in written form satisfactory to franchisor to assume all of franchisee's obligations under this agreement.

B. Franchisee may sell his interests in the franchise to another party, provided that the following conditions are met:

(1) the assignee is of good moral character, meets franchisor's normal qualifications for franchisees of franchisor, will comply with franchisor's training requirements, and enters into any and all direct agreements with franchisor that franchisor is then requiring of newly franchised persons;

(2) all monetary obligations of franchisee hereunder are fully paid, and franchisee executes a general release of all claims against franchisor, its officers and directors;

(3) The assignee pays franchisor for its legal, training, and other expenses in connection with the assignment;

(4) franchisee has first offered to sell his franchise to franchisor upon the same terms as the purchaser has offered franchisee in writing, and franchisor has refused the offer or failed to accept it for a period of thirty (30) days;

(5) franchisee shall reaffirm a covenant not to compete in favor of franchisor.

C. Franchisee may assign and transfer his rights hereunder to a corporation without, however, being relieved of any personal liability, provided that the following conditions are met:

(1) the corporation is newly formed and shall conduct no other business but the franchise business, which shall continue to be managed by franchisee;

(2) franchisee owns the controlling stock interest in the corporation and is the principal executive officer thereof;

(3) the articles of incorporation, by-laws and other organizational documents of the corporation shall recite that the issuance and assignment of any interest therein is restricted by the terms of this agreement, and all issued and outstanding stock certificates of such corporation shall bear a legend reflecting or referring to the restrictions of this agreement;

(4) all stockholders of the corporation guarantee, in written form satisfactory to franchisor, to be bound jointly and severally by all provisions of this franchise agreement;

(5) franchisee shall not use any mark in a public offering of his securities, except to reflect his franchise relationship with franchisor.

15. Termination

If franchisee defaults under the terms of this agreement and such default shall not be cured within thirty (30) days after receipt of written notice to cure from franchisor, then, in addition to all other remedies at law or in equity, franchisor may immediately terminate this agreement. Termination under such conditions shall become effective immediately upon the date of receipt by franchisee of a written notice of termination. Franchisee shall be considered to be in default under this agreement if:

(1) franchisee fails to open the business within the time specified in Section 4 of this agreement, above;

(2) franchisee abandons the franchise;

(3) franchisee attempts to assign this agreement without prior written approval of franchisor;

(4) franchisee misuses or makes an unauthorized use of the mark in a manner which materially impairs the goodwill of franchisor;

(5) franchisee has made a material misrepresentation to franchisor before or after being granted the franchise;

(6) franchisee discloses or reproduces any portion of the franchisor's operating manual to any unauthorized party;

(7) franchisee fails to abide by his covenant not to compete as provided in this agreement;

(8) franchisee fails to comply substantially with any of the requirements imposed upon franchisee by this agreement.

16. Rights and Obligations of the Parties Upon Termination or Expiration

A. On termination or expiration of this agreement, franchisee shall do or cause to be done the following:

(1) promptly pay all amounts owed to franchisor which are then unpaid;

(2) immediately cease to use any and all marks and names, and any other trade secrets, confidential information, operating manuals, slogans, signs, symbols, or devices forming part of the franchise system or otherwise used in connection with conduct of the franchise outlet;

(3) immediately return to franchisor all advertising materials, operating manuals, plans, specifications, and other materials prepared by franchisor and relative to the franchise system.

B. Covenant Not to Compete

Franchisee, its officers, directors, and shareholders agree during the term of this agreement, or upon expiration or termination, or non-renewal for any reason, they shall not have any interest as an owner, partner, director, officer, employee, manager, consultant, shareholder, representative, agent, or in any other capacity for any reason for a period of two (2) years after the occurrence of said event(s) in any business or activity involving the retail sale of widgets or proposing to engage in the sale of widgets.

Franchisee acknowledges that this covenant is reasonable and necessary and agrees that its failure to adhere strictly to the restrictions of this paragraph will cause substantial and irreparable damage to franchisor. Franchisee hereby acknowledges, therefore, that any violation of the terms and conditions of this covenant shall give rise to an entitlement to injunctive relief.

17. Enforcement and Construction

A. Severability

The paragraphs of this agreement are severable, and in the event any paragraph or portion of the agreement is declared illegal or unenforceable, the remainder of the agreement shall be effective and binding on the parties.

B. Notice

Whenever, under the terms of this agreement, notice is required, the same shall be deemed delivered if delivered by hand to whom intended, or to any adult person employed by franchisee at franchisee's place of business, or upon deposit in any U.S. depository for mail delivery, addressed to franchisee or franchisor at their respective principal business addresses.

C. Specific Performance

Nothing contained herein shall bar the franchisor's or franchisee's right to obtain specific performance of the provisions of this agreement and injunctive relief against threatened conduct that will cause it loss or damages, under customary equity rules, including applicable rules for obtaining restraining orders and preliminary injunctions.

D. Governing Law

This agreement is entered into and shall be construed in accordance with the laws of the state of _____, as of the date of execution of this agreement.

E. Successors

This agreement shall inure to the benefit of and be binding upon the executors, administrators, heirs, assigns and successors in interest of the parties.

Appendix E

The Top 100 Franchisors

Rank	Franchisor	Founded	Outlets
1.	McDonald's	1955	13,900
2.	7-Eleven Stores	1927	12,000
3.	Kentucky Fried Chicken	1972	10,200
4.	H&R Block	1955	8,800
5.	Century 21	1972	7,000
6.	Pizza Hut	1958	6,000
7.	Dairy Queen	1940	5,000
8.	Domino's Pizza	1960	4,600
9.	ServiceMaster	1947	3,875
10.	Jazzercise	1972	3,800
11.	Wendy's	1969	3,650
12.	Budget Rent A Car	1960	3,600
13.	Baskin-Robbins	1945	3,450
14.	Hardee's	1961	3,000
15.	Electronic Realty Associates	1971	2,840
16.	Taco Bell	1962	2,760
17.	SUBWAY Sandwiches	1965	2,400
18.	Diet Center, Inc.	1970	2,330
19.	Midas Muffler	1956	2,200
20.	Little Caesar's Pizza	1959	2,000
21.	Arby's	1964	2,000
22.	Chem-Dry	1977	1,840
23.	Western Auto	1909	1,800
24.	Realty World	1974	1,760
25.	Dunkin' Donuts	1950	1,735
26.	Holiday Inn	1952	1,600
27.	Dollar Rent a Car	1966	1,600
28.	Goodyear Tire Centers	1896	1,570
29.	Church's Fried Chicken	1953	1,500
30.	Long John Silver's	1969	1,500
31.	American International	1969	1,500
32.	Rainbow International	1981	1,450
33.	RE/MAX	1973	1,400
34.	National Video	1980	1,400
35.	Denny's	1953	1,390
36.	Jani-King	1969	1,300
37.	Fantastic Sam's	1974	1,275
38.	PIP Printing	1965	1,120

39.	Packy the Shipper	1976	1,120
40.	Sonic Drive-Ins	1954	1,100
41.	Ben Franklin Stores	1877	1,100
42.	TCBY/The Country's Best Yogurt	1981	1,075
43.	One Hour Martinizing	1949	1,000
44.	Nutri System	1971	1,000
45.	Kwik Kopy	1967	1,000
46.	Almost Heaven Hot Tubs	1971	975
47.	Coast to Coast Stores	1928	965
48.	Quality Inn/Choice Hotels	1941	950
49.	Jack in the Box	1951	940
50.	AAMCO Transmission	1963	920
51.	Jiffy Lube	1979	920
52.	Coverall	1979	900
53.	Pearle Vision	1962	860
54.	St. Hubert Bar-B-Q	1936	850
55.	Sir Speedy Printing	1968	830
56.	Minuteman Press	1973	820
57.	Godfather's Pizza	1973	810
58.	Culligan Water Conditioning	1936	806
59.	Adventureland	1981	800
60.	Computerland	1976	800
61.	Becker Milk Company	1957	784
62.	Bob's Big Boy	1936	780
63.	Carvel	1934	750
64.	Roto Rooter	1935	750
65.	Orange Julius	1926	745
66.	Medicine Shoppe	1970	740
67.	Meineke Discount Muffler	1972	720
68.	Decorating Den	1970	720
69.	Popeyes	1972	715
70.	Ponderosa Steakhouse	1965	700
71.	Days Inn	1971	700
72.	Pizza Inn	1960	690
73.	Novus Windshield Repair	1972	685
74.	Winchell's Donut House	1948	680
75.	Thrifty Rent-a-Car	1962	668
76.	ServPro	1967	650
77.	Kampgrounds of America	1961	640

78.	Shoney's	1959	625
79.	Duraclean	1930	615
80.	Bonanza	1963	610
81.	Mister Donut	1955	610
82.	Mr. Build	1981	605
83.	Mail Boxes Etc. USA	1980	600
84.	General Business Services	1962	600
85.	Sizzler	1959	600
86.	Ramada Inn	1954	590
87.	Western Sizzlin	1962	590
88.	Captain D's	1969	590
89.	Uniglobe	1979	580
90.	Ziebart	1954	575
91.	Roy Rogers Restaurants	1968	570
92.	Speedy Muffler King	1956	560
93.	am/pm Minimarkets	1980	550
94.	Round Table Pizza	1959	550
95.	Ice Cream Churn	1974	530
96.	A & W Restaurants	1924	525
97.	RAX Restaurants	1967	520
98.	Supercuts	1976	510
99.	American Speedy Printing	1976	508
100.	Snelling and Snelling	1951	500

Index

PRIMA'S START-YOUR-OWN-BUSINESS LIBRARY
Choose one or several!

The Complete Franchise Book, 2nd ed., by Dennis L. Foster $14.95
Now you can benefit from the pithy advice and guidance of one of America's foremost franchise consultants. Each step, from answering a newspaper ad and choosing the right company to negotiating a fair contract and opening your doors, is covered in detail.

How to Become a Successful Weekend Entrepreneur, by Jennifer Basye $14.95
Learn how to earn an extra $100 or more every weekend. Includes special money-making ideas for moms at home, teenagers, computer whizzes, and retired folks. Turn your Saturdays and Sundays into paydays!

How to Become a Successful Consultant in Your Own Field,
by Hubert Bermont   (Hardcover) $21.95
Here is the help you need to make the transition from employee to consultant. Topics covered include what it takes to be a consultant, how to get hired, how to determine what to charge, how to operate a consulting business, and how to avoid pitfalls and mistakes.

How to Start Your Own Business on a Shoestring and Make up to $500,000 a Year,
by Tyler Hicks $13.50
Over 1,000 business ideas to spark your interest and action. Tried and tested strategies for building wealth.

Mail-Order Success Secrets, by Tyler Hicks $14.95
Is owning your own business your goal? Then mail order is the low-cost, high-profit way to go. Among the areas covered are how to start your business, where to find your product, how to get low-cost publicity, the overseas mail-order market, tapping into the 800-number boom, and more. Includes real-life examples as well as Ty Hicks' insights after nearly twenty-five successful years in the mail-order business.

199 Great Home Businesses You Can Start (and Succeed in!) for Under $1000,
by Tyler Hicks $17.50
Helps you classify the type of business that would best suit you — people, nonpeople, stay-at-home, or go-outside — and then offers dozens of possible businesses you can build. From gift baskets to seminar promotion, personal shopping services to medical claims processing, Hicks has the right business for you.

Importing into the United States, 2nd ed., U.S. Department of Commerce $17.50
The official guide to importing products from abroad. A must for anyone involved in the import business. Includes chapters on the entry process; invoicing; determining duty assessments; and requirements, restrictions, and prohibitions. Contains samples of standard forms.

FILL IN AND MAIL . . . TODAY

PRIMA PUBLISHING
P.O. BOX 1260BK
ROCKLIN, CA 95677

USE YOUR VISA/MC AND ORDER BY PHONE:
(916) 624-5718 (M–F 9–4 PST)

Dear People at Prima,

I'd like to order the following titles:

Quantity	Title	Amount
_____	_____	_____
_____	_____	_____
_____	_____	_____
_____	_____	_____
_____	_____	_____
_____	_____	_____

Subtotal _____

Postage & handling $ 3.95

Sales tax _____

TOTAL (U.S. funds only) _____

Check enclosed for $_____ (payable to Prima Publishing)
Charge my ☐ Mastercard ☐ Visa

Card no. _____ Exp. date _____

Signature _____

Your printed name _____

Address _____

City/state/zip _____

Daytime telephone _____

YOU MUST BE SATISFIED, OR YOUR MONEY BACK!!!

Thank you for your order